SERENDIPITY

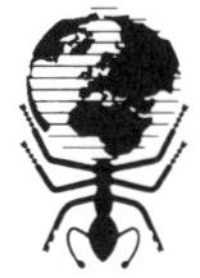

SERENDIPITY

The Afterlife of the Object

CAROL MAVOR

REAKTION BOOKS

For Sloane,
because you still believe in magical thinking

Published by
Reaktion Books Ltd
Unit 32, Waterside
44–48 Wharf Road
London N1 7UX, UK
www.reaktionbooks.co.uk

First published 2024

Printed and bound in India by Replika Press Pvt. Ltd

A catalogue record for this book is available from the British Library

ISBN 978 1 78914 950 0

CONTENTS

We ought to use time
Like emperors of the mind:
Do magic things that the future,
Surprised, will find.

BEN OKRI

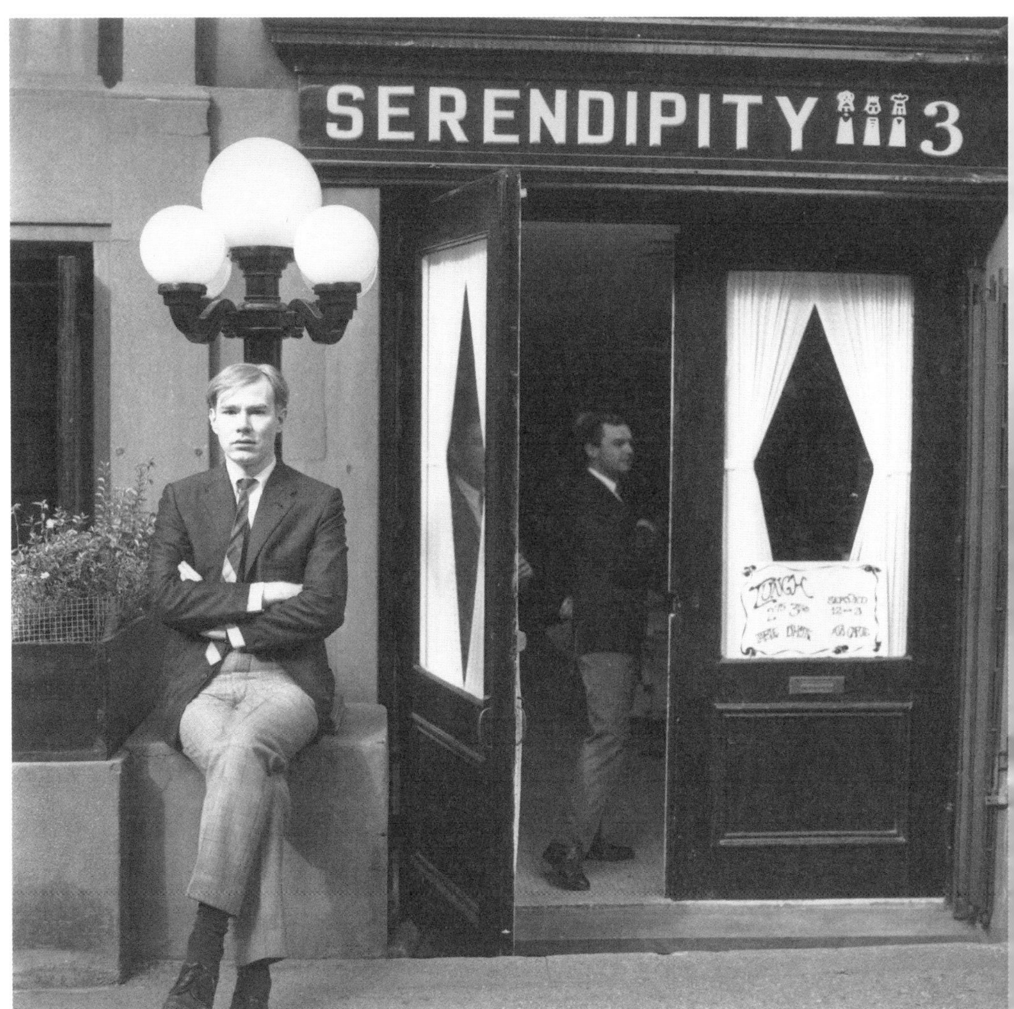

Andy Warhol in front of Serendipity 3, *c.* 1962, with Stephen Bruce, co-founder of the café, behind him in the doorway, photograph by John Ardoin.

PREFACE

My Early Education in Serendipity

My thoughts about 'happy accidents' began in the summer of 1980.

Kevin and I went to MOMA to see the Picasso retrospective. I bought a bubble-gum-pink T-shirt from the museum shop – with Picasso's famed signature emblazoned across my chest – which I wore with high-waisted trousers the colour of Baskin-Robbins 31 Flavors mint-chocolate-chip ice cream (minus the chocolate chips). Like I said, it was 1980.

The spray-painted graffiti on the subway cars dazzled us. We went to the Mudd Club, known to us through the famous song by the Talking Heads with the very long title of 'Life During Wartime (This Ain't No Party . . . This Ain't No Disco . . . This Ain't No Foolin' Around)'. David Byrne's post-apocalyptic words (gloomed by notes of what he was thinking about when writing the lyrics – Walker Percy, Patty Hearst, the Baader-Meinhof gang) were unhinged by the pure joy of actually being at the Mudd Club. 'This is the Mudd Club,' danced my heart to its own beat. We did not see Andy Warhol, but we might have.

And, on the advice of our college friend Jeannie Freilich, we went to have a frozen hot chocolate at Serendipity 3: an overly sweet café originally started by Stephen Bruce, Calvin Holt and Patch Caradine. The trio called themselves 'the princes of Serendip'. The café was made famous by Andy Warhol, the most famous of all the Pop artists. Early in his career, Warhol used Serendipity as both a studio and a pop-up art gallery. Painted over the entry door, between 'SERENDIPITY' and the number 3, are a trio of chess piece royals – in a playful nod to *Alice's Adventures in Wonderland*. Their *Arabian Nights*-like crowns signal the Sri Lankan story 'The Three Princes of Serendip'.

Inside the café, Warhol overtook tables so that friends and strangers could add colour to his books and prints any way they desired. Warhol watched, with his crazy hair and impish smile, sipping frozen hot chocolate served with a cherry and too much whipped cream, alongside bites of lemon icebox pie. No one worried about staying inside the lines. They coloured with joy.

Serendipity soon became a Warhol studio/party space: a practice version of the Factory. From 1953 until 1960, Warhol used Serendipity to exhibit his early artist's books, including *A Is an Alphabet* and *Love Is a Pink Cake*, as well as to give away copies of the limited editions to promote his talents. By the time I got to Serendipity, it was a pilgrimage site for any young art student interested in contemporary art.

During the summer of 1980, Kevin and I also visited Jeannie at her childhood home. We got a taste of the Beverly Hills scene. I have a vivid, sensate memory of Jeannie's mostly silent mother, who seemed to float rather than walk. When we first met, she came out wearing a cadmium-orange silk kaftan and a very

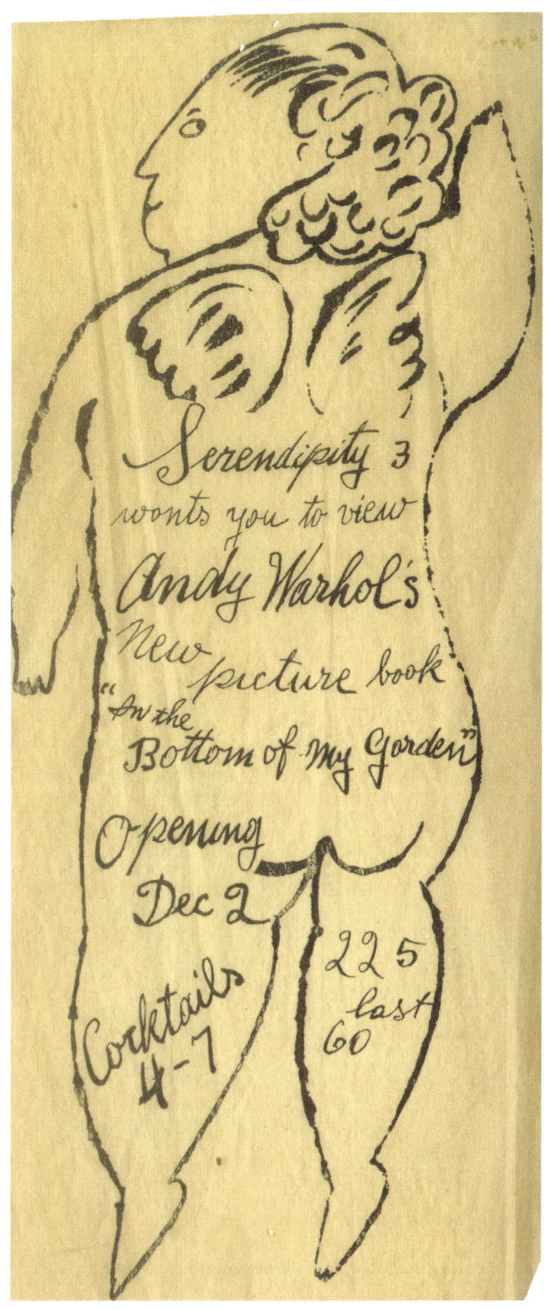

Warhol's hand-drawn invitation to an opening at Serendipity 3 for his new picture book *In the Bottom of My Garden*, c. 1954.

fragrant white gardenia tucked behind her ear. I remember her as a vision of oranges and reds, hovering like the pure colour of a Rothko stained canvas or an LA sunset: an apparition of sorts with the strong cold scent of gardenia – flowery exotic, creamy coconut.

Almost immediately, Mrs Freilich took me aside into the family's living room to show me a painting that she wanted me to see. She pointed to a perky butterfly at the bottom of the painting, a line drawing in thin black oil paint, which I would later understand as Japonisme. Pointing to the butterfly, she asked:

'Do you know what that means?'

'No,' I said with humiliation, as it was clear that I should know.

'It's James McNeill Whistler's famous signature: see, he's combined his initials, "J" "M" and "W", into a stylized butterfly. So, now you know: this is a painting by Whistler.'

At that time, I had never heard of Whistler. I was a studio art major and I had yet to learn the history of art, beyond the artists that influenced my own creative practice. I have forgotten the subject of the large, no doubt impressive, painting altogether. I only remember the butterfly. Like Whistler, I would become absorbed by butterflies. In this book, you will find Whistler's painting of three little butterflies flitting around the head of girl-child Cicely Alexander in his *Harmony in Grey and Green* (1872–4) – two are butter-yellow and one is white-grey-blue. And there is a fourth, pressed to the grey wall, pinned like the work of the lepidopterist: Whistler's cipher signature. A sign which I became an apprentice to, long ago, and which is only now emerging out of its chrysalis. Like Nabokov's boyhood memory of 'keeping a hawkmoth's pupa in a box for something like seven years' – so that he finished high school 'while the thing was asleep' – and then finally it hatched, like an epiphany, during a journey on a train.[1]

My source is serendipitous: Mrs Freilich's quiz.

The Freilichs also had a real Renoir print in their guest powder room.

For her graduation from college, Jeannie's parents had given her a real Picasso print: all I remember is the minotaur. (I keep saying 'real' but of course the entire *mise-en-scène* was anything but.) Picasso's man-bull may have been caressing a woman. I seem to remember it hanging above Jeannie's dresser in her girlish bedroom furnished in white French Provincial – although that may be my imagination at play. I am likely remembering my own girlish bedroom.

The film stars Robert Wagner and Natalie Wood lived across the street, although Wood had already mysteriously drowned. People would stand on Jeannie's lawn to take photos of the couple's house. Like the crowds of people who came to the Louvre to see the stolen *Mona Lisa*, to see the blank wall, to see what was gone.

Warhol would have loved visiting Jeannie's house, just as he loved going to Serendipity in New York.

While eating my frozen hot chocolate at Serendipity, the word 'serendipity' lodged gently into my head, along with *supercalifragilisticexpialidocious*, but I never went deeper . . . until I realized that my method for writing about art was based in part, if not wholly, on serendipitous encounters. Actually, the realization was not mine. It was Marina Warner's. After I completed a reading from my book, *Aurelia: Art and Literature Through the Mouth of the Fairy Tale*, at the London Review of Books Bookshop, Marina astutely commented that my approach was that of serendipity.

A happy accident or two, which took place during the summer of 1980.

INTRODUCTION

From a Smashed Thimble to Two Hares Falling Out of Breath

Serendipity (both the word and my book) gives life to objects *after* their physical production, from a smashed thimble to two hares falling out of breath. It also includes:

- Horace Walpole's 'Strawberry Hill' and Serendipity 3, the latter Andy Warhol's favourite New York café
- Caravaggio's *Inspiration of St Matthew* and Hugo Simberg's *The Wounded Angel*
- Anne Frank's diary and my mother's audio recording, discovered after her death
- Vladimir Nabokov's *Lolita* and Diego Velázquez's portrait of María Teresa, Infanta of Spain
- Sally Mann's photograph of a tree in Mississippi and Steve McQueen's film *12 Years a Slave.*

Serendipity makes unexpected, happy, accidental discoveries. Art provokes interpretation, but also resists it. Writing historically about works of art is unavoidably about the unknown, what is lost, what is melancholic. In response, this book breathes new life into the past by pocketing the air of serendipity.

Serendipity

The word 'serendipity' was coined in 1754 by Horace Walpole, who lived from 1717 until 1797. The *Oxford English Dictionary* defines it as 'the faculty of making happy and unexpected discoveries by accident', noting that even scientific discoveries often depend on the serendipitous, 'the chance observation falling on a receptive eye'.

Walpole formed the word out of a Persian-Italian fairy tale entitled 'The Three Princes of Serendip'. In a letter written on 28 January 1754 to his chum Horace Mann, Walpole explains that he had made 'a "critical discovery" about the Capello arms in an old book of Venetian arms' by means of 'serendipity'.[1] Using the usual excesses of unimportant incidents – sometimes fascinating, sometimes dull – which are characteristic of his letters (hence my heavy use of ellipses), Walpole writes:

> This discovery, indeed, is almost of that kind which I call *Serendipity*, a very expressive word . . . I shall endeavor to explain to you . . . I once read a silly fairy tale called *The Three Princes of Serendip*: as their Highnesses travelled, they were always making discoveries, by accident and sagacity, of things which they were not in quest of: for instance, one of them discovered that a mule blind in the right eye had travelled the same road lately, because the grass was

> eaten only on the left side, where it was worse on the right side . . . now do you understand *Serendipity*?[2]

Serendipity is almost magic ('Walpole was fond of the *Arabian Nights*'[3]), but not beyond explanation.

Of note, 'serendipity occurs only once in all of Walpole's writings.'[4] The *Oxford English Dictionary* notes that the word was formerly rare but gained wide currency in the twentieth century.

Walpole was a fastidious, affected, effeminate and sentimental satirist-novelist-artist-gossip-collector. In 1764 he published a novel, *The Castle of Otranto*, which is still widely regarded as the first piece of gothic fiction.[5] He was a tireless letter writer, writing some 4,000 epistles. He was also a dandy, fop, macaroni. As the novelist Laetitia Matilda Hawkins (a younger contemporary of Walpole) wrote:

> [Walpole's] entrance into a room was in that style of affected delicacy, which fashion had made almost natural, [a] *chapeau bras* [a bicorne hat] between his hands as if he wished to compress it, or under his arm; knees bent, and feet on tip-toe, as if afraid of a wet floor. His summer dress of ceremony was usually a lavender suit, the waistcoat embroidered with a little silver, or of white silk worked in the *tambour* [a popular embroidered net lace of the period], partridge silk stockings, gold buckles, ruffles and lace frill. In the winter he wore powder . . . His appearance at the breakfast table was proclaimed, and attended, by a fat and favourite little dog . . . and favourite squirrel [both of whom] partook of his breakfast.[6]

Walpole is most famous for spearheading the Gothic revival with his villa in Twickenham, London, which he called Strawberry Hill. (Before he renamed it the villa was known as 'Chopp'd Straw Hall'.) From 1749 onwards, Walpole concocted his giant, sprawling bright-white gingerbread castle – his 'lover to whom he was singularly faithful' (his Galatea, his Eliza Doolittle).[7] Fond of the diminutive when it came to Strawberry Hill, he called his paramour his 'nutshell', his 'babyhouse full of playthings', and described his little nothing as 'the prettiest bauble you ever saw'.[8] Walpole was a true artist, if an odd one, turning his new *jou-jou* – much of it made out of papier-mâché – into what his rivals would call a 'Gothic mousetrap'.[9] The style of his castle is known as 'Strawberry Hill Gothic'. For Walpole the word 'gothic' does not mean 'a vision of dark and terrifying masses, but rather a world of airy and intricate effects combined with solemnity and shadow'.[10]

To Gothicize with Strawberry-Hill sagacity is to go from room to room, thought to thought, as dark to light and light to dark. Interior walls of fairy-tale red and white. 'Gloomth' staircases. 'Gloomth' is a second word invented by Walpole for the effects of his own Gothic paper castle. As he notes in a couple of letters: 'one has a satisfaction in imprinting the gloomth of abbeys and cathedrals on one's house' – and Strawberry Hill 'is now at the height of its greenth, blueth, gloomth, honeysuckle-and-syringahood'.[11]

Mysterious Bluebeard rooms.

Using his hungry curatorial eye, Walpole overfilled Strawberry Hill, like readying a goose for *foie gras*, with objects, beautiful and strange, captivating and dull.

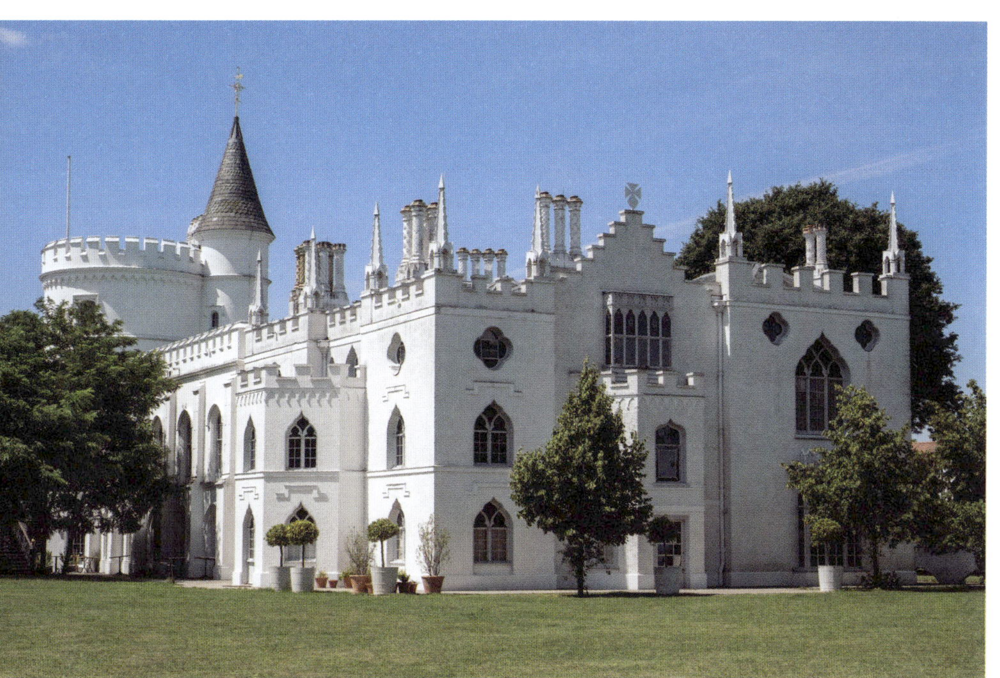

Strawberry Hill, exterior.

- The hair of Mary Tudor in a gold locket (1784).
- A large Chinese goldfish tub (*c.* 1730), in which Walpole's favourite cat, Selima, drowned.[12]
- A pair of gauntlet gloves that had once belonged to James I (1603–25) – crimson leather, trimmed with silk, metal and lace.
- The red hat of Cardinal Wolsey, sixteenth century, felt silk.
- Queen Bertha's ivory hair comb, embellished with a carved lion, a winged horse and a pair of goats standing on their hind legs, late twelfth century.

By the year of his death in 1797, Walpole had ensnared a collection of no fewer than 4,000 objects, excluding his mammoth collection of books, prints and drawings – he had a library of some 7,300 books).[13] He relished his self-inflicted collectomania.

I have long been drawn to Walpole's book of swan marks from the sixteenth century: the text is filled with mysterious abstractions and ciphers made with pen and black ink on skin-coloured vellum. As far back as 1230, only the privileged few were granted an individual swan mark – these are intriguing 'combinations of rings, chevrons, keys, nicks, crosses, and letters' sometimes also referred to as *cigninota*.[14] Any unmarked swan belonged to the Crown, and would soon be 'scarred with the royal emblem'.[15] It was mostly mute swans (the most common species in England) – who, of course, are not mute at all – that suffered the *cigninota*.

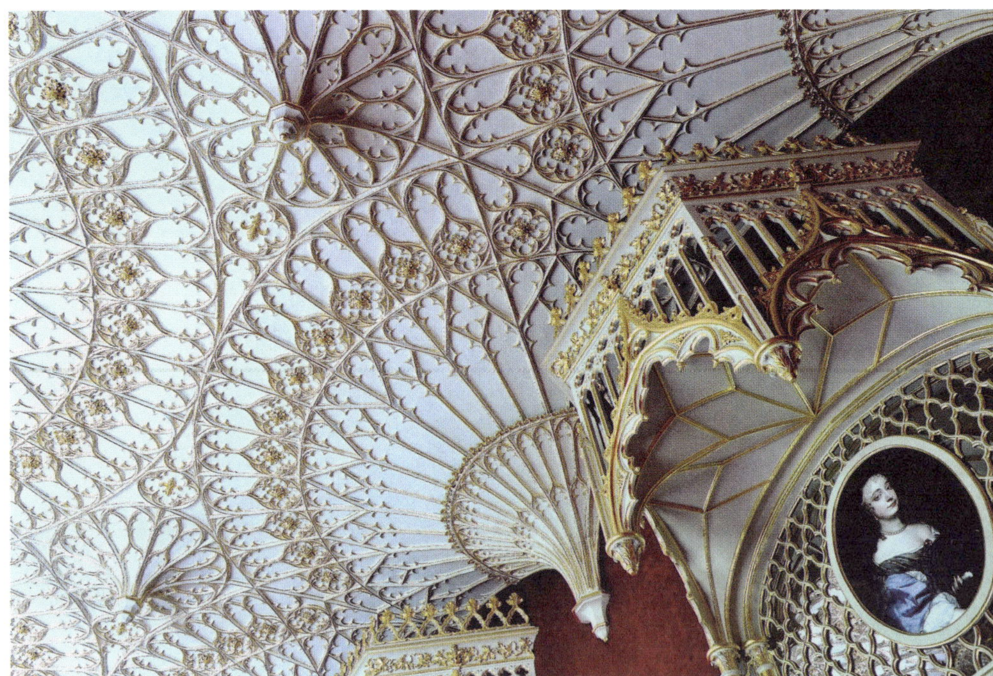

Strawberry Hill, interior.

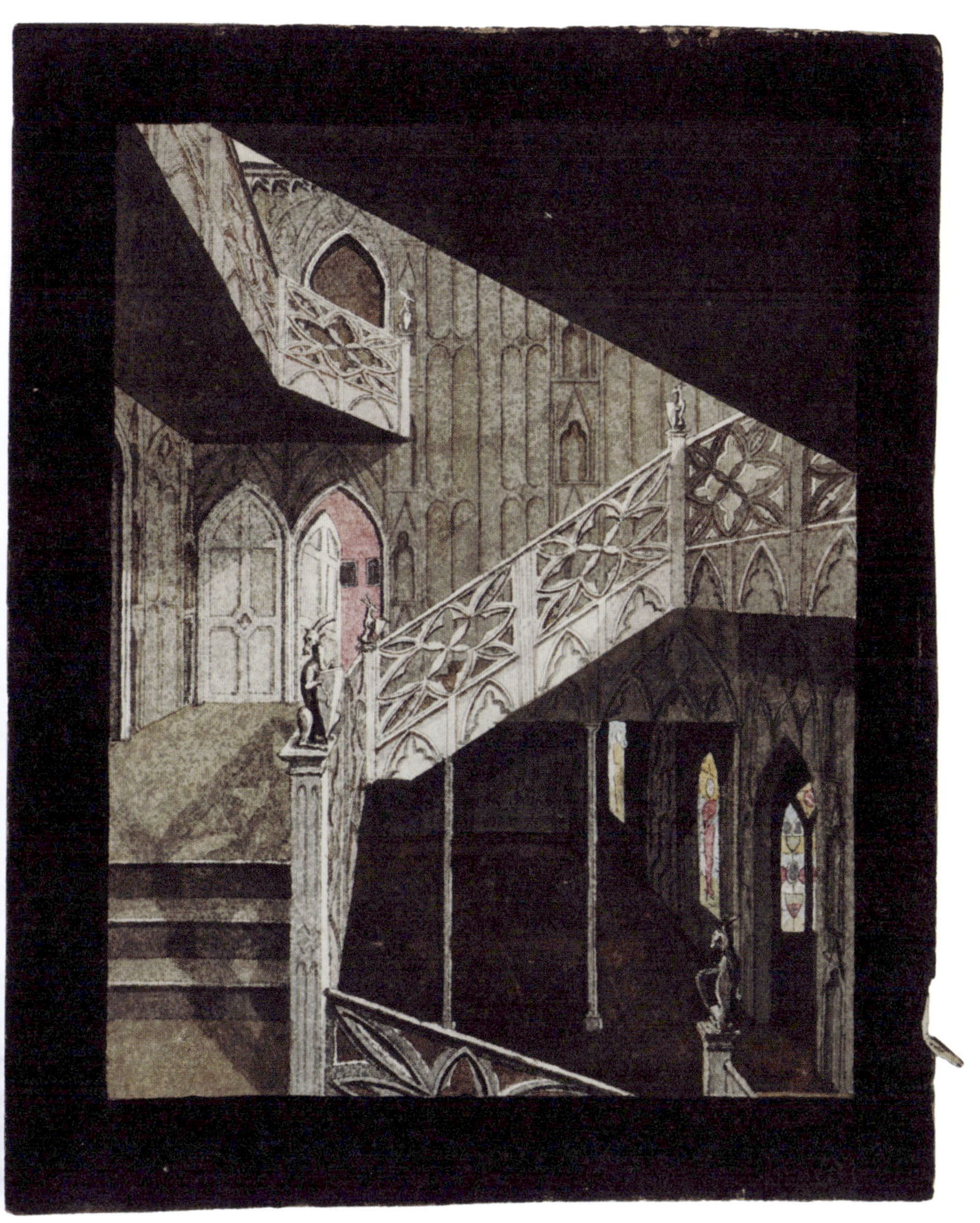

Richard Bentley, *Perspective of the Hall and Staircase at Strawberry Hill*, c. 1754, pen, ink and watercolour.

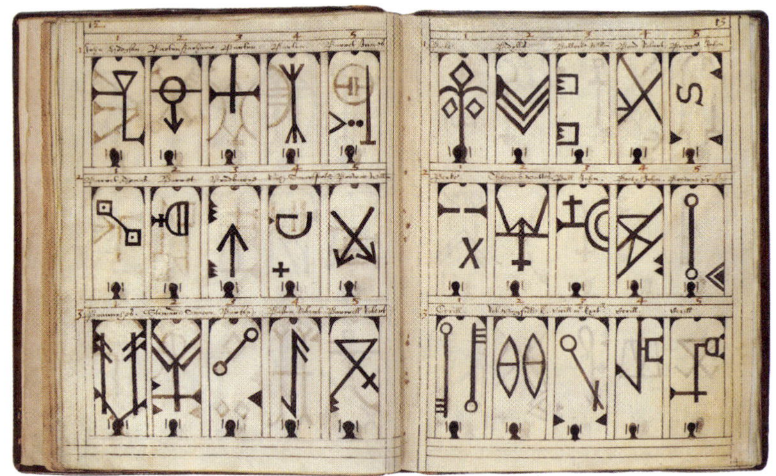

Book of swan marks, English, 16th century.

When the 'rings, chevrons, keys, nicks, crosses, and letters' fell upon my receptive eyes, I was transported back to my childhood. I recalled a present from my great-aunt Lorna: a brooch composed of a pair of silver snow skis crossed at the centre, like arrows of friendship. The skis were marked with tiny Navajo symbols. A star for night. Lightning for speed. A tree for age. A horse for family. A rolling log, which looked like a swastika, for well-being and good luck. A tiny oval egg of turquoise sat where the skis crossed in their friendship. Aunt Lorna sold and collected antiques. The object was beautiful. Mysterious. Magical. Strange. I remember, especially, the swastika-rolling log and trying to understand how one sign could mean something so dark and so light.

I have lost the brooch. (Although I often look for it.)

I remain an apprentice to reading marks on swan's beaks and silver skis.

I await discovery, which may never happen.

I dream of finding the brooch.

Walpole was a precursor to the collectomania of Andy Warhol, with his 175 cookie jars and his cardboard boxes, which he called *Time Capsules* and filled with some 300,000 objects over the course of thirteen years until his death: Studio 54 invitations, coffee sachets, a piece of Caroline Kennedy's birthday cake, a mummified foot, a seventeenth-century German book on wrestling, gay magazines and a gold dog tag from Tiffany's inscribed with the name of Warhol's dachshund, Archie.

With eccentric appetites, both Walpole and Warhol had their own gourmand taste. Their extreme differences, so pure, brighten with sameness. Just as Warhol favoured Serendipity 3's frozen hot chocolate, Walpole (who always ate sparingly, who avoided pastry, but would take a small bite of venison pie) preferred iced water.

Walpole was the Andy Warhol of his time.

Andy Warhol was the Horace Walpole of his time.

Serendipity 3 is a pop-up Strawberry Hill.

My first and only visit to Serendipity 3 – during the summer of 1980 – is where this book of happy accidents began. But back then, I did not know I would become a serendipity writer.

Afterlife

The *Oxford English Dictionary* defines 'afterlife' as 'life after death' and 'continued or renewed use'. The art historian Michael Ann Holly persuasively argues in her *The Melancholy Art* (a book to which my project is indebted) that writing historically about works of art (and, for that matter, all artefacts) is destined to be a melancholic enterprise. For 'the past is precisely that which is beyond resurrection, possibly even recognition.'[16] Objects provoke interpretation, but they also necessarily resist it, leaving a melancholic wound. Yet the interpretation and the histories that we write are dependent on falling on a receptive eye, experiencing chance encounters that animate. While what has gone missing, as Holly emphasizes, is 'nearly everything (but not quite) that once-upon-a-time breathed life into it and gave it sustenance' – her book (and mine) seeks to resuscitate the past through a productive bumping into, a kind of thinking that the literary theorist Peter Stallybrass has figured as 'against thinking'.[17] Or, as the French philosopher Jean-Luc Nancy emphasizes in *God, Justice, Love, Beauty* (key terms for the afterlife): 'sometimes what we do best is nothing, doing nothing, letting things be' – and sometimes a happy accident ascends before us.[18]

The classicist, poet, translator and essayist Anne Carson has written:

> A wound gives off its own light
> surgeons say.
> If all the lamps in the house were turned out
> you could dress this wound
> by what shines from it.[19]

If writing historically about works of art is destined to be glum – a gloomth enterprise, we might say – my book emphasizes the light of the wound.

The prose of *Serendipity* includes stories from my personal history (racial hatred in America, fears of poisoned air, my mother's depression), alongside what has been labelled variously as creative non-fiction, art writing and essay writing. The resulting 'essays' of *Serendipity* (subjective and objective) are yoked to the objects that prompted them.

In *Essayism* (2017), the writer and curator Brian Dillon remarks: 'imagine a type of writing so hard to define its very name should be something like: an effort, an attempt, a trial. Surmise or hazard, followed likely by failure.'[20] But isn't it better to fail with land in sight, than not to try at all?

As Emily Dickinson wrote – perhaps beginning this verse on a small scrap of paper with a stubby pencil – both of which she kept in one of her side pockets – the envelopes of her dress – close to her body – close to her mind, close to her heart, close to her 'writerly' hands[21] – in order to make good the immediacy of her bold writing:

> It might be easier
> To fail – with Land in Sight –
> Than gain – My Blue Peninsula –
> To perish – of Delight – [22]

I share with Marina Warner (novelist, literary theorist, essay writer and self-proclaimed 'mythographer') the view that 'art-writing at its most useful should share in the dynamism, fluidity and passions of the objects of its inquiry.'[23]

The afterlives of the objects of my book are positioned as 'inheriting pasts and enabling futures' through a serendipitous method, which locates 'the present' not as 'a vanishing instant' but rather as 'a rich temporality of living and dying.'[24] My book resists focusing on a vanished past, or, even most importantly, a vanished future. *Serendipity*'s accidental discoveries are located in what Donna Haraway refers to as the 'thick present, a thick now . . . the potent time at stake'.[25]

The limited objects addressed in this book are not always linked historically but are *historicized*. I offer histories that are true enough, in the spirit of D. W. Winnicott's famed 'good-enough mother'. According to Winnicott, a good-enough mother is not a mother who is lacking – as readers often misinterpret the term to mean. Rather, her care gives her child the tools to find (make) transitional objects (not fetishes) of their own, which lead to meaning, creative thought, curing problems. I endeavour to provide my readers with the tools to make 'good-enough' histories for our potent time at stake.

Finding Anne Frank's journal in the Secret Annex after the Second World War – finding a wounded tree in Mississippi muttering sounds of the American South, mythic and real, which we can sense but will never know – finding a large flock of Dickinson's poems, many on the wings of salvaged envelopes, nested in a hidden drawer – finding a hazelnut, left by an unknown mother, along with her child at London's Foundling Hospital, as an enigmatic token for future identification – finding Walter Sickert's painting of a dead hare (in a storage closet at a small museum in Sheffield, England) as a sign of marvellous culinary-theological transignification – finding an overlooked vision of *Lolita* whose very existence turns on the fact that the book was rescued from incineration, when pulled out of the rubbish bin by Nabokov's wife Véra – all are dependent on serendipity's happenstance of layers: finding something that you did not exactly know you were looking for until you found it.

All history is about loss, and in the case of this book, much of it is tragic – but I also offer the happiness that can be found in accidental (unexpected) discoveries.

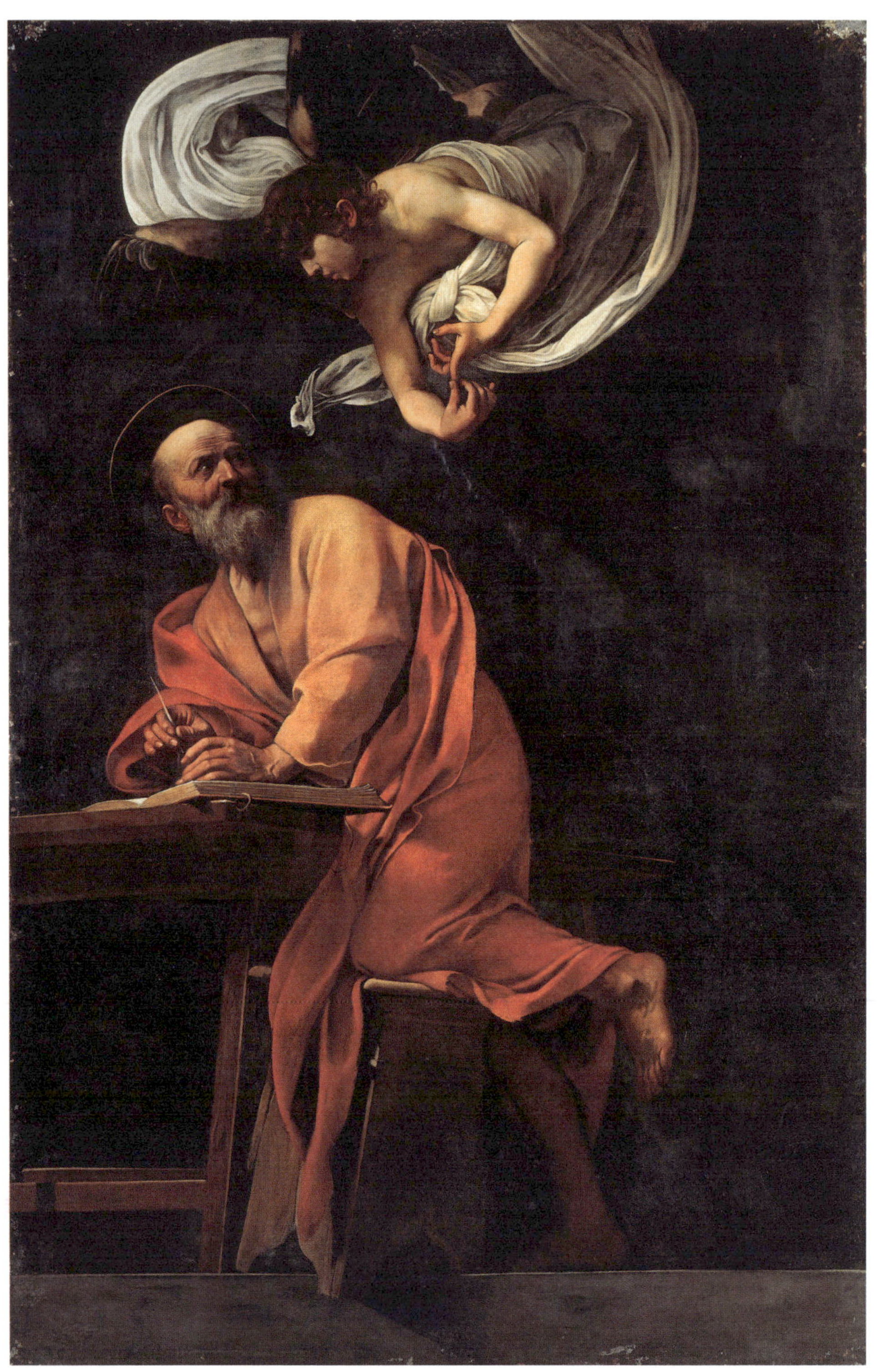

Caravaggio, *The Inspiration of St Matthew*, 1602, oil on canvas.

CHAPTER ONE

To Angelize

A moment of inspiration.

Inside the church of San Luigi dei Francesi in Rome, I stand before the Contarelli Chapel. Caravaggio's sumptuous *Inspiration of St Matthew*, of circa 1602, floats overhead, at the centre of the altar.[1] It is positioned between two other paintings by the famous Baroque master of 'bright' (*chiaro*) and 'dark' (*oscuro*), the contrast of tones known in art history as *chiaroscuro*. *The Calling of St Matthew* to the left; *The Martyrdom of St Matthew* to the right.

The *Inspiration of St Matthew* and its two companions are in darkness. Originally they would only have been seen by candlelight. I drop a coin into the slot of a metal box – which takes me to the memory of old payphones – and the dark chapel illuminates. The radiance is short-lived: only a few minutes.

A moment of enchantment, which clicks into inspiration.

I am moved.

I am lit.

I can hear the light.

The surprise of sonority.

Tendre l'oreille (to stretch the ear).

The charming angel of *The Inspiration of St Matthew* has floated down from heaven to pay St Matthew a visit.

Enhanced by the magic of the coin-operated illumination, the arbitrary vivid spotlight ('originated by Caravaggio'[2]) is not very realistic but feels believable.

Only angels can travel from heaven to this world and back again.

From light to dark to light . . .

The angel is chubby, an older adolescent who lies between child and adult. The black curls at his neck – and those threatening to cover his eyes (his hair wants cutting) – beckon my fingertips. His bee-stung lips are full. The angel hovers magically – as if he weighs nothing at all – as if he breathes air lighter than air. St Matthew has writer's block.[3] The angel has come down from heaven to inspire St Matthew *to write* 'a metaphor for the world's learning the truth from God'.[4] St Matthew is surprised, and leans back a bit on his stool. St Matthew is astonished, as I am too, by the beauty of the boy-angel. I fall in love with this heavenly creature – as Caravaggio must have as well.

The paint handling, along with the magic coin, moves me to believe.

The angel's cloud-folded drapery is a billowing bedsheet of narrative.[5] If you look closely, you will discover darkness in his huge dark, nearly black wings, which are tipped in warm orange-brown (so as to suggest the physiognomy of a giant butterfly). They are the work of a lepidopterist writ large. Theatrical. Baroque.

Wings inspired, perhaps, by a black swallowtail.

Or a red admiral; like the one who has alighted along the bottom edge of Ambrosius Bosschaert the Elder's 1607 *Glass Flask on a Marble Ledge, Flanked by a Red Admiral Butterfly and a Lizard.* (My mind jumps to Caravaggio's *Boy Bitten by a Lizard*, (*c*. 1593–4), but that's not a discovery, or serendipity – that's free association, at least so far.)

The angel is enveloped by the sheets, which bracket him, as part of the grammar of our world and also that of the heavenly sphere.

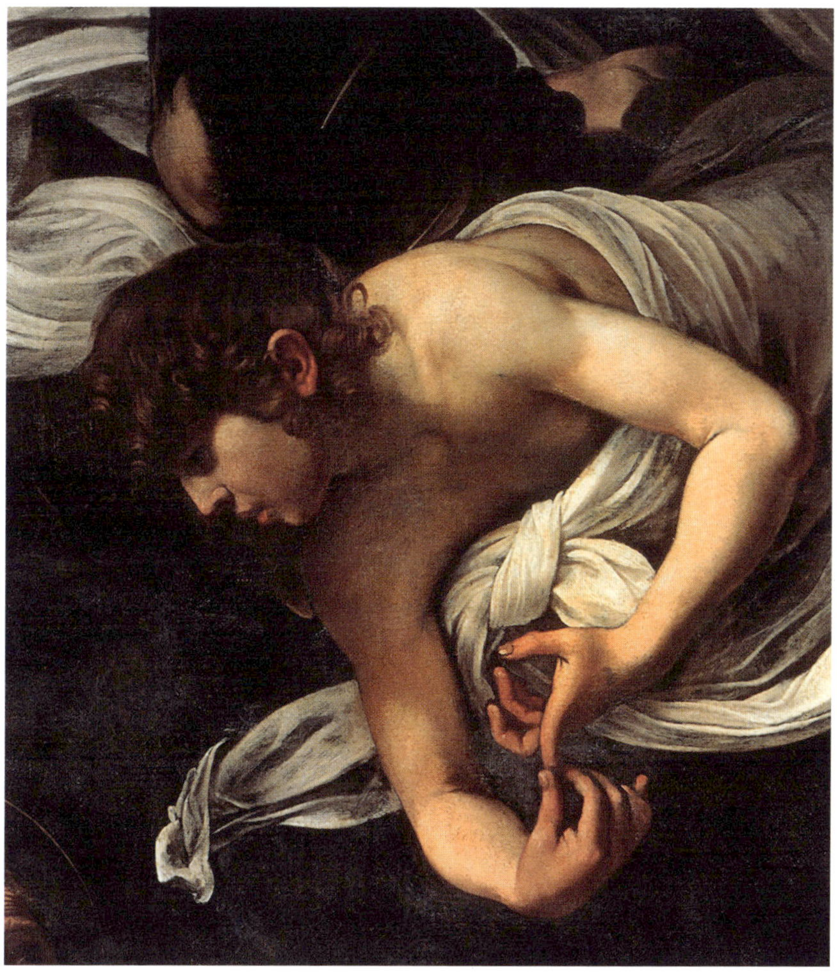

Caravaggio, *The Inspiration of St Matthew* (detail).

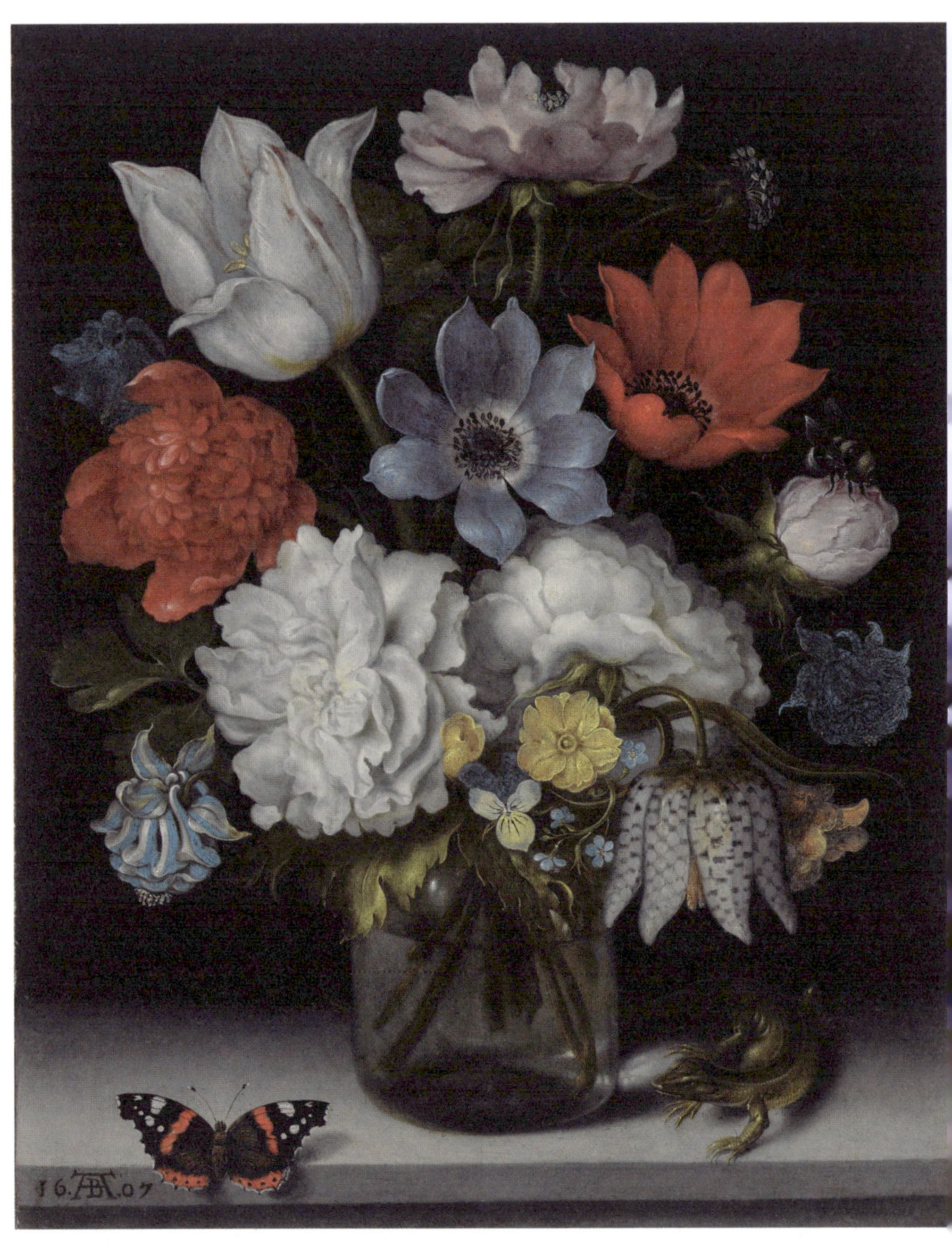

Ambrosius Bosschaert the Elder, *Flowers in a Glass Flask on a Marble Ledge, Flanked by a Red Admiral Butterfly and a Lizard*, 1607, oil on copper.

St Matthew is cloaked in this world. His velvety robe, its hue a rich citrus-orange, folds heavy with light and dark, drapes weightily down over another robe, worn close to his skin, its colour and sheen that of crème caramel. A bit of the saint's chest is exposed below his grey beard. His fabrics are not magically at play with a loss of gravity. They ground him.

The surprise of the colour of St Matthew's deliciously saturated orange draperies could have inspired Lord Leighton's secular, whimsical *Flaming June* (1895): the latter's plentiful use of yards of see-though fabric, despite 'technical mastery', appears 'slightly ridiculous'.[6] We are embarrassed to like *Flaming June*, but that is part of the pleasure. *Flaming June* is asleep; her transparent drapery, like a shedding chrysalis, exposes a bare bottom, a lovely rich thigh, a nipple. She is forever asleep. Yet the inaudible rustling of her diaphanous dress and her girl-stepping-forward Gradiva foot (made famous by Freud in 1907[7]) suggests a coming awake. A bit of sleeper magic.

St Matthew is wide awake and ready *to write*. But perhaps he is unsure about where to begin. The angel is counting on his fingers.[8] With his right thumb he holds down his left index finger. He appears to be on step two, having already held down his left thumb for step one. The angel and the saint are in the middle of things *to write*.

To write is an intransitive verb expressing an action that does not pass over to an object. An intransitive verb does not take a direct object. Other examples would be *to die*; *to be born*; *to fall*; *to sleep*; *to walk*; *to swim*; *to fly*. The case of the intransitive form of the verb *to write* is of special interest to Roland Barthes: here he finds the distance between the one who writes (the *scriptor*) and language as dissolved into the 'middle voice'.[9] In other words, that middle space where who is writing what becomes muddled.

With Barthes' hand on St Matthew (in the hands of Caravaggio), even the viewer turns into a writer. *To write* today (claims Barthes in a post-structuralist 1966 essay, one year before he will publish 'Death of the Author') is 'to make oneself the centre of the action of speech . . . as the agent of action'.[10] We become 'immediately contemporary with the writing'.[11]

Seeing *The Inspiration of St Matthew*, as guided by Barthes, is *to write* hand in hand with St Matthew: caught in the act(ion) of writing, or perhaps more accurately of trying *to write*.

The verb 'inspire' comes from the Latin *inspīrāre*, to blow or breathe into. The angel's white bedsheet of folded and creased fabric appears to be blown into by winds, perhaps the strong breath of God himself.

To inspire, then is *to resuscitate. To animate.* To bring to life. Like history, including art history, itself. The French historian Jules Michelet (1798–1874) claimed that history needs to be told, fulfilled, completed – but also to be 'consumed, devoured, ingested, so as to resuscitate the historian'.[12] In other words, the historian tries to resuscitate the past. For *our* book this is the after-life of the object, through writing. Our writing is not the past, but it is, perhaps in its finest form, a middle voice between artist and writer, reader and writer, between past and now.

Michelet was a life-long inspiration to Barthes. In 1942 Barthes studied the historian with devoted seriousness while being treated for tuberculosis in Switzerland. There Barthes read Michelet's multi-volume *Histoire de France* (1833–67), transcribing his

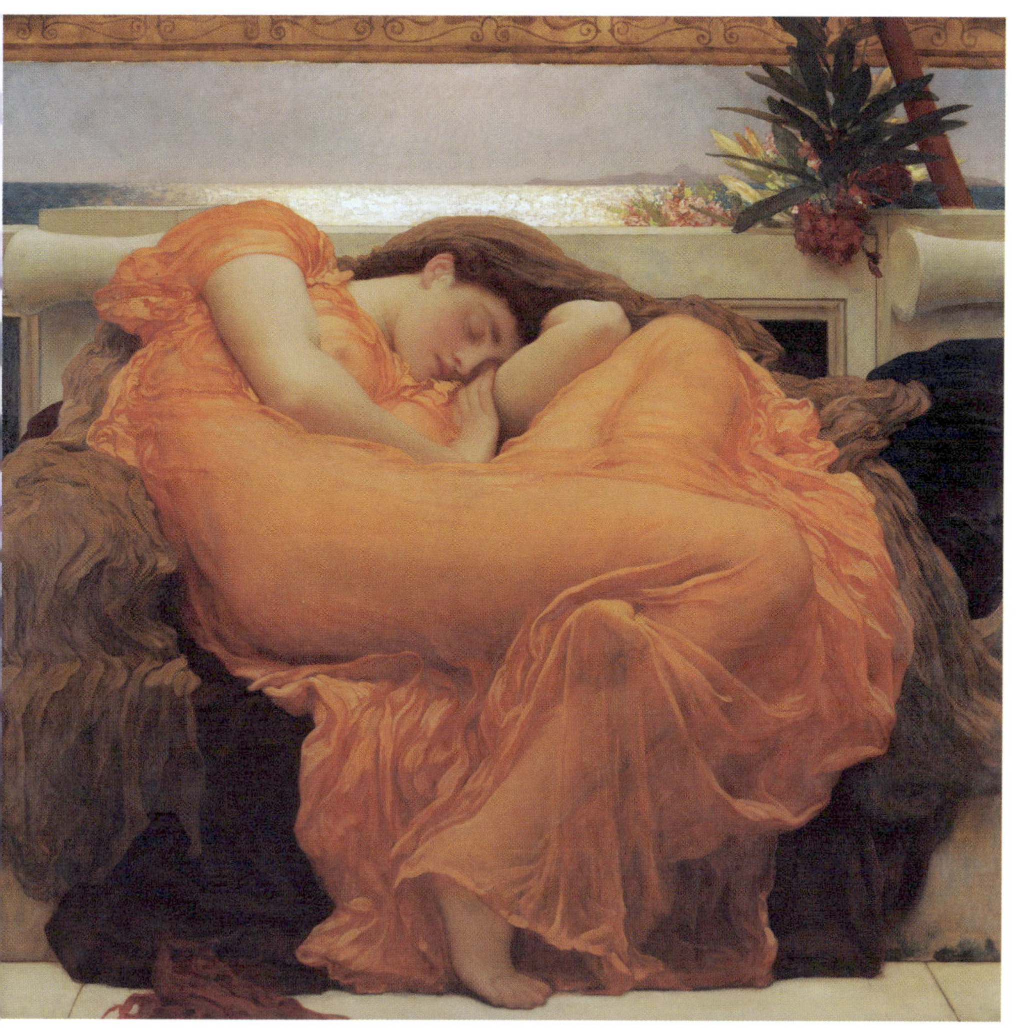

Frederic Leighton, *Flaming June*, 1895, oil on canvas.

thoughts on nearly a thousand notecards. You might say that Michelet breathed (after)life into Barthes' tubercular lungs. And with Barthes' publication of *Michelet* (1954), the famed post-structuralist breathed new life into the famed French historian.

Knowledge inspires the writer of the afterlife, what the seventh-century Greek poet Sappho refers to, at least in Anne Carson's translation, as the 'aftertime'.

In this spiteful fragment, Sappho writes:

> Dead you will lie and never memory of you
> will there be nor desire into the aftertime – for you do not
> share in the roses
> of Pieria,[13] but invisible too in Hades' house
> you will go your way among dim shapes. Having been
> breathed out.[14]

Piera is the birthplace of the Muses: 'daughters of Zeus and Mnemsoyne (Memory) and normally held to be nine in number'.[15] 'The roses of Pieria are the roses of the Muses, inhabitants of the mountain of Macedonia; those deprived of their attentions are ignorant and will be invisible after death.'[16] To not be inspired by the Muses (the goddesses who preside over learning and the arts), Sappho writes, is to not be remembered. We could say that it is to not have an afterlife (an aftertime).

Sappho's writing comes to us as fragments preserved on papyrus. In her translation of Sappho, Carson has chosen not to fill in the missing pieces, what Michael Ann Holly might call the 'wounds'.[17] Instead, Carson 'uses a single bracket to give an impression of missing matter, so that] or [indicates destroyed papyrus or the presence of letters not quite legible somewhere in the line . . . Brackets are an aesthetic gesture towards the papyrological event.'[18]

Here is one extreme example of Carson's translation with all of the wounds:

]
]
]
]
] running away
] 'bitten
]
]
] you
] makes a way with the mouth
] beautiful gifts children[19]

The brackets give mouth (resuscitation) to Sappho. We breathe mouth to mouth with Sappho: we have no choice but to be caught in the act(ion) of breathing as writing, or perhaps more accurately of trying *to breathe, to write.*

Angelization (Irigaray)

The French feminist philosopher Luce Irigaray is a wild writer who inspires. Coupling difficult philosophical texts (Plato, Freud, Spinoza, Merleau-Ponty et al.) with a new poetics, she radically imagines gender differently. In 'Sexual Difference', the chapter that

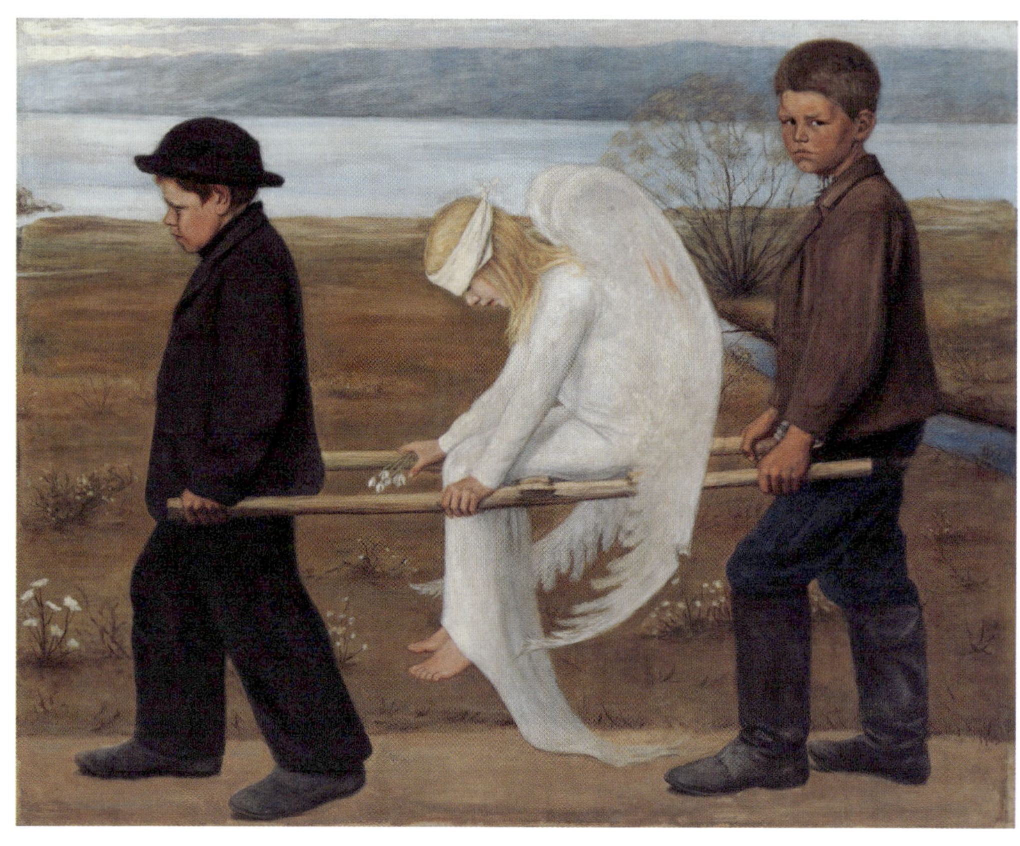

Hugo Simberg, *The Wounded Angel*, 1903, oil on canvas.

opens her book *An Ethics of Sexual Difference* (*Éthique de la différence sexuelle*, 1984), she turns to angels to 'herald a new birth, a new morning', a new experience of sexual difference: '*wonder*'.[20] For Irigaray, the womb is an envelope – a chrysalis, a shimmering space – which is transgressed to make new life (birth). She likens the female body to the envelope of space, between God and earth, the afterlife and mortal life, through which only angels can travel, fly. In her words:

> Swift angelic messengers . . . transgress all enclosures in their speed, [to] tell of the passage between the envelope of God and that of the world as micro- or macrocosm. They proclaim that such a journey can be made by the body of man, and above all the body of woman.[21]

Irigaray's angels are very positive, life-affirming, moving:

> The angel is that which unceasingly *passes through the envelope(s)* or *container(s)*, goes from one side to the other, reworking every deadline, changing every decision, thwarting all representation. Angels destroy the monstrous, that which hampers the possibility of a new age: they come to herald the arrival of a new birth, a new morning.[22]

The Wounded Angel

Hugo Simberg's *The Wounded Angel*, 1903, depicts a young angel who has injured her left wing: a small triangle of white feathers is missing, as if bitten out. She has a bandage over her eyes. Are they also wounded? Or is the bandage protecting her from the unavoidable emotional damage of seeing life on earth? In the words of Irigaray: 'In a certain way nothing is as sensitive, especially to touch, as my sight.'[23] For our eyes are easily affected by physical touch – just as feelings are touched, sometimes unbearably so, by what we see (or cannot see).

The angel has fallen out of her envelope. She can no longer pass through from heaven to earth and back again. She is wounded. The boys have found her. The unusual, specific details of the painting – an angel with a slightly broken wing, blindfolded (as in George Frederic Watts's *Hope*, 1866), holding snowdrops in her right hand (symbols of healing and rebirth), being carried on a stretcher by two boys, one wearing a black hat, the other looking at us – are cast in a sense of reality. A closer look reveals that her blindfold is above her eyes – but her eyes are closed. As if to look might keep her from returning to heaven.

The image does not look real. The place is recognizably real to the Finnish: the shore of Töölönlahti Bay. This angel is 'real but painted. Real but miraculous; with miracle' – to echo T. J. Clark on Giotto's Arena Chapel angels.[24]

But this wounded angel has not materialized out of Giotto's joyous blue; she has fallen from the sky. When Simberg displayed the painting for the first time, there was simply a long dash where there should have been a title. This was the artist's grammar, a way of saying there is no single correct interpretation. Each viewer creates his own meaning.[25]

The discovery of the angel by the boys must have been serendipitous. Lance Olsen has imagined it this way:

> [The boy without the hat] happens to glance up and sees her lying in the meadow thirty or forty meters away. Initially he believes he is looking at the remnants of a thawing snowdrift. Then he realizes the shape is completely wrong for that. Nor are there any other swaths of snow in view. So, he convinces himself that he must be looking at an enormous bird. A swan[26] perhaps, shot recently by a hunter. Yet the truth is that he has never seen a bird this big.[27]

The boys have found her like 'an extinct species of bird' – some sort of portmanteau creature . . . swan and girl . . . a *swirl*.[28]

'The manner in which she curls into herself makes her wings arch up behind her like gigantic feathery parentheses separating her from the surrounding text of the world.'[29] She is of our sentence, but also of another sphere, an altered line of thinking. What strikes the hatless boy is 'that angels with their six appendages and tremendous wings are closer in essential physiognomy to butterflies, beetles, and bees than to mortals.'[30] As Caravaggio knew.

The angel tells the boys how she got here, her voice in italics: '*I simply reached down one day, in a manner of speaking, in a metaphorical sense, that is, and tore my wing. I tore my wing, but . . . it didn't hurt. Not in the least.*'[31]

Her wing is torn: an exit wound from tearing through the envelope (poem). There's a little pinkish blood on her wings, which look like lungs.

The painting was vital for Simberg. The painter had been ill for a long time, including a stay in hospital for over six months, due to meningitis (a disease that affects the lungs). But because he wanted to complete his painting (which would become, arguably, the most favoured work of art by the Finns) he managed to fight for his breath. The artist got the idea for his painting in the landscape on long walks, which he did on the shores of Töölönlahti near the Helsinki Hospital.

The wings of the wounded angel look like lungs. Wings as lungs give flight to the breath of life.

To inspire is to resuscitate.

Touched by an angel.

Serendipitously.

CHAPTER TWO

Moeder, Maman, Mom
Anne Frank, Chantal Akerman, Dorothy Aileen Ashcraft

'We lay on our bed . . . and I fed you plums
the colour of bruises.'
JEANETTE WINTERSON, *Written on the Body*

A bruise marks the distance and closeness of the encounter between an adolescent daughter and mother. A bleeding under the skin. Tender to the touch. Dark as the night, womb, underground. Blue as the sky, the veins that feed us, my mother's eyes. Wounds that keep us thinking about what happened. As Margaret Atwood writes in her poem entitled 'What Happened':

Meanwhile on several
areas of my skin, strange bruises glow
and fade, and I can't remember
what accidents I had, whether I was
badly hurt, how long ago.[1]

The past is irretrievable, but writing can provoke the bruising – give life's blood to the afterlives of those we mourn, including History herself.

A bruise is a wound that lies hiding under the skin.

'Moeder, Maman, Mom' (dark, sweet, tender, fleshy, tough-skinned, stony-hearted) is fed by three secret journals *bruisy* with the maternal and adolescence.

The first journal is Anne Frank's famed diary, known in various edited and more complete forms as *The Secret Annexe* (*Het Achterhuis*) and *The Diary of a Young Girl*, and will be familiar to you; perhaps it is already precious to you.[2]

The second journal is Sidonie Ehrenburg's relatively unknown diary. Sidonie was the grandmother of the Belgium filmmaker Chantal Akerman (1950–2015), best known for her handsome three-hour masterpiece *Jeanne Dielman, 23 quai du Commerce, 1080, Bruxelles* (1975). (*Jeanne Dielman* has affected me more than any film I have ever seen.) Sidonie's journal, discovered after she was murdered at Auschwitz, is featured in Akerman's 24-minute split-screen video entitled *Marcher à côté de ses lacets dans un frigidaire vide* (To Walk Next to One's Shoelaces in an Empty Fridge) of 2004.[3] Akerman's mother gave her the diary in 1984.

The third journal is Dorothy Mavor's completely unknown audio diary. (At least up to the time of this book.) Dorothy was my mother. Her audio diary is very short: only nine minutes and two seconds long.

Bruises to keep

Anne wrote her journal in Dutch (her mother tongue) for two years between the ages of thirteen and fifteen, while hiding in Amsterdam from the Nazis. Anne tells 'Kitty' (the name she gave to her journal) all her secrets. Anne is a moody adolescent (in many ways typical of all girls of her age). She has to struggle to keep writing under the shadow of terror. She does her best to refuse what she calls 'turning the Secret Annexe into the Melancholy Annexe'.[4] Mother is a constant irritant to her. Father is 'the most adorable father' she 'has ever seen' [7].

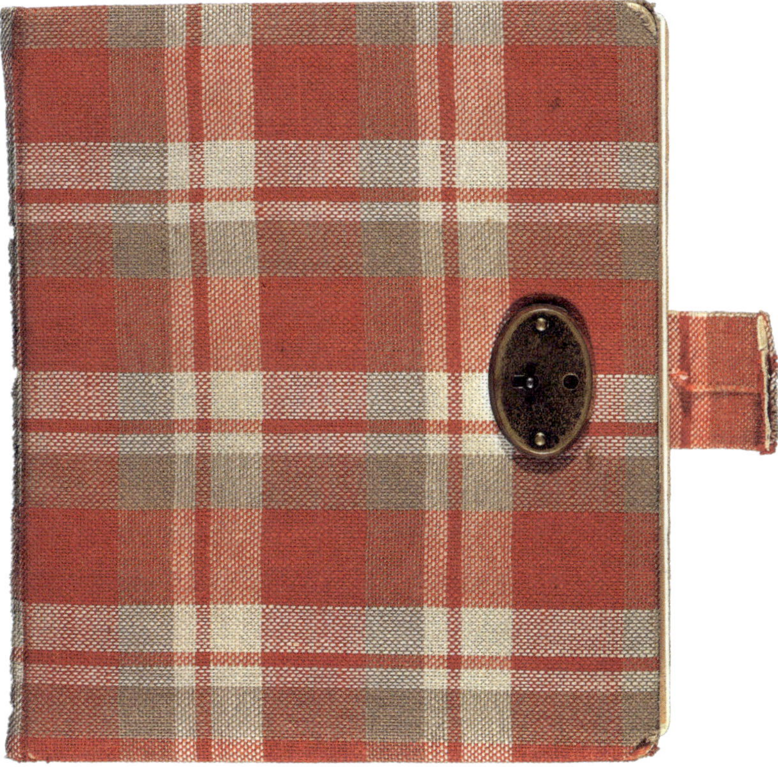

Anne Frank's diary 'Kitty', 1942.

> ANNE: I can imagine Mother dying someday, but Daddy's death seems inconceivable. It's very mean of me, but that's how I feel. I hope Mother will *never* read this or anything else I've written [51].
>
> ANNE: 'Paper is more patient than people' . . .
>
> I imagine the kind of mum I'd like to be to my children later on. The kind of mum who doesn't take everything people say too seriously, but who does take *me* seriously. I find it difficult to describe what I mean, but the word 'mum' says it all. Do you know what I've come up with? In order to give me the feeling of calling my mother something that sounds like 'Mum', I often call her 'Mumsie'. Sometimes I shorten it to 'Mums': an imperfect 'Mum'. I wish I could honour her by removing the 's'. It's a good thing she doesn't realize this, since it would only make her unhappy [153–4].

The Diary of a Young Girl, 'the symbol of a wounded generation',[5] is a book that everyone seems to read as an adolescent in high school – and then it is most often put away, almost hidden away. In a drawer or under a bed. Or tucked into a bookshelf and never turned to again. Or even stuffed into a cardboard box of childhood things and stored in the attic.

In its English translation, I see Anne's name hiding in the title itself: *Anne*-xe.

*

Akerman's grandmother was an artist, with 'golden hands'.[6] Like Anne's, Sidonie's journal was also short-lived. Sidonie began writing it in 1920 when she was only thirteen years old. Her last entry was written in 1922. In *To Walk Next to One's Shoelaces in an Empty Fridge*, Chantal uses the diary as a transitional object, a plaything. Sidonie's diary serves as a mouthpiece to speak the unspeakable: Chantal's mother Nelly's own experiences at Auschwitz.

> Nelly moved to Brussels 'in 1938 from a small town near Krakow. But strangely enough, in 1942 or 1943, she was taken back to Auschwitz, which was just 30 miles from where she grew up . . . Her parents died there and a lot of her family.'[7]

In *To Walk Next to One's Shoelaces in an Empty Fridge*, Sidonie's journal is barely seen and is instead heard through the voice of Nelly struggling to remember her Polish (her mother tongue) and to translate it into French on the spot for her daughter Chantal. We watch the split-screen video in black and white, going in and out of focus, like taking your reading glasses on and off. The mother and daughter look often into each other's eyes. Chantal asks her mother to read the first page. The video, like *Jeanne Dielman*, is a filmic love letter to her mother.

> NELLY: 'All right, let's see if I can see with your glasses. Otherwise, mine are on the table there . . . Look her [Sidonie's] handwriting is already lovely . . . Look how small the writing is. Do you see? And look at this . . . The writing that I admire, so tiny . . .'

Sidonie's journal, written with hopeful adolescent suffering between the years 1920 and 1922, begins: 'I am woman!' Chantal and Nelly note the exclamation point with pleasure.

*

My father and I found her secret hidden in a plastic cassette.

My mother made the tape on her mother's birthday. My mother's mother was born in Tennessee.

My mother's mother was thirteen and pregnant on her wedding day.

My mother's childhood memories are American Southern Gothic disturbing: twisted as the uncontrollable kudzu vines that ate the South, overtaking everything in its path. The Jack-in-the-Beanstalk vine. The strangling vine.

My mother's memories are the stuff of Flannery O'Connor.

Desperate Dorothy Allison poverty: 'shoes that went to paper in the rain.'[8]

> DOROTHY: Today is February 4th, 1992. It is my mother's birthday, and if she were alive today, she would be eighty-two years old. But she's not alive. And I'm alive. So, what should I talk about?[9]

Unlike Anne and unlike Sidonie, and, in turn, Nelly, my mother was barely touched by the war. Her wounding (incomparable) was cotton-picking familial. Her abuse was smothered in grey gravy. Her peril included eating greens boiled and drained four times, in hopes of getting the poison out.

Rickets.

Lice.

But like Nelly, whose experiences at Auschwitz greatly affected Akerman's childhood, so my mother's affected mine.

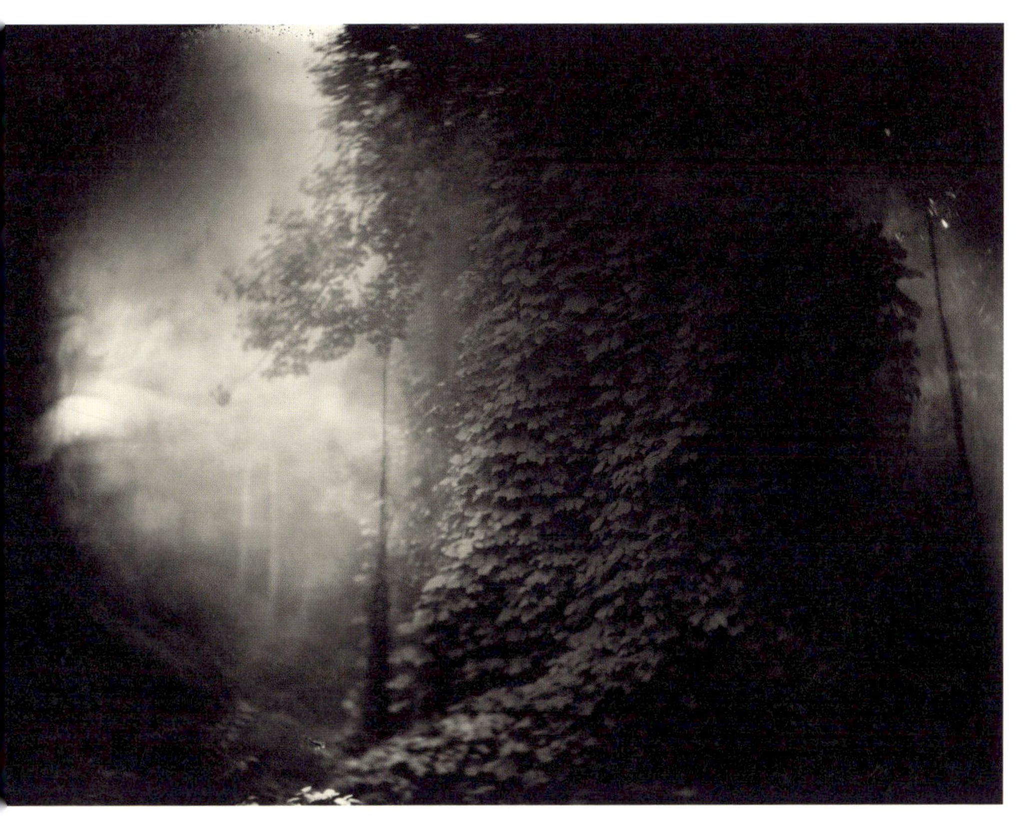

Sally Mann, *Georgia, Untitled (Kudzu)*, 1996, tea-toned gelatin silver print.

In an interview, Akerman explains:

> my mother was totally different from the mothers of my friends. She would never separate from me. In a way, my life belongs to her . . . My mother was so resentful that she did not have a career because after the war she was broken. She remembered her late mother [Sidonie], who had painted and drawn and made couture clothes, and she saw in me a continuation of her.[10]

My mother's fears of separation were based on being left behind, ignored, unseen. She was paranoid – fearing it would happen again.

While Nelly encouraged her daughter to make something of her life, my mother was more like Akerman's father, who wanted her to stay slim and get married. My mother wanted me to be just like her: a problem magnified by the fact that she was not sure who she was.

And unlike Akerman and more like Anne, when I was an adolescent, my mother was a constant irritant to me.

Around my swollen eye, a bruise the size of a girl's heart is blossoming. At first, it was a pale-blue hydrangea. Then purple lilacs. Now a black-pansy, as if printed.

If I am not careful, the bruise will heal, turning to weeping willow branches, whose pale green will be tinged with a hint of the blue that comes with the onset of summer. Then yellow-green moss. Then yellow freesia. Then nothing.[11]

Nothing cannot happen.

The pain and colour of the bruise must remain.

'But now there is hope, and pain is implanted with hope,' writes Marguerite Duras.[12]

Bruises to keep.

But there were and there still are

ANNE: I hope I will be able to confide everything to you [1].

So begins Anne's journal.

Anne's red plaid diary, like a schoolgirl's skirt, which hits just above bruised knees, unfolds the stories of her life in the Secret Annexe. The diary was a gift for her thirteenth birthday: 'I'll begin from the moment I got you, the moment I saw you lying on the table among my other birthday presents' [1].

I have seen her precious diary, with its pages delicately, unashamedly open, in its clear glass box in the Anne Frank House.

A sleeping beauty who keeps the world awake.

'Kitty', as Elie Wiesel lacerates, is not a book: it is 'a wound'.[13]

When reading *The Diary of a Young Girl*, we become Anne. We too, 'long to ride a bike, dance, whistle, look at the world, feel young', believe we are 'free' [153]. We want what Julia Kristeva calls 'adolescent reverie'.[14] We want to be adolescents.

'Kitty is ourselves, the reader.'[15]

I discover pages written with Anne's beloved fountain pen, with its 'thick nib', which had a 'long and interesting fountain-pen life' [145]. The pen was a gift from her grandmother when she was nine. It travelled with her to the annexe when she was thirteen, but met its demise when Anne was fourteen. Falling accidentally into the stove, as in some horrific fairy tale, it burned. 'Not a trace

16. Oct. 1942.
Vrij

Beste Jet,
Als Emmy een krabbel ertusschen door krijgt be
jij ook geen stiefkind, dus hoe gaat het er m
Alweer een beetje van de schrik bekomen
ik hoop van wel. Hier is gelukkig no
alles bij het oude. Ik heb vandaag bijste
gemaakt van de Fransche onregelmatige
werkw. Dat is een precies en vervelend
werkje maar ik wil het graag afmaken
Ik heb nog niets aan Nero gedaan mis
schien Maandavond nog. maar het is Vr
dag dus dat is critiesch. Mama is weer
in een rotbui. We hebben gehoord dat d
familie Hohnke is gaan schuilen, gelu
kig maar. Ik ben nu Körner aan het
lezen, die schrijft erg leuk. Nu tot de
volgende keer Jettie-lief van

Anne Fran

en zo in → een spiegel

Nu kijk ik ← in een kinderwagen

Dik is ← Ook snoezig hé.

Anne.

Hier heb ik zeker naar de harlekijn gekeken.

Anne

18 Oct. 1942
Zondag.

Lieve Marianne, 18 Oct
Zo
gisteren is het
schrijven er weer bi
ingeschoten. Ten eers
omdat ik de lijst v
Franse werkwoorden
afmaken en ten twe
Omdat ik ook nog a
werk had. Ik heb w
2 boeken van Kleim
kregen, De Arcadia. Da
deed over een reis naar

Dit is een foto, zoals ik me zou wensen, altÿd zo te zÿn. Dan had ik nog wel een kans om naar Holywood te komen. Maar tegenwoordig zie ik er jammer genoeg meestal anders uit.

Anne Frank.
10 Oct. 1942
Zondag.

Anne Frank's diary,
where she writes about the fountain pen.

of the gold nib was left. "It must have melted into stone," Father conjectured. I'm left with one consolation, small though it may be: my fountain pen was cremated, just as I would like to be some day' [146].

As a child, Sarah Kofman pinched her father's fountain pen from her mother's purse. Rabbi Bereck Kofman (Sarah's father) was picked up by the Vichy police from their home on rue Ordener on 16 July 1942. The pulsing heart of the fountain pen writes even in brokenness (like Anne herself):

> I took it one day from my mother's purse, where she kept it along with some souvenirs of my father. It is a kind of pen no longer made, the kind you have to fill with ink. I used it all through school. It 'failed' me before I could bring myself to give it up, patched up with Scotch tape; it is right in front of me on my desk and makes me write, write.
>
> Maybe all of my books have been the detours required to bring me to write about 'that'.[16]

Anne's diary ends abruptly on 1 August 1944, her fountain pen vanished: 'if only there were no other people in the world' [334].

But there were and there still are.

A joy that cannot be extinguished

NELLY [reading Sidonie's journal in Polish and translating into French]: I can't tell all my secrets, all my hopes and all my thoughts, in a loud voice. Aloud. I can only suffer in secret my little journal.

CHANTAL: [turning to her mother, looking into her mother's eyes, the eyes that had seen Auschwitz, the eyes that had seen Sidonie]: And this is the only thing you have left?
NELLY: Yes.

And then Chantal shows Nelly that she has written in Sidonie's journal.

CHANTAL: There, it's you who signed it, that's your writing Maman
NELLY: Why did I sign?

Nelly does not remember writing in her mother's journal. In the video, we never see what Nelly wrote.

Then, we watch Nelly's head move gently back and forth as she silently discovers and examines where Chantal has also written in the diary. They laugh quietly together.

In the video, we never learn what Chantal wrote in Sidonie's journal.

Nelly gently takes Chantal's chin in her hand and kisses her daughter. *Smack*. A big laugh out of Nelly – and tears. She wipes her runny nose.

CHANTAL: It's incredible . . .
NELLY: But how did you find it?
CHANTAL: I found it in a drawer. Obviously, I had no idea of what was written in it. I only saw that you had written in it, so I wrote in it too. I must have been about ten years old . . . and a few years later, Sylviane found it and also wrote

in it . . . She must have been seven or eight years old.

NELLY: Yes she wrote something too.

NELLY: So . . . It's wonderful. Treasure it, it's all we have left . . . My little darling [*poupée*], I am so happy I have lived for this day.

In the video, we never see what Sylviane (Chantal's younger sister) wrote in Sidonie's journal.

What Nelly, Chantal and Sylviane all secretly wrote in Sidonie's journal remains a hush-hush secret to the viewers of *To Walk Next to One's Shoelaces in an Empty Fridge*. Their writing in maternal milk is never held up to the light of a warm candle to make the invisible visible. Yet between Nelly and Chantal we witness a joy that cannot be extinguished.

'That's the way I feel – perhaps I am wrong – I've been wrong before.'

DOROTHY: I want to record a message.
I want to record a message.

These are the first two lines of my mother's audio journal. A one-day diary. Her singular repertoire. As an adolescent, I remember her writing a few notes in lined notebooks, like you would use for university. But they are gone. All we have left is her voice: which is a lot.

It is as if I am hearing her voice for the first time. Not only because my mother speaks with such uncharacteristic lucidity, but because I listen to her without seeing her face, without seeing the almost disturbing liquid clarity of her pale aquamarine-blue eyes, coupled with her high forehead and pronounced cheekbones, which figure so prominently in the old-fashioned roundness of her face.

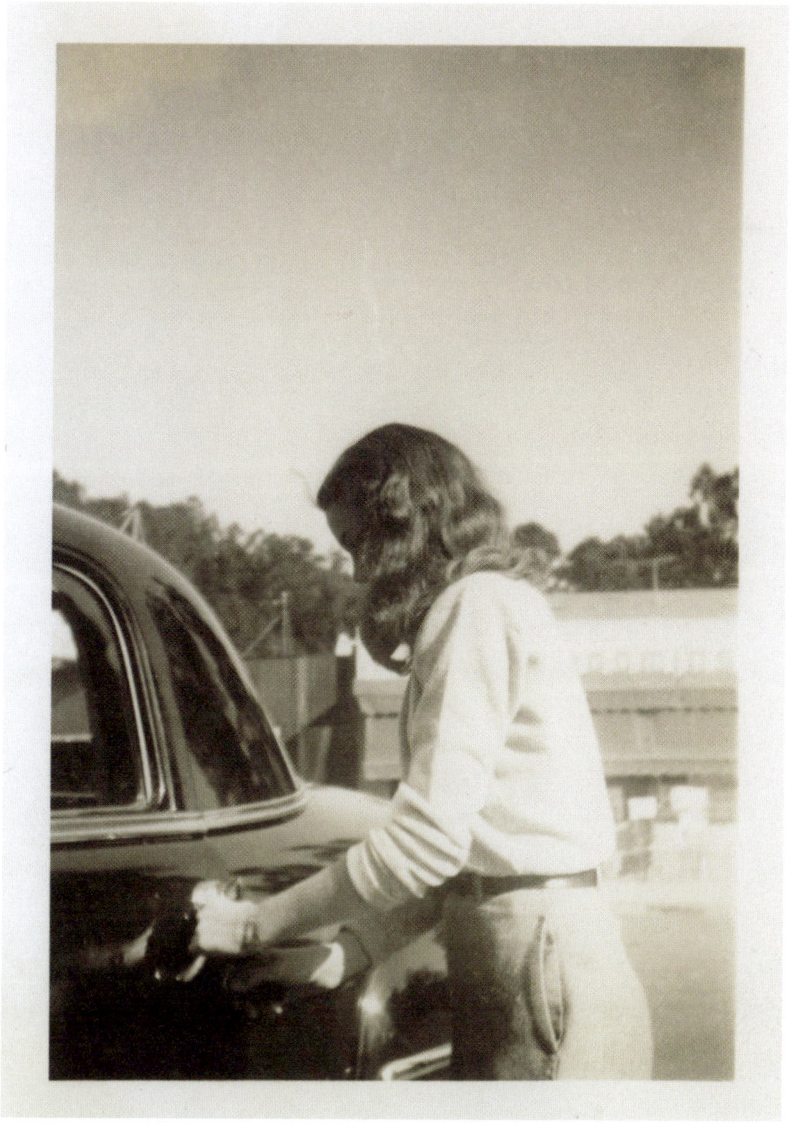

Dorothy Mavor, family snapshot, *c*. 1955.

The voice is hers, but unfamiliar. It is a kind of 'writing aloud'.[17] I admire it.

In her, I hear 'Marcel' Proust hearing his grandmother's voice on the telephone for the first time: 'It is she, it is her voice that is speaking, that is there. But how far away it is!'[18]

That day when my mother spoke into the small microphone of her cassette recorder, I was already 35, living on the other side of the United States, a mother of two children.

I first heard my mother's recorded voice while driving in the car with my father. My mother was dead. The only tape player my father had after her death (now an outdated technology) was in the old Volvo.

We listened as we drove through the blandness of North Carolina suburbia – where housing developments have levelled the ever-abundant pine trees, exposing the red clay soil, like lacerations. We both felt the grain of her voice against the murmuring of what was left of the woodland.

Beginning with the first lines of her nine minutes and two seconds, my mother speaks of wanting – a wanting that cannot be fully expressed. I repeat her desperate repeating lines again.

> DOROTHY: I *want* to record a message. I *want* to record a message.

My mother was a bored middle-class housewife. She went to university for the first time when I was in high school – she graduated, tried her hand at working, including being a teacher – but nothing was fulfilling, nothing stuck.

DOROTHY: Someone should help me . . . somehow I should be able to help myself. But I . . . just go around constantly doing the same thing every day, never changing, never changing anything. Never changing anything.

She is suffering from desire for desire.[19] She is dangerously waiting for nothing.

The last line comes abruptly.

DOROTHY: That's the way I feel – perhaps I am wrong – I've been wrong before.

I experience the 'unbearable' realism of 'film'

The house where Anne was hidden was a place of nesting secrets, like Russian dolls. Anne's journal was an infant house enclosing her most intimate thoughts; her teenage body was a child-house that enclosed the diary; the Secret Annexe was a mother-house (where she lived with her sister and parents, along with Mr and Mrs van Pels and their son Peter, as well as the dentist Fritz Pfeffer) – and Prinsengracht 263 was a father-house that contained them all, all the way back down to Anne's tiny heart. One beating inside the other, inside the other, inside the other, inside the other . . .

ANNE: I hid inside myself, thought of no one but myself and calmly wrote down all my joy, sarcasm and sorrow in my diary [157].

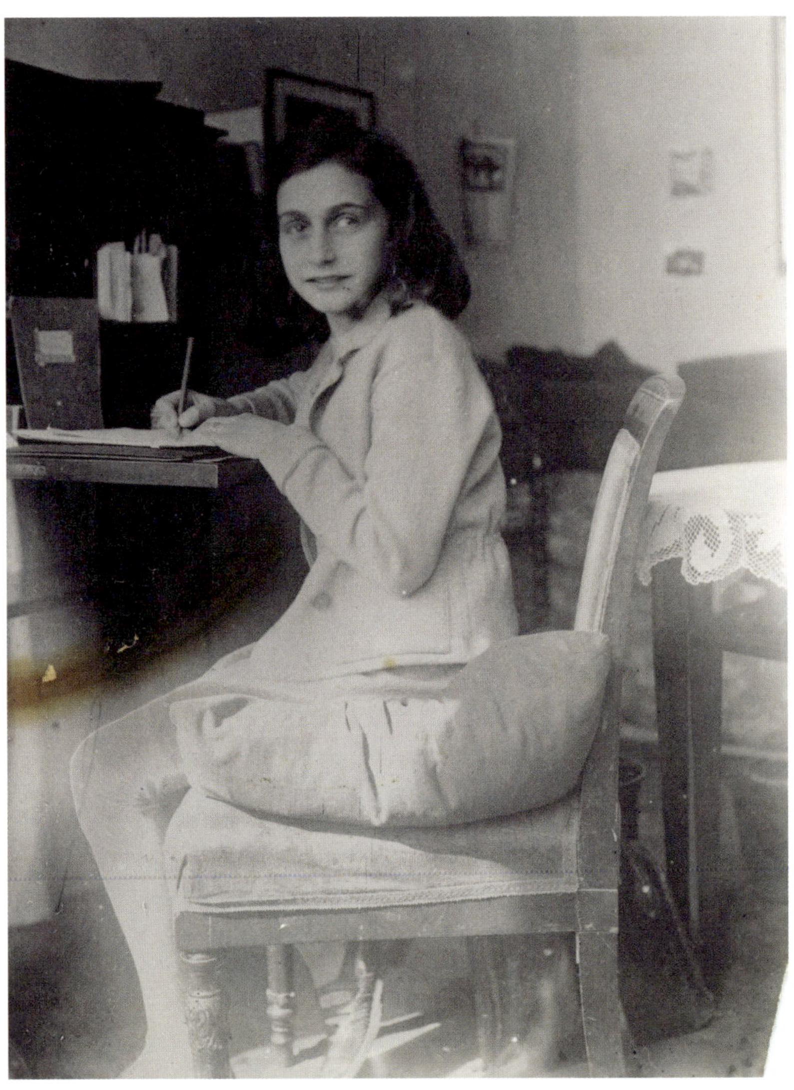

Anne Frank writing at her desk, *c.* 1941,
before the family went into hiding.

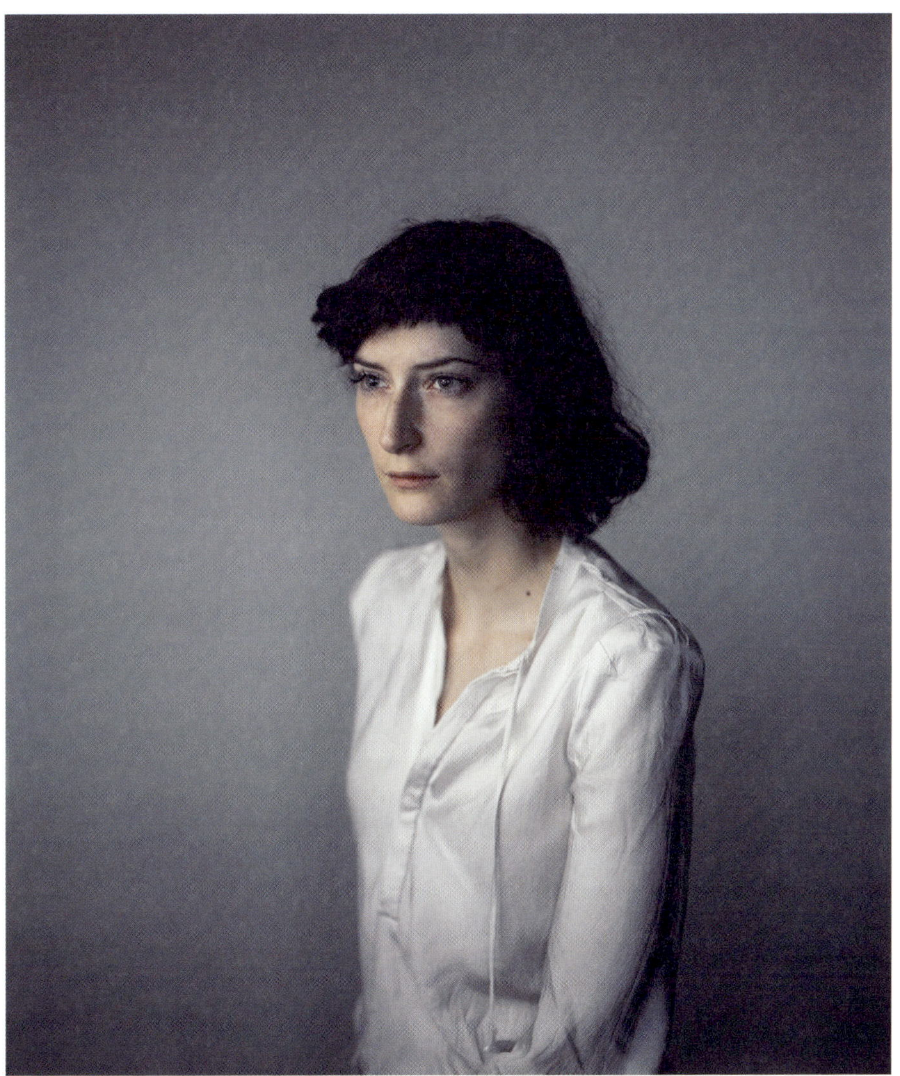

Richard Learoyd, *Jasmijn, to the Light*, 2008, unique Ilfochrome photograph.

The Secret Annexe is where Anne began her period, became a woman.

> ANNE: Whenever I have my period (and that's only been three times), I have the feeling that in spite of all of the pain, discomfort and mess, I'm carrying around a sweet secret. So even though it's a nuisance, in a certain way I'm always looking forward to the time when I'll feel that secret inside me once again [159].

And she wears heels:

> ANNE: Everywhere I go, upstairs or down, they all cast admiring glances at my feet, which are adorned by a pair of exceptionally beautiful (for times like these!) shoes. Miep managed to snap them up for 27.50 guilders. Burgundy-coloured [*wijnrood*] suede and leather with medium-sized heels. I feel as if I'm on stilts, and look even taller than I already am [129].

Her French vocabulary list, recorded when she is age fourteen, ends with the word *le sang* (blood).[20]

Women are 'the walking wounded', wrote Jules Michelet.[21]

The Secret Annexe is now a public place: a museum. Anne Frank Huis. The exterior black paint and the blocked-out glass windows are so shiny black that Prinsengracht 263 appears as a big black mirror; as if the smooth dark canal before it has stood up straight to reach for the sky.

The doors of Prinsengracht 263 are now permanently closed. Today people enter in great throngs after waiting in long queues through an entrance around the corner.

On each side of the original doors are two white placards: one with the house number '263', and the other spelling out 'ANNE FRANK HUIS'. People pose in front of the house to be photographed. Especially young girls, who pull up their short skirts to make them a bit shorter, bend a knee flirtatiously towards the camera, pull their peasant tops further off their shoulders, take off their dark glasses, smile with their freshly lipsticked mouths. *Click*.

When I first witnessed this, I was appalled. But then I remembered how Anne Frank was full of adolescent reverie: had wanted to be a movie star; liked clothes; liked Peter van Pels; liked girls:

> ANNE: Once when I was spending the night at Jacque's, I could no longer restrain my curiosity about her body, which she had always hidden from me and which I'd never seen. I asked her whether, as proof of our friendship, we could touch each other's breasts. Jacque refused. I also had a terrible desire to kiss her, which I did. Every time I see a female nude, such as the Venus in my art history book, I go into ecstasy. Sometimes I find them so exquisite I have to struggle to hold back my tears. If only I had a girlfriend!

Inside Anne Frank House, my eyes take in the adolescent objects of Anne. Like the photograph taken of her sitting at a desk on a plump pillow, writing. The picture was taken not long before she went into hiding. Her eyes meet us, the world. She is

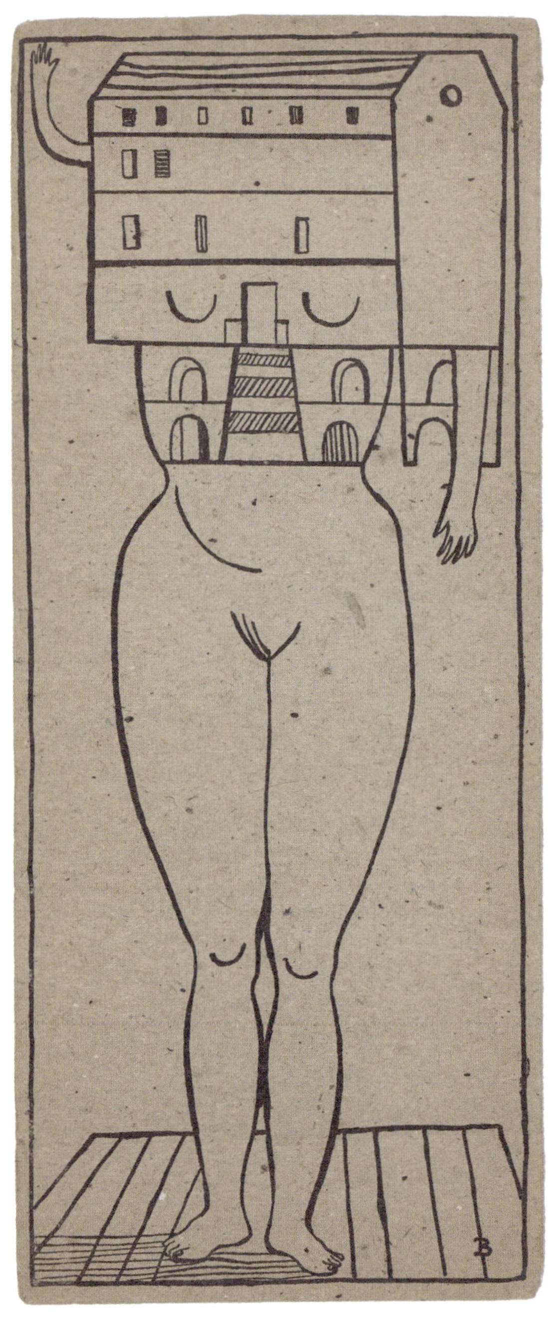

Louise Bourgeois, *Femme-Maison* (Woman House), 1947, composition used for an exhibition brochure for 'Louise Bourgeois: Paintings', Norlyst Gallery, New York, 1947.

adorable. The girl who never grew up. The girl who should have grown up.

When Richard Learoyd made his 2008 portrait *Jasmijn, to the Light*, he was thinking of the iconic image of Anne Frank, featured on book covers throughout the world. He saw the famous face of the little girl who never grew up in Jasmijn and so do I. In his words: 'One of the things I use in my work is the idea of collective photographic memory.'[22]

(There are no more photos of Anne after she went into hiding at age thirteen.)

There is a film of Anne looking out the window on 22 July 1941. Seeing her moving is overwhelmingly moving to me. I experience the 'unbearable' realism of 'film.'[23]

Femme-Maison: Witty and Monstrous

When I was twelve, my parents drove me, their only child – in our white Delta 88 Oldsmobile, with a light blue interior – from our home in Los Gatos, California, down to Las Vegas, through Arizona, New Mexico, Texas and up to Arkansas. I sat bored in the backseat, car sick, sleepy and afraid to be living outside of our usual habits and habitat. We were heading towards the 'Lewis Place' (where my mother grew up), situated in a non-town called 'Cross-Roads.' (There are some dozen places in Arkansas with the barren name of Cross-Roads.) One old timber-clad store, leaning and ready to fall. Two roads that, indeed, crossed. When our shiny, clean Olds reached the Lewis Place at the end of an overgrown unpaved skinny road, we found nothing, save for the brick fireplace and part of the chimney. Next to the ruins was a three-toed box turtle. When it peeked out of its stone habitat I saw its eye, which would have been bright red if it was a male, yellowish-brown or dull brown if it was a female. But I clearly remember it as brilliant yellow.

A turtle's shell grows with its body: a perfect fit. But the turtle's shell never falls off and is attached to its internal bones.

Louise Bourgeois' *Femme-Maison* (1947) is a woman's body attached to a shell (a little house), but rather than poking out her face like a turtle or a snail, she pushes out her legs, arms and genitals while standing very straight. With a touch of malice, Alice and her Wonderland reappear in *Femme-Maison*: witty and monstrous.

I see Chantal looking out its window, in an echo of Anne Frank

'It all came very easily, because of course,
I had seen it all around me.'
CHANTAL AKERMAN, speaking about Jeanne Dielman

Akerman built her mother's femme-maison for us a long time ago: her mother's handsome dollhouse writ large, 'autofictionally', as Jeanne Dielman.[24] In the background of *To Walk Next to One's Shoelaces in an Empty Fridge* we are reassured to see, once again, Nelly's Belgian apartment furnished with cleanliness, orderliness and 'women's time'.[25] And we are comforted to see it, yet again (just as it always was), in Akerman's *No Home Movie* (2015).

Femme-maison translates as 'housewife': the woman who supposedly does nothing.

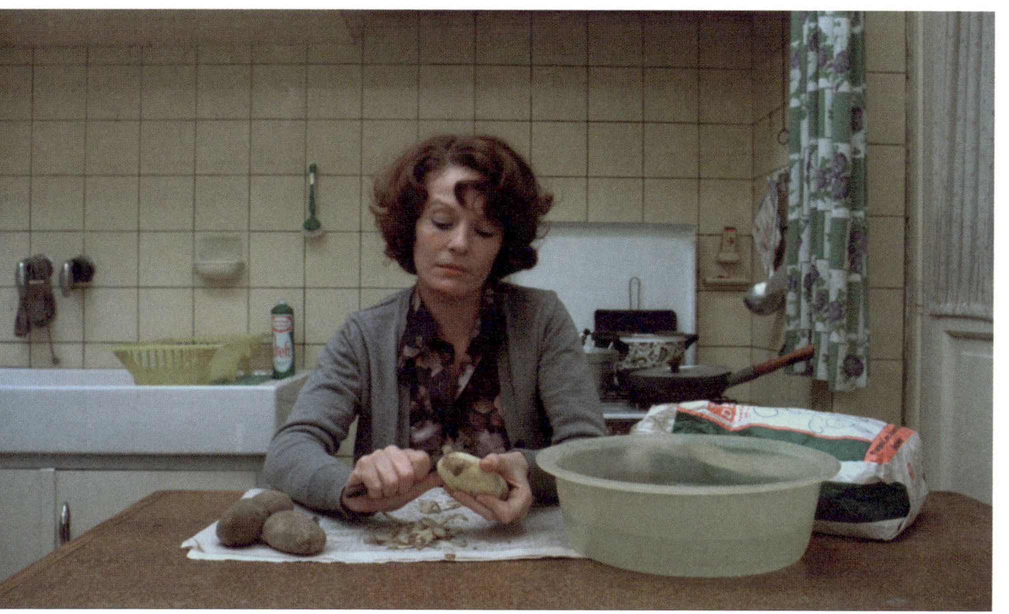

Delphine Seyrig in Chantal Akerman, *Jeanne Dielman, 23, quai du commerce, 1080 Bruxelles* (1975).

NELLY: There's only me . . . the generation that . . . has done nothing.

CHANTAL: I call it the sacrificed generation.

Nelly was sacrificed as a Jew during the war and as a woman-wife-mother in the post-war culture of 1950s middle-class life.

Nelly's domestic life and habits, through the filmic hands and eyes of her daughter, are revealed as a replacement of the strict Jewish life that the family once lived, where 'practically every activity of the day is ritualized.'[26] Both ritual practices (strict housekeeping and strict Judaism) 'bring a sort of peace . . . knowing every moment of every day brings a sort of peace and keeps anxiety at bay.'[27]

Femme-maison also translates as 'woman-house'. In it, I find a 'room of one's own'. I see Chantal looking out its window, in an echo of Anne Frank.

Nowhere toPlay

Somehow, someone managed to give my mother a Shirley Temple doll.

And she decided to bury it. Bury it in the hard Arkansas dirt, full of clay: the colour of dried blood. Death surrounded my mother, including Frankie, her brother who died of typhoid fever. My mother was 'playing' funeral. Burying Shirley in the ground must have taken a great effort.

It rained cats and dogs the night of the burial. It rained so hard that the pitter-patter on the tin roof was not a comfort to the ears. It sounded like bobcats and wolves.

When Shirley was dug up from the earth, that 'devouring mother', she was wrecked.[28]

My mother never learned to play. I have memories of my mother loving me – a caress of my hair – letting me lick the icing bowl from the cake that she made for my birthday – sewing me a dress with a green velvet ribbon along its Jane Austen bodice that tied in a bow in the back below my shoulder blades – taking me shopping for a new doll. But I have no memories of my mother playing dolls with me, imagining with me, even reading to me. My father was my imaginative playmate who played board games with me nearly every night, read *Alice's Adventures in Wonderland* with me . . . My mother, I now understand, was depressed.

She never learned how to make a Winnicottian transitional object to cope with being alone. No blanket with satin trim to rub when no one was there. No song of one's own. No soft object to become other things. No making of something out of nothing. No magic. No play. As Winnicott teaches us, play enables the child to thrive and is the first entry into spiritual life, creative life. When we feel that we have lost our selves, transitional objects – which are not necessarily material – bring joy. We need to make transitional objects as babies *and* throughout our lives.

My mother never learned to be a child. She never really became adolescent or a woman. Robbed of being a little girl, there was nowhere to *become*. Nowhere to play.

'I want to do something creative, something that would, would make me really feel good.'

CHANTAL: Maman . . .

'Maman' is the first word of *To Walk Next to One's Shoelaces in an Empty Fridge*. And then the pretend play begins. Chantal wants to make something together with her mother (the video that we are watching). Bringing out Sidonie's journal, she places it on the table in front of Nelly.

CHANTAL: Say that they find this under an armchair . . . let's say one of the people who come to visit the apartment find this and come to read it in Polish. Can you read it?

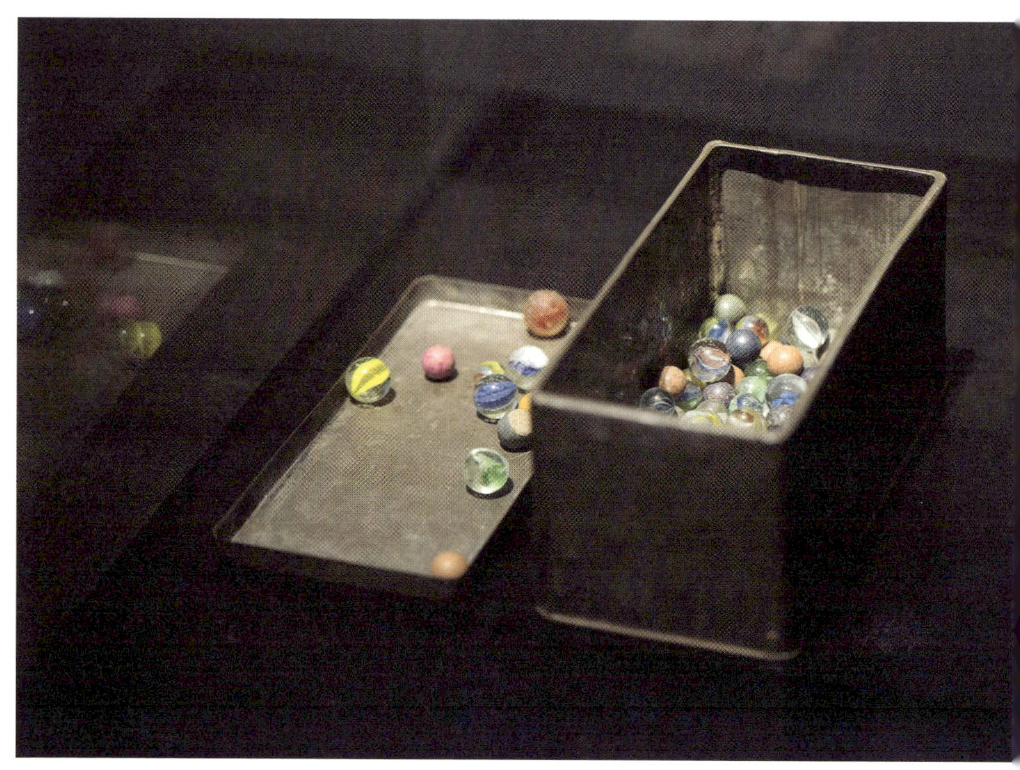

Anne Frank's marbles.

Chantal (always the 'old child') is helping her mother, by playing with her. They are making a film (art) by playing a game. Their 'toy', their transitional object, is Sidonie's journal.

Nelly, broken by Auschwitz, was broken, could not figure out what to do, how to play when she returned from the camps.

> NELLY: I was going to make models and designs and all that . . . I drew very well and now not at all. It's gone . . . I would have liked to do something of my own, that's the only thing I regret . . . You know, I did nothing . . . I was shattered, I was broken, I couldn't do it anymore.

Like my mother, broken by her childhood, who could not figure out what to do, how to play.

> DOROTHY: I keep saying I'm going to do this. I'm going to do that. I don't do anything! . . . I don't know how to get an interest for myself . . . I just feel like I want to do something creative, something that would, would make me really feel good.

Elle puts the marble in her mouth

Before going into hiding on 6 July 1942, Anne gave away her tin of marbles – her childishness roundness. The round marbles are warm with the start of summer. Anne's marbles hold all the hope of her return to a life outside of the Secret Annexe.

Life is round. It just is.[29] The pregnant belly. The bird's nest. The earth. And in all this roundness is hope.

In Alain Resnais and Marguerite Duras' *Hiroshima mon amour* (1959), a child's marble rolls through the metal bars of the small door that leads down stone stairs into the underground cavern, which serves as a household cellar. This is where *Elle* (She), the unnamed Frenchwoman of the film, was held captive by her family for sleeping with a German soldier during the Occupation. *Elle* is a prisoner in her own home. The marble bounces down the stairs, 'warm' with 'summer'.[30] The marble's heat is a metaphor, full of paradox, indicating the end of the war and the horrific temperatures at the epicentre of the nuclear bomb soon to be dropped on Hiroshima. *Elle* puts the marble in her mouth.

'I'm doing fine, except I've got no appetite'

Ernst Bloch writes that 'hunger is the basic energy of hope.'[31]

The title of *To Walk Next to One's Shoelaces in an Empty Fridge* refers to the fact that Akerman never tied her shoelaces and that the fridge in her home growing up was always empty, because she was being pushed to eat all the time. As Akerman explains:

> When I was a child, she [my mother] complained that I was anorexic so they sent me to places to get me to eat. When I look at pictures of myself, I was just a normal-looking child. It was her fantasy. Because she was starving for such a long time, she wanted to push me to eat. I wanted to eat for her, to give her pleasure, but I became anxious about it.[32]
> NELLY: [After being freed from the camps, the Americans took us] to a hospital at Borna and we were cared for there.

It was lucky I tell you, lucky because some people started to eat anything, everything they found, and they died . . . they died after . . . after all this suffering . . . they died after . . . at the Liberation.

CHANTAL: From eating too much?

NELLY: They couldn't eat . . . you couldn't eat with nothing in your stomach. So, where we were – they fed us by the teaspoon, very gently.

When Robert Antelme returned to Marguerite Duras' house for the first time after his horrific internment by the Nazis, the starving man stared at the cherry 'clafoutis sitting on a console table'.[33] And he asked for some. At the time Antelme weighed about 83 pounds – 'skin, bones, heart, liver, intestines, brains, lungs, everything' – to eat would be to die.[34] He could not eat, but he had to eat. The doctor said that the fact that Robert wanted to eat cherry clafoutis was a sign of 'a little hope', but that he could only eat gruel by tea-spoons.[35] As Duras writes: 'But one teaspoon of gruel choked him, he would cling to our hands, sucking air, and fall back onto his bed. Yet he'd swallow it.'[36]

After seventeen days, his fever dropped – he had bowel movements that smelled inhuman – 'and one morning – "I'm hungry," he said.'[37] And he began to eat everything. 'As soon as he'd eaten and his hunger could feed on itself, it [the hunger] became gigantic and frightening.'[38]

'As a teenager, I ate voraciously,' claims Akerman.[39]

Underneath the bed in her childhood home, my mother had collected and hidden three precious chocolate bars: contained in a box, like her Shirley Temple doll. They were too dear to eat.

Then one day, my adolescent mother pulled them out of their hiding place and gorged herself on all three, all at once, as fast she could, ridding herself of all that desire under her bed.

ANNE: I'm doing fine, except I've got no appetite [141].

To play

I cannot revive Anne, Sidonie, Nelly, Chantal, Dorothy.

But to write history is to breathe into the dead – to push onto their stony hearts – to hope.

George Frederic Watts has painted Hope with 'golden hands', sitting on the round earth: a huge beautiful golden marble. She is blindfolded. Contained. Dreaming. The strings on her lyre are all broken. Save for one.

That's for you . . . to play.

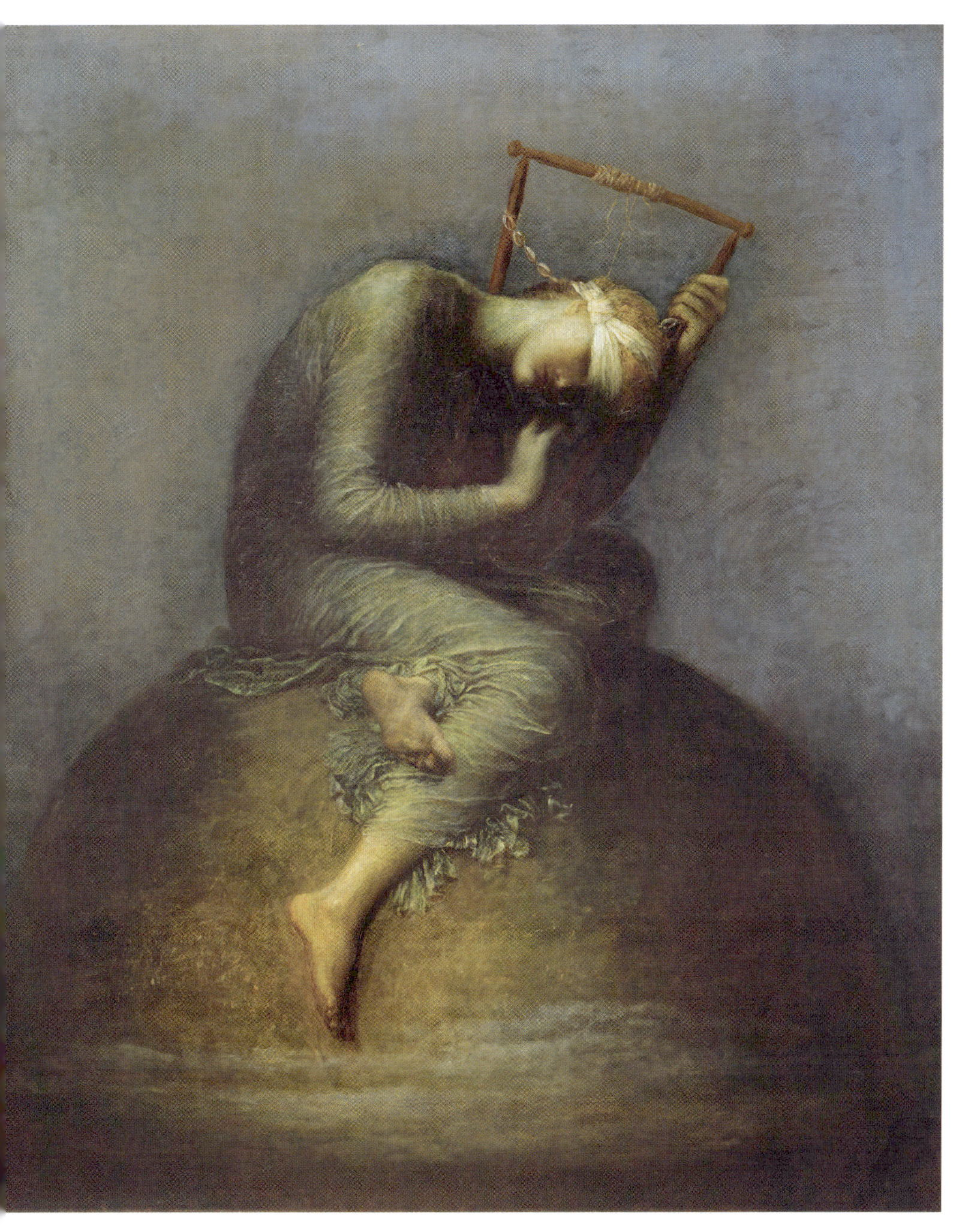

George Frederic Watts, *Hope*, 1886,
oil on canvas.

POSTSCRIPTUM

Written After: Moeder, Maman, Mom *or,* I sang so hard I almost exploded

As Chantal Akerman writes of her grandmother's adolescent diary:

> of my grandmother there remains her young girl's notebook. My mother gave it to me. She said, it will protect you. She gave it to me when I was in need of being protected and she felt powerless. She gave it to me instead of talking. She gave it to me, that's the point. It's been mine since 1984, I think. In fact everything changed in 1984. I sang so hard I exploded. Since then I explode from time to time.[1]

I now reluctantly offer you the precious words of Nelly, Chantal and Sylviane that each tenderly inscribed upon the pages of Sidonie's journal. I say 'reluctant', because of the power that the unrevealed inscriptions hold in *To Walk Next to One's Shoelaces in an Empty Fridge*. They remain in hiding. Like the Winter Garden Photograph, so prominent, but never shown in Roland Barthes' *Camera Lucida*.

In any case, these pages are already out there in the world, if a bit hard to find. I think it is best for you to have it here.

I can only hope that 'Chantal' might agree.

These are the words that Nelly wrote in Sidonie's journal in 1945:

> *This is the diary of my poor mother who disappeared so early, at the age of 40. I will never forget her young girl's life, and I will always think of her as the best mother who ever lived. I am sorry that I did not love her more and love her better than I loved her. She was so good and so understanding that she will remain in my heart always, singular and unique, and no one will ever replace her for me. My dear little mother, <u>protect</u> me.*
>
> *Nelly*

These are the words Chantal wrote in 1960, when she was around ten years old, in response to her mother's 1945 inscription:

> *Dear Mama,*
> *You can't imagine how I felt reading what you wrote in those few lines. I hope you feel <u>protected</u> and loved by all and that you are happy.*
>
> *Chantal*

These are the words that Chantal's younger sister Sylviane wrote around 1963, in answer to her older sister's 1960 message:

> *Dear Mama,*
> *I also felt something in my heart reading what you had written. No one can replace you dear Mama, I would have loved to know your beloved mother. Your daughter who loves you so much.*
>
> *Sylviane*[2]

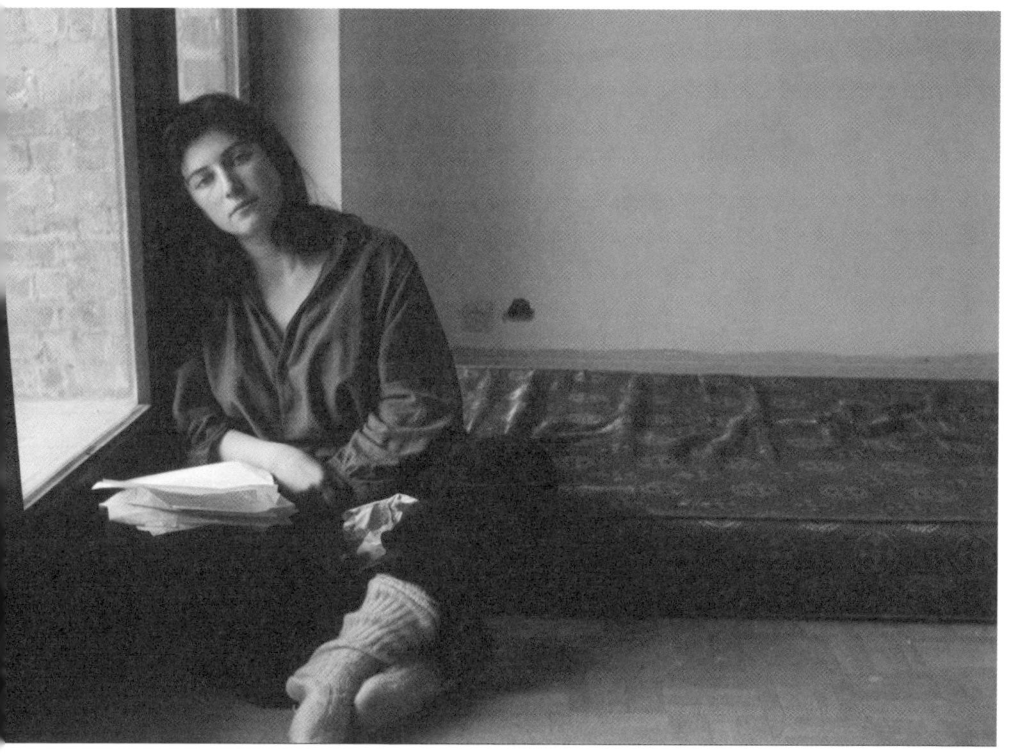

Chantal Akerman in her film *Je tu il elle* (1974).

CHAPTER THREE

Sally Mann's Scarred Tree

Tête-à-Tête with Proust's 'Three Trees'

Allow me to speak of cake, before I get to the trees.

Near the start of *Swann's Way*, the first volume of Marcel Proust's *In Search of Lost Time*, 'Marcel' has his famous chance meeting with a bit of madeleine dipped in lime tisane.[1] This is the novel's first embodiment of 'involuntary memory'. Marcel had not tasted madeleine dipped in lime tisane since he was a child.

> My mother, seeing that I was cold, offered me some tea, a thing I did not ordinarily take. I declined at first, and then, for no particular reason, changed my mind. She sent for one of those squat, plump little cakes called 'petites madeleines', which look as though they had been moulded in the fluted valve of a scallop shell . . . I raised to my lips a spoonful of the cake. No sooner had the warm liquid mixed with the crumbs touched my palate than a shiver ran through me and I stopped, intent on the extraordinary thing that was happening to me. An exquisite pleasure had invaded my senses . . . this new sensation having had the effect which love has, of filling me with a precious essence; or rather

> this essence was not in me, it *was* me. I had ceased to feel mediocre, contingent, mortal . . . And suddenly the memory revealed itself.[2]

The memory is of childhood Easter holidays spent with Aunt Léonie in Combray, outside of Paris. The old grey house – all the flowers in the garden – M. Swann's Parc – the water lilies on the Vivonne – the whole of Combray sprang into being from Marcel's 'cup of tea'.[3]

The encounter is serendipitous. Marcel did not ordinarily take tea – at first, he (even) declined the refreshment. Yet the morsel of madeleine soaked in a warm teaspoon of tea will turn out to hold the key of 'Art' itself – what Marcel would like his readers to experience in reading his *Search*: a novel about writing a novel. The rest of the book is a search for Art – a sensation of bliss, of love, of ceasing to feel immortal – prompted by involuntary memory.

In the second volume of the *Search*, entitled *Within a Budding Grove*, Marcel encounters another one of the multiple involuntary memories that punctuate the *Search*: the sighting of the 'three trees'. Gilles Deleuze maintains that this is the most profound of all of the involuntary memories taken up in the *Search*, because its source remains incomplete. It is ours to take to make meaning from.

More on Marcel's 'three trees' to follow, but first let me tell you how I fell for a tree: a scarred tree that lives in Mississippi.

To you

'I tell you. I fell in love with a tree. I couldn't not.'[4] It spoke to me and I started falling. I fell for a tree.

I happened upon my tree in a photograph taken by Sally Mann in 1998. It is a tea-toned gelatine silver print, made like photographs of the nineteenth century from a glass-plate negative coated in wet collodion: *Deep South, Untitled (Scarred Tree)*. It is a large photograph (38 × 48 inches).

Its bark is scarred with a slash that marks its wound as mouth.

A botched attempt to cut it down.

A grimace of refusal.

The roots of my tree sink their great claws into the ground, like the majestic toes of an aged, but still heroic, regal lion.

A wire fence with wooden posts blurs its way behind my tree. On this fence hangs an unknowable small dark mass, like a tiny dress: it beckons me with its littleness.

A vagueness made of trees resides behind the blurred fence.

I think I see a swing hanging from a branch, just peeking its way into the left frame of the photograph. But I may never know. Nevertheless, I hear the creak of the strong unseen branch that holds the swing – that waits for the child to come.

The child that I once was emerges from me. Takes a turn. Holds her head down and stretches her legs out – strong and straight – to go higher.

I hear the squeaking song of the metal swing, which hung from a chain, in the lonely backyard of our yellow house on Milligan Drive in San Jose, California.

Recalling this memory makes my stomach jump.

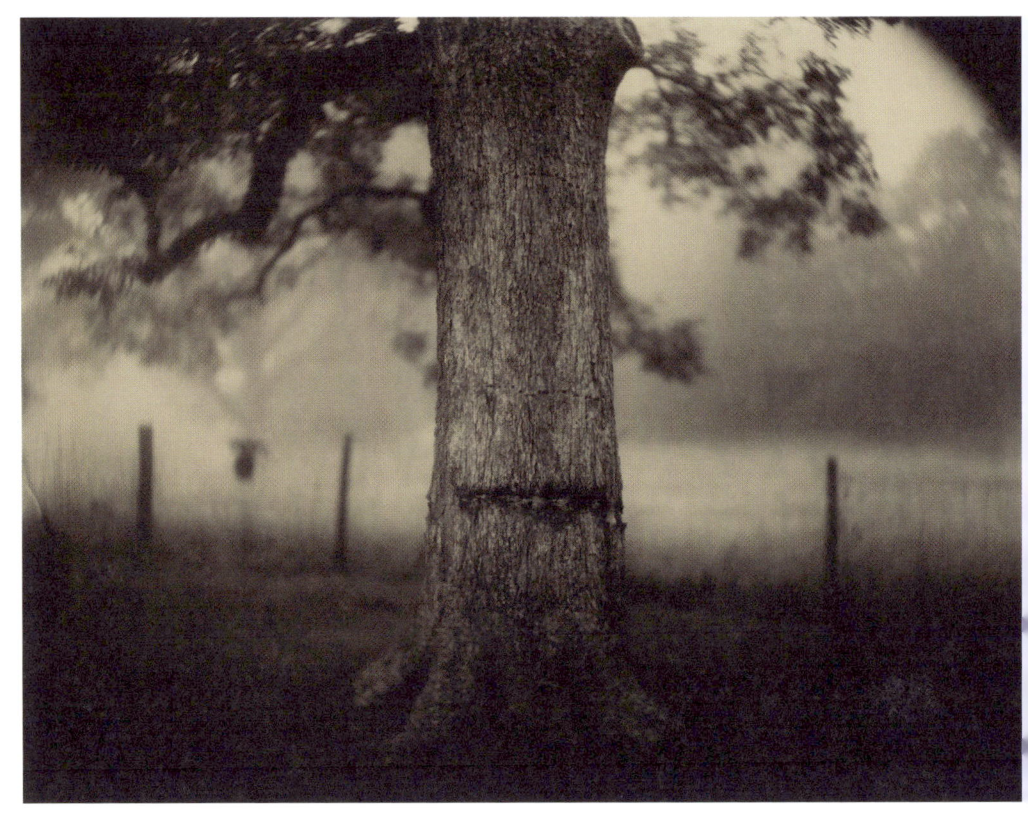

Sally Mann, *Deep South, Untitled (Scarred Tree)*, 1998, tea-toned gelatin silver print.

The colour of Mann's *Scarred Tree* audibly breathes the hushed warm-coolness of morning fog: silvery brown, creamy yellow-grey and almost grey-brown black.

Mother Land Mist.[5]

Mother Land Missed.

In 1997 Mann received training for the very complicated and tricky wet-collodion process. Mann describes using the syrupy solution of nitrocellulose in ether and alcohol as a 'cranky process' fraught with difficulties, including those inherent in using potentially explosive materials.[6] As Mann learned the ceremonial steps of the process, she discovered that it was the happy accidents, the flaws, that she liked. This significantly altered her art.[7]

She had always been open to serendipity, eagerly embracing the fleeting glance of a teenage girl, the unexpected gestures of her children, the light flares, uneven focus and spatial ambiguity cause by her camera and lenses. But now chance became a determining element in the creation of her art.[8]

The *Scarred Tree* lives among a forest-album of other trees from Mann's pictures of Georgia, Mississippi and Virginia, in her series entitled *Deep South*. The *Scarred Tree* is my chosen one. The one that chose me. The one that speaks to me. The one that murmurs sweet (nothings) to me.

'To be listening', writes Jean-Luc Nancy, 'is to be inclined toward the opening of meaning, hence to a slash, a cut in un-sensed indifference.'[9] I am inclined towards the slash of my tree.

The *Scarred Tree* spoke to Mann before it murmured to me. And undoubtedly to others as it grew from a sapling into its current large, gnarled, scarred self. As Mann wrote to me:

> I'm keen to hear what you say about the trees. They've always had plenty to say to me and any chance I get to be in the same sentence with Proust, I'm happy.
>
> The scarred tree materialized from a heavy morning fog in the backyard of an old antebellum home where I was staying down in Mississippi. I had come in late the night before, too dark to see anything, and was blearily squinting out the window as it materialized, like Wallace Stevens's jar on a hill in Tennessee, commandingly. Imagine my dawning realization of its massive power, metaphorically and physically, and my mad scramble to find shoes, socks, camera, film, tripod, etc., etc. . . . as though it was going anywhere!? I didn't want to lose the fog and didn't.[10]

When trees speak, they murmur. To murmur is to talk in a hushed and indistinct voice.

To Mann, who listens to the sound of the trees, this Mississippi tree murmured the words of Wallace Stevens's poem: 'Anecdote of the Jar' (1919).

> I placed a jar in Tennessee,
> And round it was, upon a hill.
> It made the slovenly wilderness
> Surround that hill.
>
> The wilderness rose up to it,
> And sprawled around, no longer wild.
> The jar was round upon the ground
> And tall and of a port in air.

It took dominion everywhere.
The jar was gray and bare.
It did not give of bird or bush,
Like nothing else in Tennessee.

Mann took the photograph of the tree with her mammoth, wooden, bellowed, antique-view camera. The glass plate negatives were grand in their 8 × 10-inch scale. She wore the photographer's black hood over her head (like a makeshift tent – like a child's blanket over a table to make a place to hide and be); the camera stood tall on its anthropomorphic tripod legs. And Mann saw the tree on the ground glass, upside down and backwards. As if it were the nineteenth century.

The ground glass of Mann's field camera is Wallace Stevens's glass jar, which magically gifted Mann with the upside-down and backwards scarred tree.

Likewise, Mann's camera lens – a 'good ruined lens' that is game for happy accidents – is also Stevens's glass jar.[11] Mann doesn't buy a 'tack-sharp lens that would take the perfect picture, that's in focus from end to end'.[12] She uses a broken antique lens. As she explains:

> A lens is made up of several different pieces of glass, which are supposed to stay glued in the right relationship to each other. But my most prized lens has just one of the pieces of glass askew, so when the light comes in it, it's refulgent. It just bounces all around and does this great sort of luminescent thing on the glass.[13]

Before a scarred tree, she placed a jar in Mississippi.

Before a scarred tree, she placed a camera in Mississippi.

Before a scarred tree, she placed a camera, not in Tennessee, but in Mississippi.

Her camera is a Winnicottian magical transitional object, between reality and imagination.

The jar is turned into a tree.

Its hollow shape, both a wordless mouth and an ear ready to listen.[14]

Taking on language, the tree grew roots and branches.

It found its way into a book.

A codex.

Latin *caudex*, for 'trunk of a tree'.

And it is here that the *Scarred Tree* rustles and murmurs something familiar, yet unknown, to me.

To you.

The tree, the table, the floor

'Mur-mur' replays the same meaningless sound to make a word. It is a remarking. It is an echo of the 'fort-da' game theorized by Sigmund Freud and played by his toddler grandson Ernst. By symbolically turning his ma-ma into a toy – wooden spool on a string, a yo-yo, a wooden doll, a ma-ma-Pinocchio – Ernst imaginatively threw his jou-jou, his ma-ma, back and forth, imaginatively controlling her comings and goings. When the wooden spool was away from him, he pretended that she was gone (saying 'fort'). When the spool was near him, he pretended that she was here (saying 'da').

Such transitional objects, according to Winnicott, which include transitional phenomena (like immaterial sounds), are our first creative thoughts (before traditional language) – when we begin to make something out of nothing. Like focusing on how a piece of string can be used to connect things – or how a song of noises (not words) resonates when we are alone in the cot. Transitional objects give way to independence, so that we can handle the absence of the mother (or father or caregiver). Through our own imagination, we can be weaned physically and emotionally.

For Winnicott, transitional objects are a part of a lifetime of making, which enables creative living . . . spiritual life. Art.

Barthes, who was well-schooled in Winnicottian phenomena,[15] published his short essay 'Toys', in his famed *Mythologies* (1957), as an unabashed nostalgic nod that favours wooden objects over plastic. The latter tend to be objects that prepare the child to accept the 'universe of adult functions'.[16] Like a doctor's medical kit, motorcycles, gas stations, cash registers, telephones. 'The toy here delivers the catalog of everything the grown-up does not find surprising: war, bureaucracy, ugliness, Martians'.[17] Conversely, a set of wooden blocks can become many things. They are meant to be built, knocked down, rebuilt without end. Wooden blocks do not envision the child as 'nothing but a littler man, a homunculus who must be furnished with objects his own size'.[18] And wood does not break. Toys made of plastic – 'products of chemistry not nature . . . crude and hygienic' – eliminate pleasure, gentleness, human touch.[19] Today, plastics have grown to such proportions that we now have invisible microplastics in our oceans and rivers, on the highest peaks of the Alps and the Himalayas, in the air we breathe, in the food we eat, in our very blood.[20]

> A wooden toy neither vibrates nor grates, it makes a sound that is both muffled and distinct: wood is a familiar and poetic substance which allows the child a continuity of contact with the tree, the table, the floor.[21]

'Makes the picture timeless'

As Barthes explains in *Camera Lucida*, cameras were once made of wood and were a kind of cabinetry. Mann has an antique camera made of wood.

> She shoots with antique view cameras from the early 1900s, the kind where you duck under a cloth to take the picture. They have hulking wooden frames, accordion-like bellows and long brass lenses held together with tape, with mold growing inside. She says she loves that. It softens the light, makes the pictures timeless.[22]

'My tree's first words to me were a mur-mur'

The *Oxford English Dictionary* defines timbre as a 'sonorous quality of any instrument or of a voice'. For a tree, its timbre is a sonorous murmur. The leaves of my tree rustle with language; it has a particular timbre. Trees as the source of timber produce the timbre of the violin, the cello, the viola da gamba.

Homonyms give me joy. They open up what Nancy calls 'listening to the beyond-meaning'.[23] *Jouissance* (total joy or ecstasy) sounds like *j'ouïs sens* (I heard meaning). A prime example of this 'listening to the beyond meaning'.[24]

Ernst took pleasure in making wood into *sense*, into yo-yo, into meaning, a further development of his likely first utterance of 'ma-ma'.[25]

First words, like the rhythmic maternal ma-ma and the rhythmic paternal da-da and the rhythmic grandparental na-na and pa-pa, are words that grow out of reduplicating sounds.

They are doubles. Like a mother and child. Like the referent and its photograph.

For Sally Mann there was Gee-Gee. Gee-Gee took care of Sally as a child and of Sally Mann's children. Gee-Gee's full name was Virginia Franklin Carter. *Reduplicatively*, she was affectionately called Gee-Gee. Mann claims her as 'an African American woman

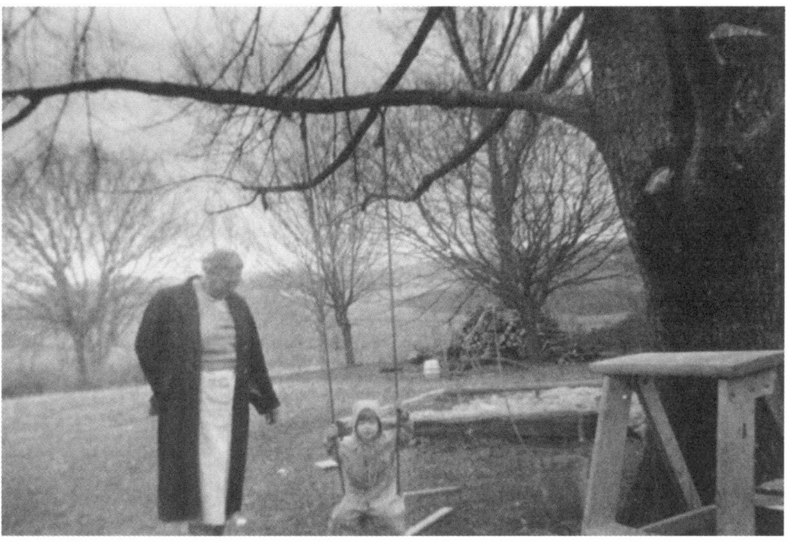

Mann family snapshot, Virginia Carter, Sally Mann and tree, *c.* 1955.

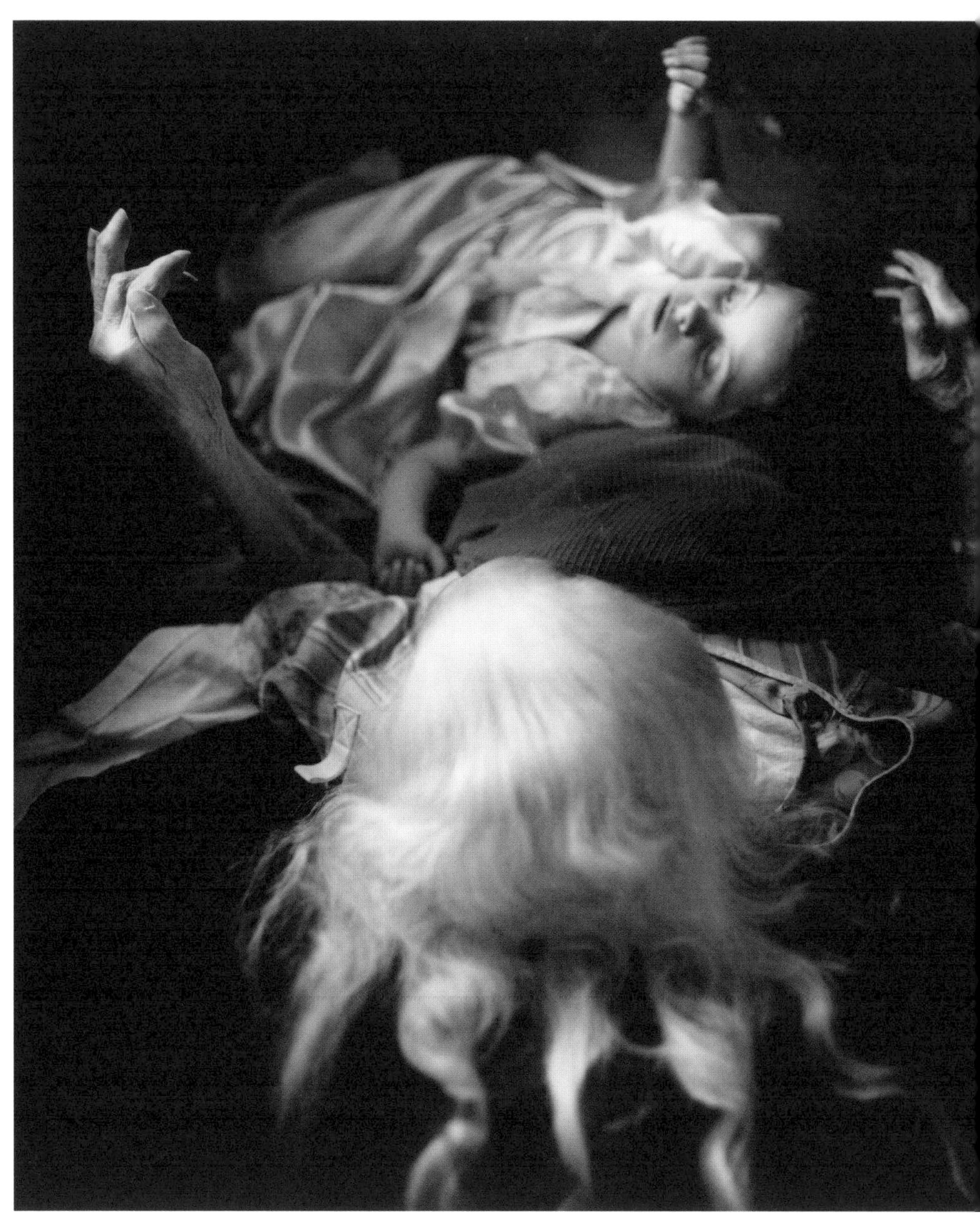

Sally Mann, *The Two Virginias #4*, 1991,
gelatin silver print.

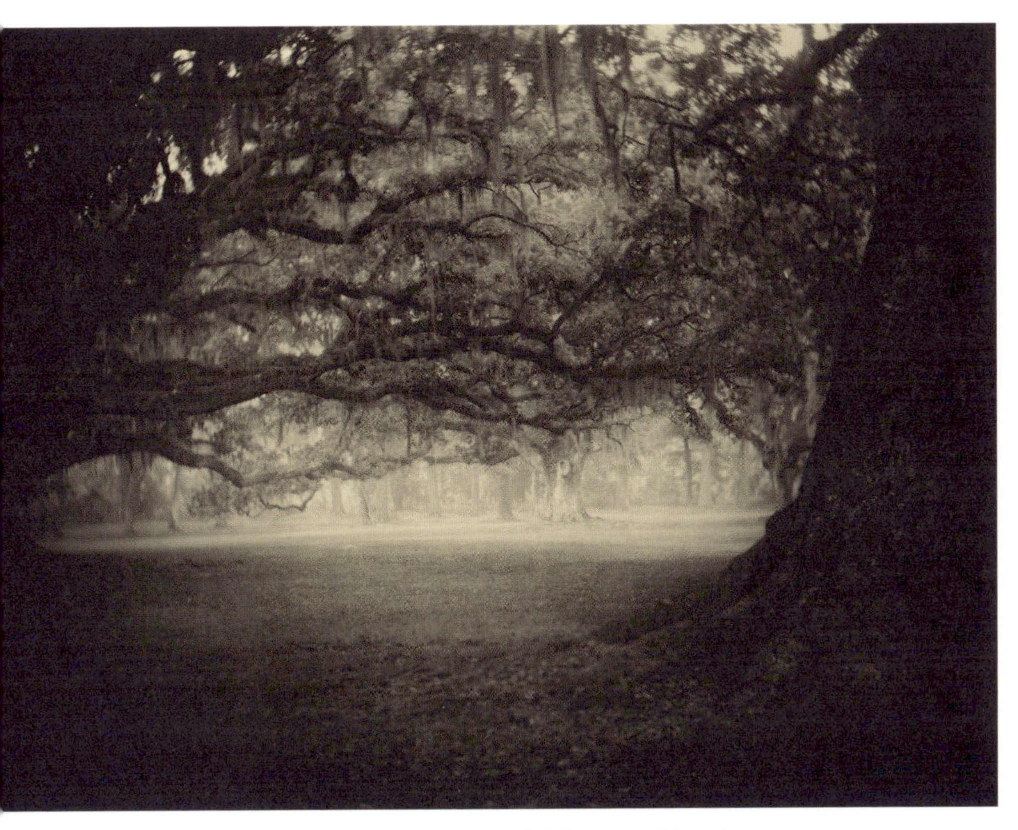

Sally Mann, *Deep South, Untitled (Fontainebleau)*, 1998, tea-toned gelatin silver print.

whom I loved past speech'.[26] In a family snapshot, Sally sits in a tree swing, while Gee-Gee pushes and guards. Far in the background of the picture, large, neatly cut branches are piled up like aggrandized toy Lincoln Logs, waiting to be built into a log cabin. A stepladder in the foreground reaches up to, perhaps, a recent amputation of a tree limb.

Mann, who lives on a farm in Virginia, who grew up in Virginia, named her daughter Virginia after Gee-Gee. Sally Mann's Virginias, one Virginia in another Virginia in another Virginia, endlessly repeat themselves. Mann's 'Virginia' is *en abyme*, like Russian nesting dolls made of wood.

'A photograph is', as Craig Owens has rightly argued, 'en abyme', not only like an image in the mirror, but also like our first reduplicative babbles – ma-ma, pa-pa – as can be deduced from the work of Roman Jakobson and later Rosalind Krauss.[27] Photographs and first words reproduce 'in miniature the structure of the text [image, sound] in its entirety'.[28]

In *The Two Virginias No. 4*, 1991, little Virginia, her mouth but a tender leaf, is but a sapling of old and twisted Virginia, whose hands have become the gnarled branches of a tree. The hair of old Virginia is Spanish moss, like the kind that drips from Mann's photograph of trees in Georgia or the kind that drips from my laurel oak trees in Florida, where I now live. The Gee-Gee at play here is not a reduplicative structure in its entirety, but is akin to Owen's *en abyme*, as experienced through the damaged, Old South lenses of Mann.

Speech is an acoustic instrument, a song of wood, to cope with 'here-gone' mama or whomever or whatever you are longing for.

My tree's first words to me were a mur-mur.

'Razor-sliced to accomodate her pain'

Living in the South often means slipping out of temporal joint, a peculiar phenomenon that I find nourishes and wounds. To identify a person as a Southerner suggests not only that her history is inescapable and formative but that it is also impossibly present. Southerners live uneasily at the nexus between myth and reality.

SALLY MANN, *Deep South*

The American South is a myth.

A tree is a myth.

Stories of the American South come from the mouth of my tree.

As Barthes writes in 'Myth Today':

> Every object in the world can pass from closed, silent existence to an oral state. Open to appropriation by society, for there is no law, whether natural or not, which forbids talking about things. A tree is a tree. Yes, of course. But a tree as expressed by Minou Drouet is no longer quite a tree.[29]

Likewise, a tree, expressed, exposed, by Sally Mann is 'no longer quite a tree'.

Mann's *Scarred Tree* is a tree that is dipped, wounded, nourished by the Old South, including the life of Gee-Gee: the granddaughter of a former slave and the daughter of a woman most likely raped by a white man.[30]

The mur-mur, the glug-glug of a scarred tree, a ma-ma 'past speech'.

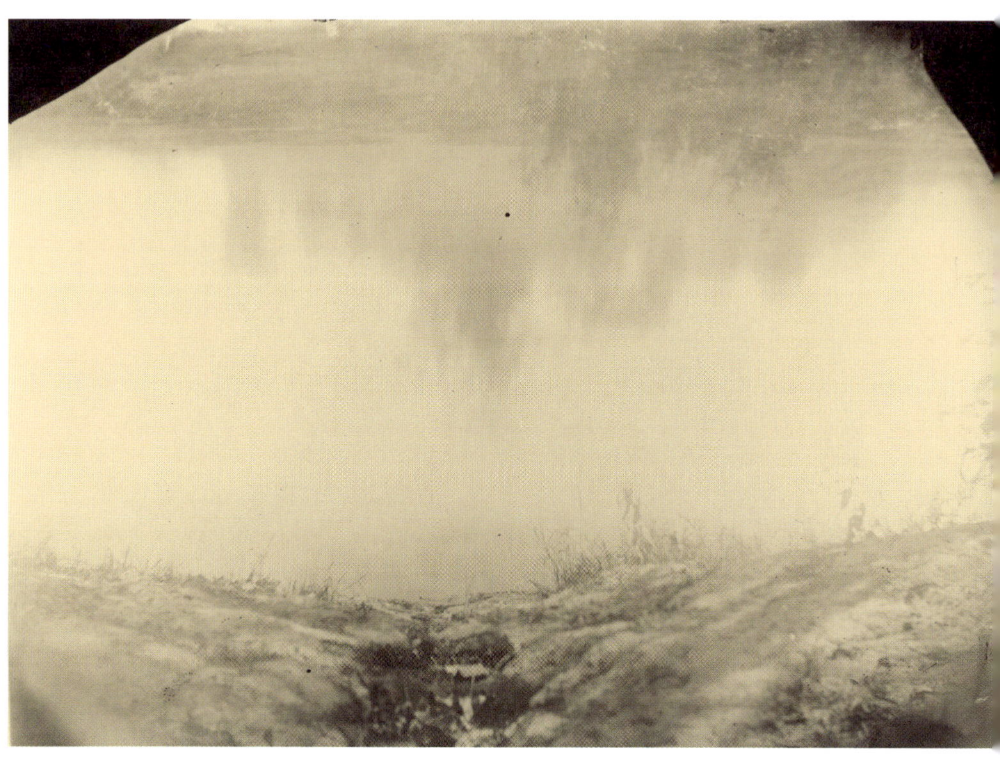

Sally Mann, *Deep South, Untitled (Emmett Till River Bank)*, 1998, tea-toned gelatin silver print.

Gee-Gee's hands were bigger than those of Mann's father, 'with nails glowing like pale beacons at the tip of her fingers'.[31] She wore Mann's mother's old stockings 'whose gossamer runs enlarged into ladder-rungs as the day went on, the seams wobbling crazily' – and Mann's father's discarded shoes, 'razor-sliced to accommodate the corns on her toes'.[32]

Murmuring in the mouth of the scarred tree are Gee-Gee's hand-me-down stockings, with runs enlarging and seams wobbling crazily, and her hand-me-down shoes, razor-sliced to accommodate her pain.

'Nothing but the bark'

In a different context from that of slavery in America, but one also punctured by its own unspeakable violence, Jean Cayrol explains the impossibility of describing life in a Nazi concentration camp: 'We can show you nothing but the bark.'[33]

Mann shows us nothing but the bark.

'You will never know'

Some wounds never heal. Never scar. Mann's photograph, entitled *Emmett Till River Bank* (1998), is a picture of what remains, the wet remains, of the young Black boy who was kidnapped, tortured and lynched in 1955. Here, Mann's trees are gone, save for their reflections in muddy water. Like the trees of Atget, they stand as witnesses of a crime that has already happened, as well as crimes to come.[34]

As Mann writes of Emmett Till and her picture:

> It will come as no surprise to anyone who knows my family pictures that the name Emmett means a great deal to me. The murder of Emmett Till has haunted me since I first became aware of it, early in my life. Till's murder, which shocked most of sentient America, took place in 1954; I was three years old at the time. [This photograph] . . . was taken one serenely mote-floating, balmy, yellowish October afternoon at the very spot from which the fourteen-year-old Emmett, naked and necklaced with a cotton-gin fan, was heaved into the Tallahatchie River. I had help bush-whacking a path to the now abandoned boat lock from the daughter of the former owner of the land. Pushing through the undergrowth at the river's edge, we stared in amazement at the humdrum, back-washy feeling of the place. How could a place so fraught with historical pain appear to be so *ordinary?* Turning from the river, we came across a piece of lined paper with schoolgirl handwriting inexplicably nailed on a tree, there in the middle of nowhere, admonishing us to Confess Your Sins to Jesus![35]

The trees blurrily mirrored in the backwashy water of the no-place where Emmett Till was killed cause me to reflect. When I look closely, I think they are gesturing to me to try to understand. Mann's trees can be heard as an echo of that moment in Proust's *Search* when Marcel (while travelling in a carriage) is struck by the image of the three trees. The trees are strange and poignant to him. The trees are familiar, giving rise to bodily feelings, yet they are untied to a knowable specific memory. They are pleasurable, but full of something sad. The only thing certain is the fact that they are trying to tell him something. Marcel sees them as 'waving their despairing arms, seeming to say [to him]: What you fail to learn from us today, you will never know.'[36] Likewise, these trees in the backwashy water of the no-place where Emmett Till was killed are also 'waving their despairing arms, seeming to say to me: What you fail to learn from us today, you will never know.'[37]

'Collodion was used in surgery during the civil war to bind wounds'

The word 'tree' is not made out of wood, with leafy branches. Words, unlike trees, have no indigenous origin. The word 'tree' has nothing to do with trees. Words, as everyone knows, are arbitrarily connected to the things they represent. This commonsense concept was deeply rooted as semiotic theory long ago in Ferdinand Saussure's 1916 *Course in General Linguistics*. He famously used a tree to make his point.

An exception to the arbitrary nature of language might be onomatopoeia. As Saussure admits, words like *glug-glug*, *bow-wow*, *tick-tock*, *sizzle*, *bang* and perhaps even *murmur* seem to 'prove that the choice of the signifier is not always arbitrary'.[38] Yet Saussure will go on to say that onomatopoeia is nevertheless cultural and arbitrary. He notes the often very different sounds ascribed to the cry of the animal in different cultures. Furthermore, by tracing the Latin roots to words whose meaning and sound are the same thing, he shows that onomatopoetic words, even though their sense seems to make sense, are simply cases of cultural, 'fortuitous . . . phonetic evolution.'[39]

Mann's *Scarred Tree* with its whipped-tar mouth barely open speaks to me with its own 'fortuitous . . . phonetic evolution'.

Its mouth is a wound, which strangely nourishes.

Its mouth is a slit that has given birth.

Its mouth is a large swollen eye bitten by a wasp.

Its mouth is a cut stitched up.

Its mouth makes sounds stronger than vision. As Nancy writes:

> The sonorous, on the other hand, outweighs form. It does not dissolve it, but rather enlarges it; it gives it an amplitude, a density, and a vibration or an undulation whose outline never does anything but approach. The visual persists until its disappearance; the sonorous appears and fades away into permanence.[40]

I hear the rolling smell of Sally Mann's dark room (womb) on wheels that she takes out into the trees. It is a heady bouquet of collodion, ether, grain alcohol, silver nitrate, ferrous sulphate, plain sodium thiosulphate.[41]

And I hear the voice of Mann. She murmurs metaphoric things to me. I listen. I hear that 'collodion was used in surgery during the Civil war to bind wounds.'[42]

A kind of *jouissance* to this arbitrariness times three

Jean-Paul Sartre's masterpiece, *Nausea* (1938), is a philosophical novel on the non-meaning of the world. The narrator, Antoine Roquentin, lives in a place called Bouville (which translates as Mudtown). Life is random and meaningless, to the point of nausea. While Roquentin will never reach a resolved understanding of life, he is able to accept the arbitrary nature of reality through his encounter with the absurdity of a chestnut tree in a municipal park. Focusing on the strange root of a chestnut tree ('soft, monstrous masses, in disorder – naked, with a frightening, obscene nakedness'), Roquentin proclaims: 'I had found the key to Existence, the key to my Nausea, to my own life. In fact, all that I was able to grasp afterwards comes down to this fundamental absurdity.'[43]

Sartre, like Saussure, used a tree to make his point. Likewise, you could say that Sartre's chestnut tree was a recasting of Proust's 'three trees', from the point of existentialism. Although Sartre, the anti-Proust, would deny it.

Saussure asks us to reflect on the arbitrariness of language. Sartre asks us to reflect on the arbitrariness of existence. Proust focuses on the impossibility of a fully recovered meaning as, in fact, the most meaningful kind of meaning. All three (Proust, Saussure, Sartre) focus on the arbitrary meaning of the tree. There is a certain joy, a kind of *jouissance*, to this arbitrariness times three.

'One day devoured'

My mother grew up dirt poor during the Depression in Arkansas picking cotton that the family could not sell.

My mother's family had a little money when 'Daddy' had a job at a lumber mill. He made some money from the trees. Yet, as we all know, and as my mother would later tell me over and over: 'Money does not grow on trees.'

In this book's first chapter, I wrote of my mother playing funeral as a kid. So many people were always dying, children too. One time, taking the play so far as to make a small cardboard coffin for her one and only doll: a Shirley Temple doll.

Let me tell you a little more.

Shirley was the kind of doll that can open and shut her eyes. You could hear the tiny clicking of the lids when Shirley was turned from upright to lying down.

You already know that while playing funeral, my mother buried her doll. And that while Shirley was underground – my mother forgot about her and it rained, as it does nearly every afternoon in an Arkansas summer. The rain, so loud and relentless on the family's tin roof, eventually triggered my mother's memory with its pounding drops, like the beat of a calligraphic poem by Apollinaire, *metred* in black raindrop letters, but it was too late. The doll, once cherished, was ruined before my mother could *unbury* her. She found her remains in the sludge under the big oak tree. Shirley was covered in the tobacco spit of the deluge. Her eyes pasted shut with gunk. It was so trivial, yet too big for words. My mother loved that doll 'past speech'. But I have yet to tell you that Shirley's grave site was under the Lewis Place's big oak tree. My mother's tree.

When I visited the Lewis Place, the house was devoured, save the remains of the fireplace. But the big oak tree, *she* was there. I have no photographs of the tree. I cannot reproduce my mother's tree. It only exists for me. Even if I could, it, it would be nothing for you but an indifferent tree, one of the thousand manifestations of the 'ordinary'. In it, for you, no wound.[44]

A tree is a tree. Yes, of course. But my mother's tree that grows on the Lewis Place is no longer quite a tree.

The big oak was my mother's other mother. The good mother with time on her hands. The good mother who was not a child herself. The good mother whose branches, like arms, held young Dorothy in order to escape her vengeful sisters, her spiteful brother, her terrible uncles.

Perhaps my mother wanted her mother-tree to hide Shirley underground – protect her with big strong nutritive roots.

Perhaps I was wrong when I claimed that 'my mother never learned to play.'

In the shadow of my mother's tree, I hear the word for mother in German.

Mutter.

As Mann writes:

> When the land subsumes the dead, they become the rich body of earth, the dark matter of creation. As I walk the field of this farm, beneath my feet shift the bones of incalculable bodies; death is the sculptor of the ravishing landscape, the terrible mother, the damp creator of life, by whom we are one day devoured.[45]

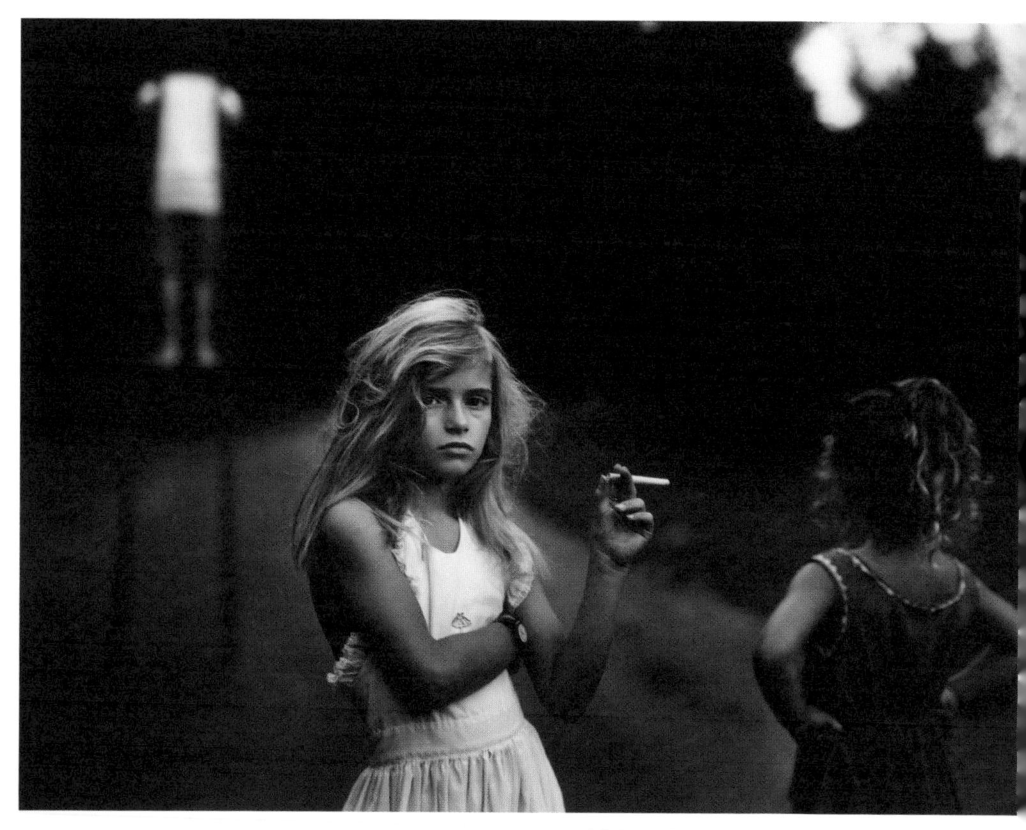

Sally Mann, *Candy Cigarette*, 1989, gelatin silver print.

'What, am I hearing light?'

By the end of Proust's long, long *In Search of Lost Time* (indeed, in the final paragraph), Marcel has grown old and is terrified by the thought that he has become so stretched as to be ready to fall: 'as though men spend their lives perched upon living stilts which never cease to grow until sometimes they become taller than church steeples, making it in the end both difficult and perilous for them to walk and raising them to an eminence from which they suddenly fall.'[46]

Stilts, of course, are made of wood.

In a 1989 photograph, Mann has pictured daughter Jessie with a candy cigarette. Behind Jessie is a dark mass of trees. Because of Jessie's studied mimicry of older women who smoke, she looks as if she truly is holding a real cigarette.

Jessie's ruffled dress is backless: it is 'little girl' and woman at once. It is her sartorial ego,[47] just as the cigarette is child's candy and adult vice at once. Little sister Virginia stands with her back towards us, her arms akimbo. But it is the child on the wooden stilts who interests me: Mann's son Emmett. He represents something to me, akin to Barthesian 'punctum', but unlocatable. Like Proust's image of the three trees, the boy on stilts overwhelms me with 'profound happiness' tinged in sadness.[48] He conceals something that I cannot 'grasp, as when an object is placed out of reach, so that our fingers, stretched out at arm's length, can only touch for a moment its outer surface, without managing to take hold of anything.'[49] Yet I can hear the sonorous wooden clump-clump with every step taken, as the boy on tall, tall wooden legs inches his way away from us, until . . .

I look at this nearly transparent figure, stretching into the future, and I cry out: 'What, am I hearing light?'[50]

Trees felled as humans

I was in a hurricane in North Carolina; her name was Fran. Huddled inside my home with too much glass, I heard the pound of rain, the train of winds that did not stop all night long, the blast of lightning. I also heard the sound of giant trees – falling trees – the fall of trees that had been there long before my lifetime – before the life of my mother, before the life of my grandmother, before the Civil War, before the end of slavery. The trees were being ripped out from the wet ground by their very roots. They were plucked from earth – as if they were meaningless lives, as if they were soldiers in America's civil war, as if they were Africans axed from their own land and piled on a wooden ship, using cruel mathematical precision to fill the boat as full as possible.

Humans as felled trees.

Trees felled as humans.

'Sense opens up in silence'

And the LORD God commanded the man, saying,
Of every tree of the garden thou mayest freely eat:
But of the tree of the knowledge of good and evil,
thou shalt not eat of it: for in the day that thou eatest
thereof thou shalt surely die.

GENESIS 2:9

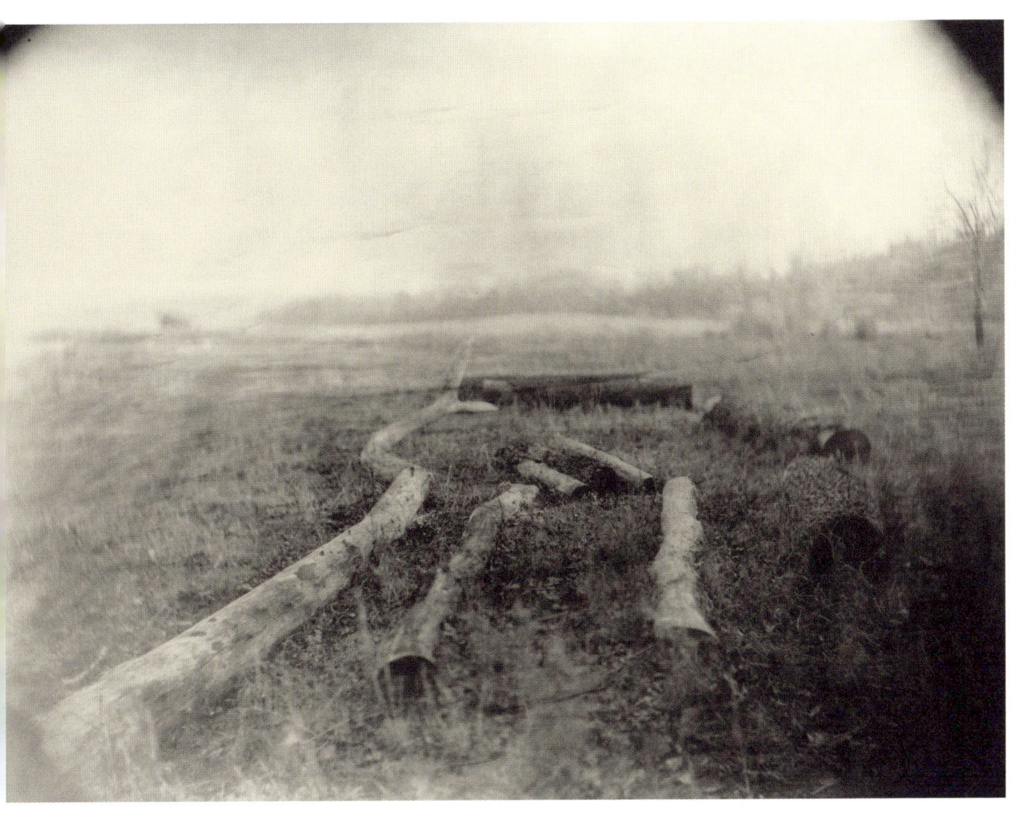

Sally Mann, *Georgia, Untitled (Snake Log)*, 1996, tea-toned gelatin silver print.

A tree is knowledge: that is part of its threat.

Come spring and summer, many of the trees of the south-eastern United States are covered with layers and layers of Adam-and-Eve kudzu aprons, covering up knowledge, their otherwise secret trunks and branches, like genitals to be hidden, as if the poplars and the oaks and the maples had discovered shame in their wisdom.[51] Eve ate the fruit from the Tree of Knowledge and kudzu ate the South, a Jack-and-the-Beanstalk foot-a-night vine, or, in top condition, the mile-a-minute vine.

A tree is a library full of leaves of knowledge. That is why Charles Rennie Mackintosh constructed his gorgeous, gloomy, wild but ordered library at the Glasgow School of Art, like a Gaelic forest. Timbered with dark wood, it was (until it recently burned down for a second time) a woodland supported by wooden columns that retained their treeness as they stood erect and reached towards the lights above (like stars peeking through a dark canopy of trees) towards an opening of meaning. It was a silent place, like most libraries. As Nancy writes: 'Sense opens up in silence.'[52]

'Nature is a haunted house – but art – a house that tries to be haunted'

Proust lovers, myself included, are hooked on the madeleine as the most poignant sign of *In Search of Lost Time*. But the little scallop-shell-shaped cake, the sign of involuntary memory, which magically returned Marcel to the time of his childhood through a rush of forgotten memories, really did not work that well. The experience was over after a nibble. Marcel could not make it happen again. Gilles Deleuze has argued that Proust's presentation 'cites the madeleine as a case of failure'.[53]

Apart from the madeleine, the three trees are forever unattached to any roots. Thereby, according to Deleuze, the three trees are the most profound of Marcel's involuntary memories.

Proust's three trees are roaming, wandering, roving, peripatetic, nomadic and dark; so much so that Marcel even begins to doubt their very materiality:

> Were they merely an image freshly extracted from a dream of the night before, but already so worn, so faded that it seemed to me to come from somewhere far more distant? Or had I indeed never seen them before . . .?[54]

Marcel is made dizzy by the three trees. A sense of vertigo. Where had he seen this madeleine-imposter before?

The three trees will remain forever obscured, and that is their power. As Marcel acknowledges: 'I was never to know what they had been trying to give me nor where else I had seen them.'[55]

Perhaps the only way to really see the trees is to cover one's eyes, as Marcel does, in order to better understand his vision: 'I put my hand for a moment across my eyes.'[56]

Cover your eyes and listen to the trees.

The three trees are never over. Their meaning is never resolved. Never swallowed. Never finished. They just keep growing. Their *appeal* to us is never-ending.

'Nature is a Haunted House – but Art – a House that tries to be haunted.'[57]

Some tree ring of the past outside of my life

I am an only child. My mother, my father and I: we are three trees. A family tree. My mother gave birth to me in California, far from Arkansas. She had left the South to try to forget that she ever lived there. Then, to the surprise of my parents and friends, I ended up moving to the South to teach at the University of North Carolina. It is the oldest public university in the United States. Many of its original stones were laid by slaves. Soldiers who fought on the wrong side during the Civil War are buried on campus in the Old Chapel Hill Cemetery. My parents eventually came across the country and moved to the South to be with me.

When my mother developed Alzheimer's, she began to hate the sound of the trees.. 'The ears do not have eyelids.'[58]

The murmur of the trees shuddered her with all of the horror and the beauty, all of the horrible beauty of her Southern childhood. As if in a bad dream, she could only live in the past: an unforgettable South. Unspeakables by an uncle. No shoes. Nothing to eat. She stopped speaking to me. She only sang to me: admonishing me to confess my sins to Jesus. I did not know her songs. I had never heard them before. She sang them to me – she sings them to me – from some tree ring of the past outside of my life.

Like the rustle of the wings of the angel of serendipity

I look at my tree. Its scar murmurs the sound of the axe. Again and again, I hear: 'the birthing cry, the birth of the cry – call or complaint, song, rustling of self, until the last *murmur*.'[59]

I look at my tree in the 'almost religious expression' – the 'liquid expression' of wet collodion, seen through Mann's camera lens of uncertainty.[60]

The focused scar is a mouth, an eye, a wound, sound, silence. The soft dark velvet corners at the top of each side are a glimpse of the open curtains, setting the stage for the tree.

Or, the dark sky hovering at the edges of the light of the moon at night.

At the top of a tree we see a limb that has been cut close to the trunk. It reaches out to me.

The tree feels this limb as a phantom limb of pain.

Of joy.

Of relief.

Of peace.

Of me.

When she began working with wet collodion, Mann found herself praying to 'the angel of uncertainty' to bestow on her plates 'essential peculiarities, persuasive consequence, intrigue, drama, and allegory'.[61]

Mann is playing with Marcel's good 'angel of certainty'. After the long course of a waking dream – in which, through 'confused gusts of memory' – Marcel visits a 'series of rooms in which [he] had at one time or another slept', so as to find himself in a changing state of 'uncertainty' as to where he was – the 'good angel of certainty' flies down and makes all the surrounding objects in his current bedroom 'stand still'.[62]

Mann's angel of uncertainty is a game of inversion.

Inversion is a pastime that circles throughout the *Search*. As Barthes notes: 'Inversion – as *form* – invades the entire structure of *La Recherche*.'[63]

I think, specifically, of Marcel and his first boyish crush on the boyish Gilberte-girl, whose refulgent blue eyes are later noted in the book to be strikingly black. One will never know whether the young Jewess's blue eyes were really black or whether Proust was critiquing the antisemitism of the time. Or whether it was a *happy accident*, which takes the readers of the *Search* back to the madeleine first given to Marcel by his Jewish mother.

Like the waving arms of the three trees.

Like the muttering mouth of the scarred tree.

Like the rustle of the wings of the angel of serendipity.

CHAPTER FOUR

Making Poems Out of What Is Not There: The Envelopes of Emily Dickinson and London's Foundling Hospital

> I . . . am small, like the Wren, and my Hair is bold, like the Chestnut Bur
>
> – EMILY DICKINSON

This morning, I woke up to a very still world, save for the notes from the birds.

Looking out from my writing desk – through the wavy old glass of my Victorian house – in my green writing room – the hue of Werner's 'the neck of Eider Drake' – I see Hullard Park – with its rows of mature white cherry trees – all in blossom. The flowers are the colour of Werner's 'breast of the Screech Owl'.[1] The feather-snow-blossoms will soon fall, their short lives over, making drifts of English spring. Scarcely, barely, lilac scent. Then they will blow away. Run away.

'Cakes reign but one day.'[2]

It is a school day. A mother and her young son stop below a cherry tree within my window view while on their way to Seymour

Park Primary School. They peer up at two birds, so high in the branches. Flirting and busying themselves with spring's nest building.

'No ladder needs the bird but skies.'[3]

They, too, hear the notes of the birds.

'"Hope" is the thing with feathers – [4]
'The "Tune is in the Tree –"'[5]

I shift in my chair.

I hear the envelope poems of Emily Dickinson.

I hear the unsung song of the enveloped infants and children of London's Foundling Hospital.

In this chapter Hope does not remain tucked inside the jar or the box, but flies out from the gummed and pinned seals of the envelope.[6]

Extemporaneous poem

Dickinson's envelope poems come as a flock of unnamed birds – darting, skimming, flashing, fluttering, dipping, swooping – between poetry and visual art. Of her 3,507 pieces of work, a sizeable number are written on reused envelopes and envelope scraps, often cut and refolded to produce 'mingled verbal and graphic gifts'.[7] Fifty-two of these envelope poems appear in all of their visual splendour in the book *Emily Dickinson: The Gorgeous Nothings*.[8]

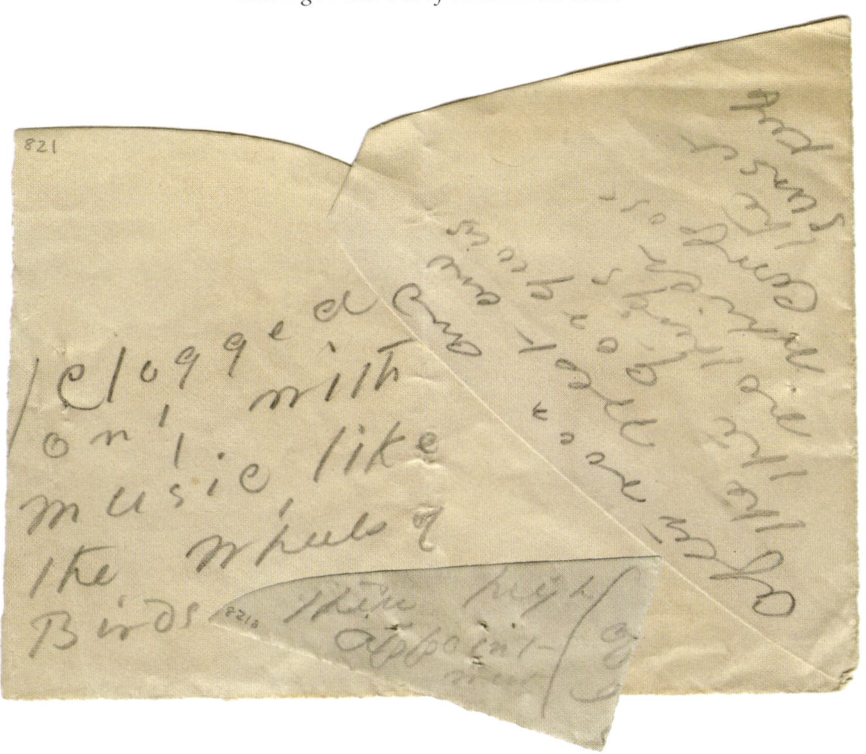

Emily Dickinson, 'Clogged/ only with/ Music, like', *c.* 1885, envelope poem.

In one such gift – a collage made of two envelope fragments – the paper is khaki-milky, the hue of Werner's 'Light Parts of Feathers on the Back of the Snipe'.[9] The words of the poem are written in strong grey with a stubby pencil – in varying hands, perhaps written on different occasions – the colour of Werner's 'Back of Nut-Hatch'.[10] The unfolded, cut and pasted object requires that it be turned like a pinwheel in order to be read.[11]

There are two wings made from one envelope: an extra piece of envelope-seal has been attached as makeshift tail ('their high Appointment of I'), enabling the wings to fly.

Here it is a possible *translation* from visual object to written poem:

Clogged
only with
Music, like
the Wheels of
Birds
Afternoon and
the West and
the gorgeous
nothings
which
compose
the sunset
keep
their high
Appoint
ment
of I

Yet, looking at the envelope fragment and its helpful map (facsimile), there is no indication of beginning or end.[12]

The content is the form.

The form is the content.

Like 'Wheels of Birds'.

Its wings open up 'gorgeous nothings'.

During her lifetime, Dickinson published only ten poems of her 3,507 pieces of work ('1,800 distinct poems within 2,357 poem drafts and at least 1,150 letters and prose fragments'[13]). They were all published anonymously. Publication was, as she put it, as 'foreign to my thought as Firmament to Fin'.[14] Like a

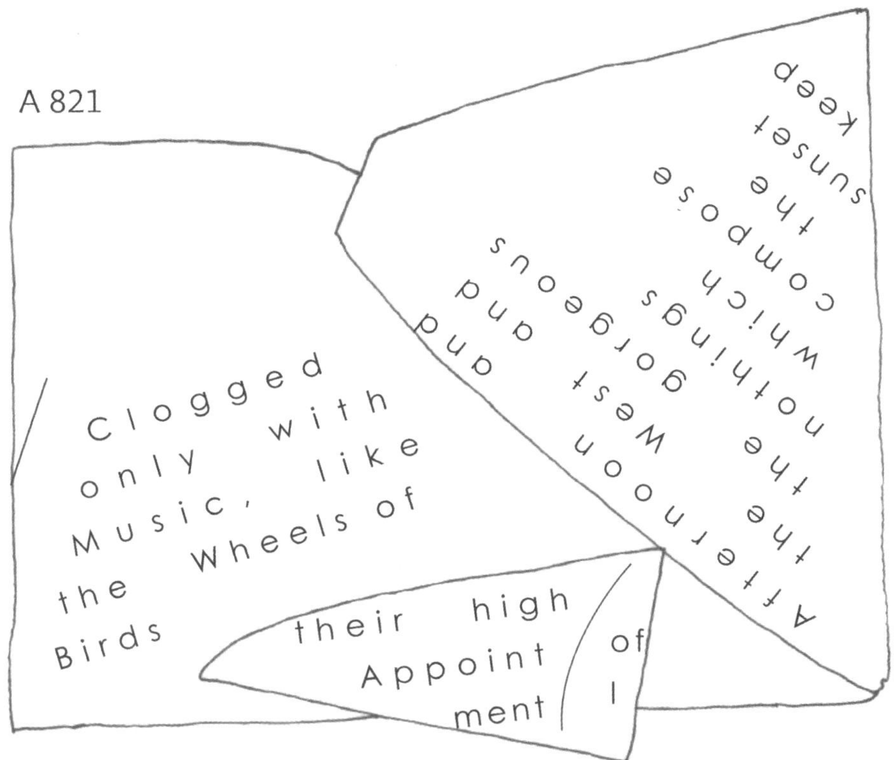

Emily Dickinson, 'Clogged/ only with/ Music, like', *c.* 1885, facsimile.

fish (out of water) in the heavens or sky. 'Not that she intended her poems to go unread – she often sent them to friends, sometimes with other enclosures: dried flowers, a three-cent stamp, a dead cricket.'[15] To her friend Helen Hunt, Dickinson sent a tiny fan 'pathetic in its smallness'.[16] (Dickinson's enveloped tokens make their own poems out of form – like the envelope poems themselves and, as we shall see, like tokens enveloped in billets at London's Foundling Hospital.)

A poem sent to the Bowleses, 'wryly nudging them to write', begins:[17]

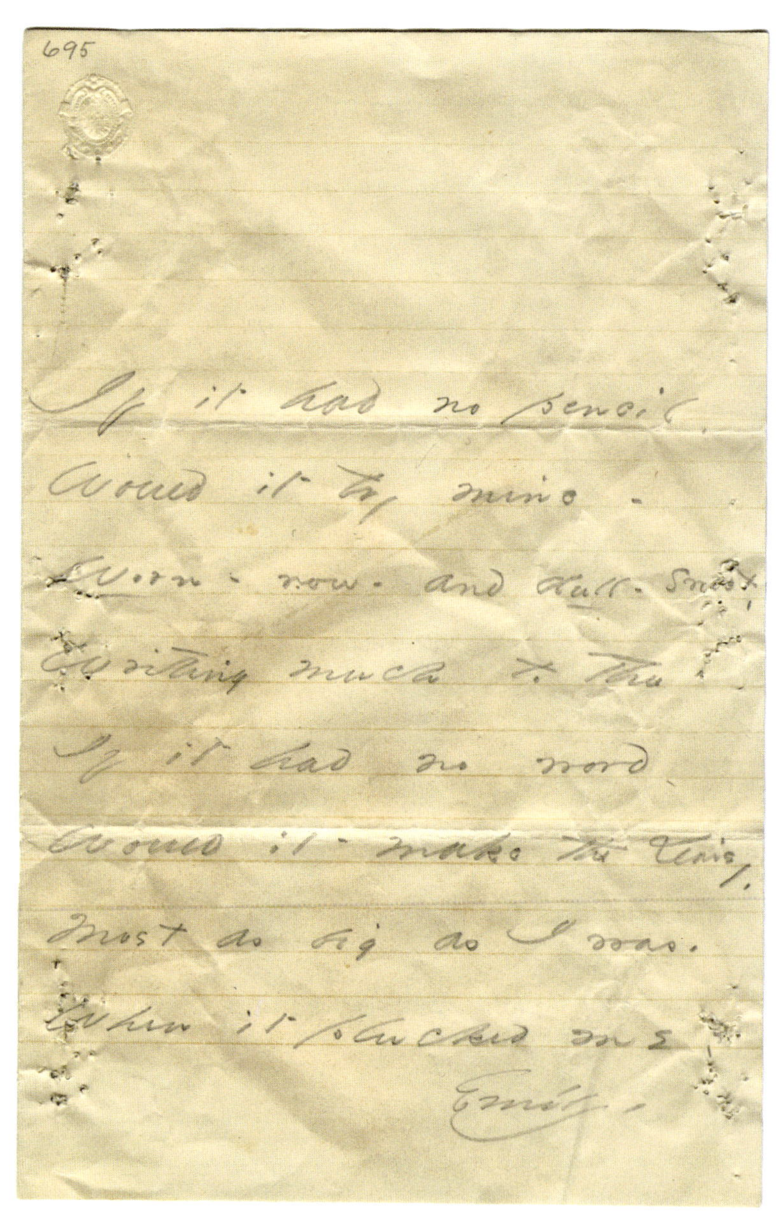

695

If it had no pencil,
Would it try mine –
Worn – now – and dull – sweet,
Writing much to thee.
If it had no word –
Would it make the Daisy,
Most as big as I was.
When it plucked me?
Emily.

Emily Dickinson, 'If it had no pencil',
letter/poem to Samuel Bowles, *c.* 1864.

If it had no pencil,
Would it try mine –
Worn – now – and – *dull* – sweet,
Writing much to thee.[18]

'The poem was enveloped in a letter folded into thirds horizontally, pinned closed at each side.'[19] The letter is riddled with tiny exit holes where the pins once held the makeshift envelope together, as if she were preparing fabric to sew a pocket in a dress.

Inside was one of her stubby pencils – 'Worn – now – and – *dull* – sweet'.[20] One presumes it came straight from her dress pocket.

As Jen Bervin writes:

> All of the envelope poems are written in pencil. Unlike a fountain pen, a pencil stub, especially a very small one, fits

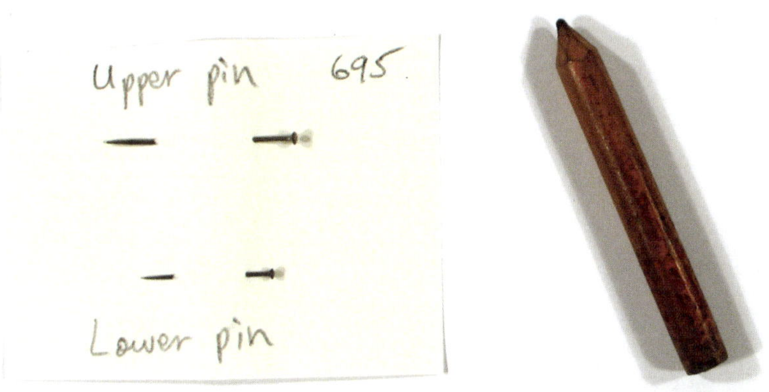

Pencil and two pins from one of Dickinson's letters to Bowles. Originally, the pencil was pinned inside the letter, which was folded to make a crude envelope.

neatly, at the ready, in the pocket of a dress. In an early letter to her brother, Austin, she wrote 'This is truly extempore, Austin – I have no notes in my pocket,' suggesting that there were typically jottings accumulating there. Dickinson's one surviving dress has a large external pocket on the right side, where her hand would fall easily at rest. The economy of the pocket is worth considering. An envelope is a pocket.[21]

Pencils sketch.
The etymology of 'sketch' is 'extemporaneous poem'.

Envehope

An envelope is for making interiority.

A paper envelope most often makes a place to keep something, usually with the intention of sending it through the post. Or perhaps slipping it under a door. A letter. A card. A valentine. A breakup. A filing for divorce.

Postcards are envelope-less. Bare.

A chrysalis is an envelope holding the wet-butterfly-letter before she creeps out and hangs down from a twig to dry. 'She is very damp and bedraggled.'[22] It takes her about twenty minutes to get ready and dry. To unfold. To turn handsome. To fly to the firmament.

She leaves behind the envelope-chrysalis, which holds nothing but air.

Making something out of nothing.

Marcel Duchamp proclaims the force of 'nothing' in his *50 cc of Paris Air* (1919): a glass chrysalis of Paris air.

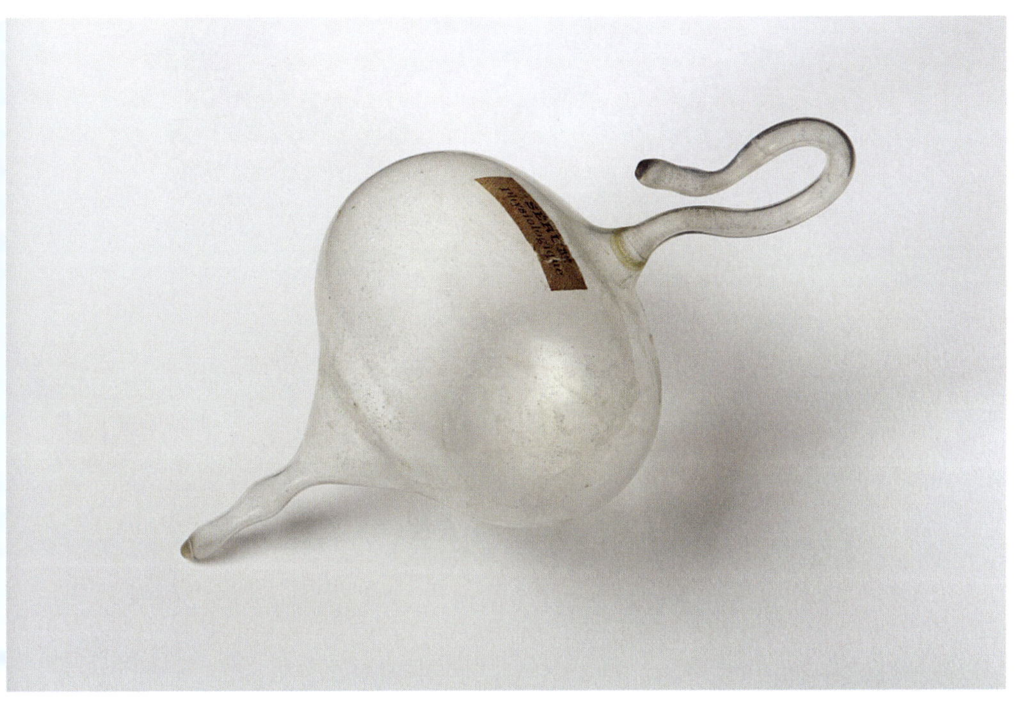

Marcel Duchamp, *50 cc of Paris Air*, 1919, glass ampoule.

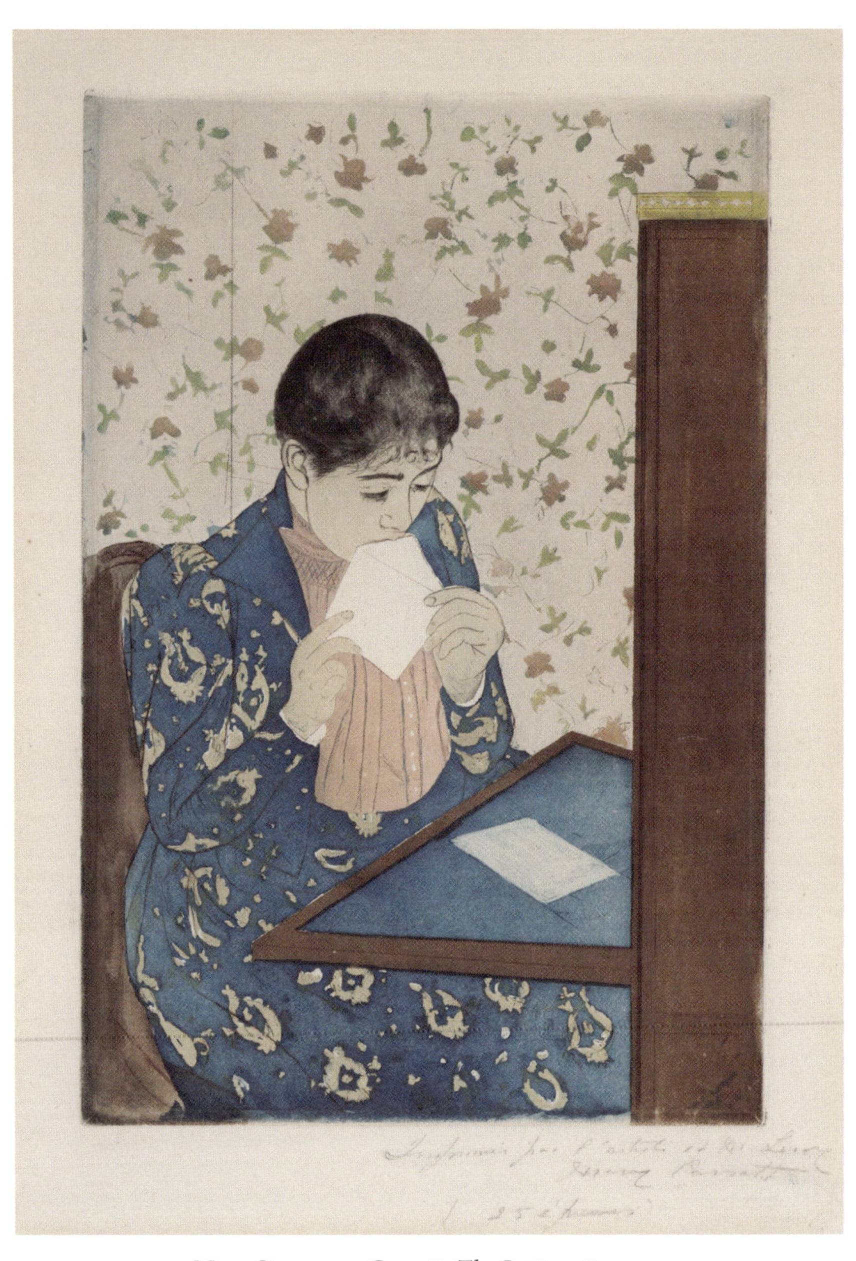

Mary Stevenson Cassatt, *The Letter*, 1890–91, colour drypoint and aquatint.

When this glass envelope – this 'found object', an ampoule from a pharmacist in Paris – was accidentally broken, the Paris air flew off.

I have a favourite envelope image, made by the American-French Impressionist Mary Cassatt, known for her supra-interiorized paintings and prints of women inside the home or in walled-off gardens – always enveloped (as Griselda Pollock masterfully argues in her *Vision and Difference* (1988)). The image is Cassatt's print: *The Letter* (1890–91). One notes that the woman is licking the envelope before inserting the letter that rests on her blue writing desk. But perhaps there is another page or pages already inside the envelope? There is no name on the envelope. Neither is there an address.

Nothing inside.

Nothing outside.

This beautiful flat print, with solid spaces of colour and pattern, is influenced by the period's rage for Japonisme (the French enthusiasm for the printmaking of the Edo period). Cassatt admired and collected prints by Kitagawa Utamaro, which 'hung on her glass enclosed veranda at her chateau.'[23]

Cassatt's *The Letter* might be more aptly named *The Envelope* – for the latter is where all of the action takes place. We see a woman licking the gum of the envelope. The licking holds the envelope open. Jane Gallop playfully equates the licking with a kiss.[24] An open-mouthed (French) kiss. Yet the empty space of the print, with its flat areas of colour and flat design, has its own simplicity. The green leaves of the wallpaper are 'neck of the Eider Drake' green – the same green as my writing room. The woman's dress is 'Wing Feather of Jay' blue – patterned with the 'Wings of the Goldfinch.'[25]

A meditative space.

No pen can be seen.

She licks the envelope like a wound, to keep it open and clean.

It is not inconceivable that Cassatt saw Kitagawa Utamaro's *Hinazuru of the Keizetsuro*, from his series 'Comparing the Charms of Beauties'.

In Utamaro's print, the courtesan's hands are felt but unseen: her left hand is outside the frame; her right hand is hidden, but suggestive in its absence. Is she cupping, or even fondling her left breast through her luscious creamy-cocoa-coloured kimono? With her coral-coloured painted lips (the same hue as her sensual silk *juban* (her under-kimono)), she holds a sheet of clean white tissue. Until the tissue drops, or is taken from her mouth, her lips are silenced by this gentle holding. And it is then that we will see the stain. Like those erotic lipstick kisses that have been defacing Oscar Wilde's massive memorial in Paris's Père Lachaise cemetery for decades. Sealing his grave with kisses.

The American poet Joan I. Siegel wrote a poem out of the Cassatt print, emphasizing the letter as interiorized by the envelope, like the woman interiorized by the room. The content of the letter is a hush-hush friend. Her tongue is unspeaking, in favour of sealing. She 'seals it with her tongue'.

All day it is with her like a song
even as she slices a breakfast orange,
brushes her hair,
shuts a window.
She is listening to it
when company calls

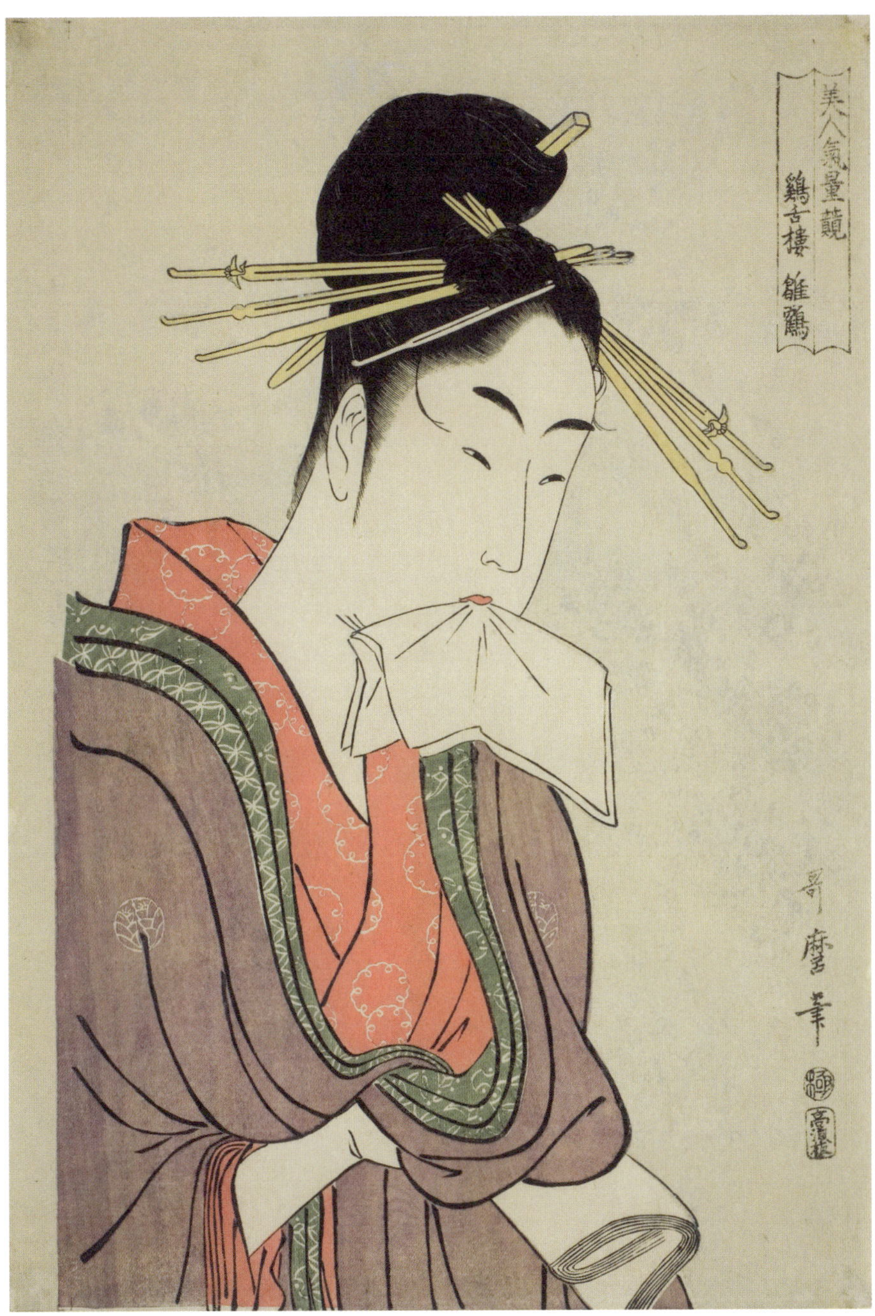

Kitagawa Utamaro, *Hinazuru of the Keizetsuro*, from the series 'Comparing the Charms of Beauties', *c.* 1794–5, colour woodblock print.

and she talks about yesterday's news,
pours tea,
says good-bye at the door.
Then, alone with it finally
in late afternoon,
she puts it on the desk,
arranges it
as though she were putting flowers in a vase.
Then she slips it into the envelope,
seals it with her tongue.

An envelope can hold contact from a lost lover, an invitation to a grand party, good marks, news of a fellowship, news from home, forgiveness, acceptance for the publication of your poem, an apology, money. All the things we might hope for. Envelopes can also hold dread, money owed, divorce papers, rejection. All the things we hope against. Unopened, the envelope makes a portmanteau: *envehope.*

'It granulates, it crackles, it caresses, it grates, it cuts'

In *Gorgeous Nothings*, Dickinson's envelopes are pinned and displayed like a lepidopterist's collection of butterflies. But they are not mute monarchs: they are aloud like birds, even when the world is still.[26]

I hold the envelope poems to my ear, like a paper conch – I hear:

> 'things that sing/ Not Birds entirely – but Minds – Minute Effulgen'[27]
> 'As Sleigh Bells/ sound/ seem in Summer'[28]
> 'And the Hoofs of/ the Clock – / Pausing in front/ of our +Sentenced/ Faces'[29]
> 'Clogged/ only with/ Music, like/ the Wheels of/ Birds'[30]

Many of Dickinson poems were written aloud. Louise Norcross, the beloved cousin of Dickinson, wrote this to the editors of Boston's *Woman's Journal* (a feminist weekly) on 26 March 1904:

> I know that Emily Dickinson wrote most emphatic things in the pantry, so cool and quiet, while she skimmed the milk; because I sat on the footstool behind the door, in delight, as she read them to me. The blinds were closed, but through the green slats she saw all those fascinating ups and downs going on outside that she wrote about.[31]

As Roland Barthes has written: 'If it were possible to imagine an aesthetic of textual pleasure, it would have to include: writing aloud . . . it granulates, it crackles, it caresses, it grates, it cuts.'[32]

'Has – holds but one sword'

Written on an envelope's wing-flap, this poem gives rise to one note from one bird, privileging sound over meaning.[33]

Here is a possible *translation* from visual object to written poem:

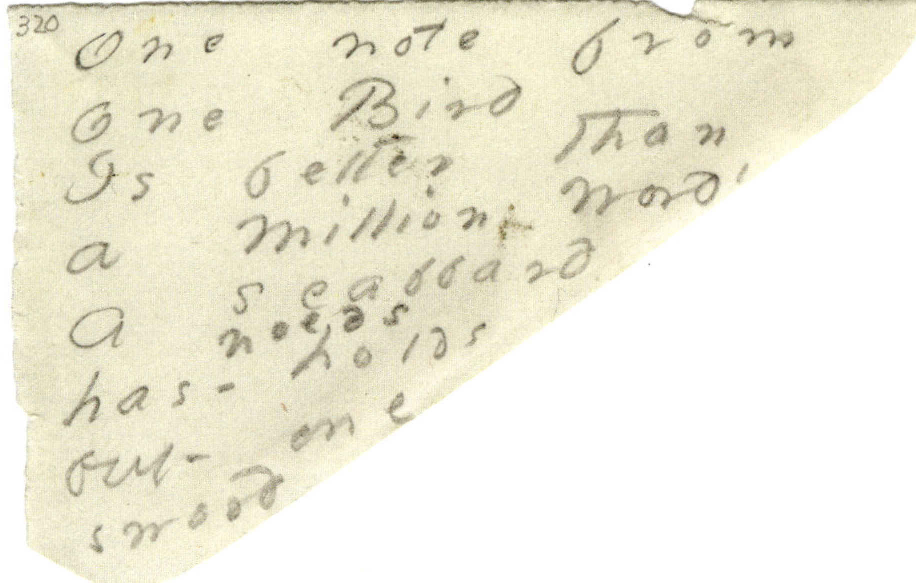
320
One note from
One Bird
Is better than
a million words
A scabbard
means
has - holds
but - one
sword

Emily Dickinson, 'One note from/ One bird', n. d., envelope poem.

One note from
One Bird
Is better than
a million words
A scabbard
      means
has – holds
but one
sword

Here is how the 'mingled verbal graphic gift' has been mapped.

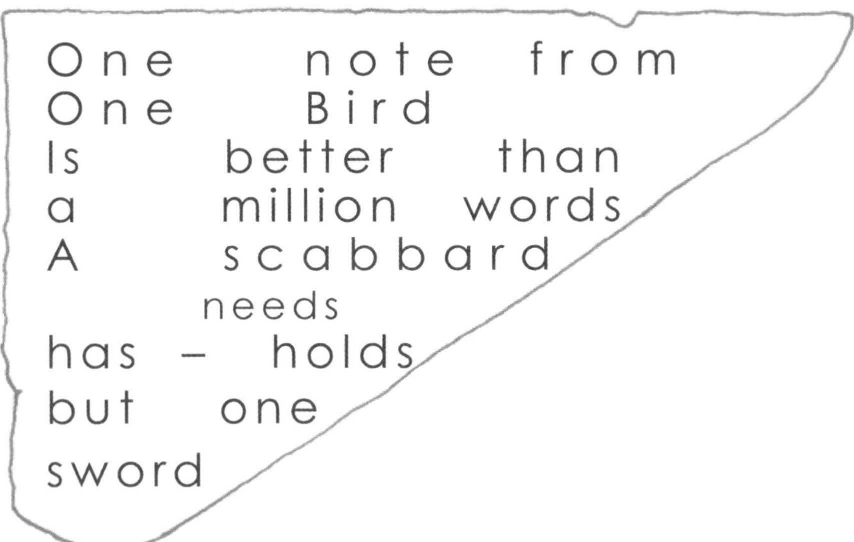

Emily Dickinson, 'One note from/ One bird', n. d., facsimile.

The tip of an envelope wing.
Flap.
The tip of the poet's pencil.
Tongue.
In concert, they pun 'note'.
A memo.
A tone.

Dickinson's 'note' is a transitional object (between object and word – between sound and word – between writer and reader), which she pushes out of the enveloped state, like a fledging from its nest. Making something out of nothing – one note from one bird is exalted as a kind of scabbard-pocket that 'has – holds but one sword'.[34]

A foundling of Hope

The envelope pictured here is a two-storey house.

Hope is not in a jar.

Hope is not in a box.

Opposite is the back of the house, addressed in an unknown hand to Mrs Edward Dickinson and Family.

Underneath is the architectural plan.

Three very long floorboard dashes divides the house into upstairs and downstairs, facilitating two stories.

The poem is two inseparable stories of form and content. Like Apollinaire's 'It is raining' calligramme, written with raindrops of black ink.

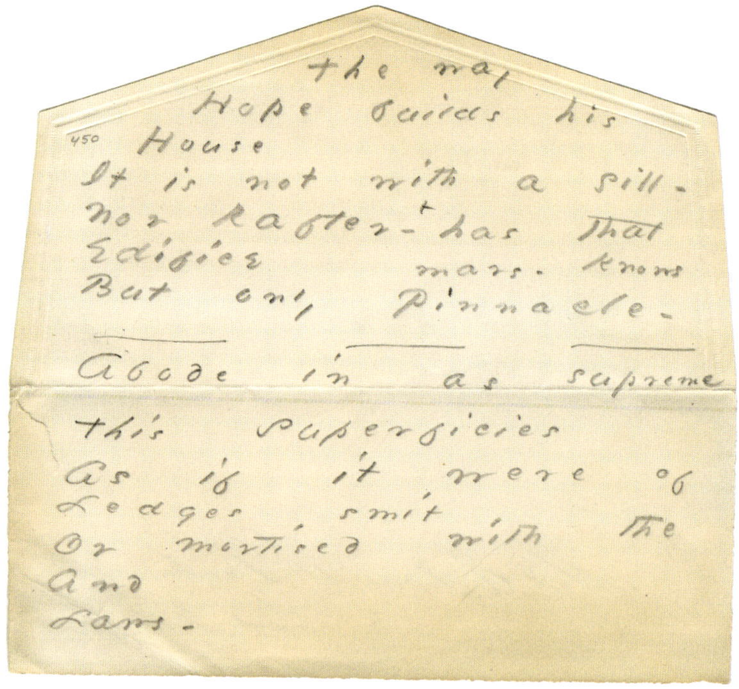

the way
Hope builds his
450 House
It is not with a sill -
nor Rafter - has That
Edifice mars. knows
But only Pinnacle -
Abode in as supreme
this superficies
As if it were of
Ledges smit
Or mortised with the
and
Laws -

Emily Dickinson, 'The way/ Hope builds his/ House',
n. d., envelope poem.

Emily Dickinson, 'The way/ Hope builds his/ House',
n. d., back of envelope, addressed in unknown hand.

A 450

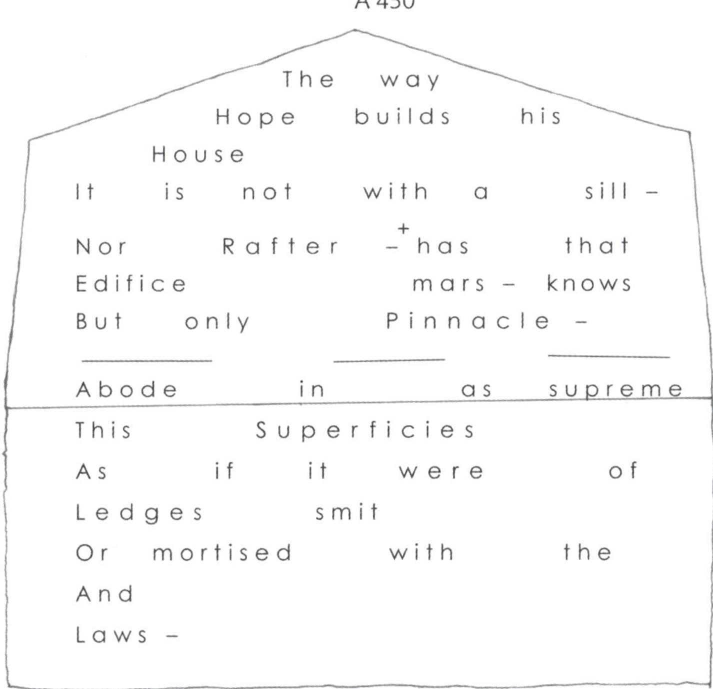
The way
Hope builds his
House
It is not with a sill –
Nor Rafter – + has that
Edifice mars – knows
But only Pinnacle –
Abode in as supreme
This Superficies
As if it were of
Ledges smit
Or mortised with the
And
Laws –

Emily Dickinson, 'The way/ Hope builds his/ House', n. d., facsimile.

For Dickinson the *found* becomes house by opening/unfolding the envelope flap. Her form of origami. (From *ori*: folding – and *kami*: paper.) The embossed trim is a decorative roof line. The bottom edge has been carefully torn, scaling it into a very satisfying house shape. Perhaps Dickinson could not find her pair of scissors, so she folded and refolded, forwards and backwards, forwards and backwards, along a straight line – making a sharp paper fissure to tear along the straight edge of a table. Or she just preferred the softness of a torn cut.

A cast-off envelope.

A *foundling* of Hope.

'We should respect the seals of others'

An epigraph of picture secrets. A rebus. According to the *Oxford English Dictionary*, the precise origin of the word 'rebus' is uncertain. It has been explained as denoting 'by things', on account of a representation with a rebus being *non verbis sed rebus*, 'not by words but by things'. This engraved medal with a small hole for tying with string or ribbon around one's neck was left with an infant at London's Foundling Hospital, presumably in the year 1759 that 'G.B' was born.

The etymology of 'infant' is certain. From the Latin, meaning unable to speak.

At this time, we know nothing more of this boy (Grant, Gregory, George . . .) or girl (Genevieve, Grace, Gretel . . .).

A foundling is 'a deserted infant whose parents are unknown, a child whom there is no one to claim', according to the *Oxford English Dictionary*. This was not the case for the children who were left at London's Foundling Hospital for more than two centuries.[35] They were left by caregivers (primarily by mothers) who were unable to care for the child, many with hope of reunification. A mending of the broken thread.

Upon admission, an entry billet was drawn up to record the approximate age of the child, gender, 'marks' and details of the clothing that the child was wearing upon arrival. Children were also given an individual serial number, which was stamped on a tag: initially made of lead, soon to be changed to pewter, and by the twentieth century plastic. These tags would be placed around the neck of each foundling. 'Marks' was an expanded category that often included a range of identifiers visible and invisible, such as whether or not a child had been christened. Or, less often, an indication of race, for example: 'a mulatto'. Race was not usually indicated, and children of colour were few.[36]

Hospital officials required that individuals (parents, guardians, relatives, midwives, parish officials) affix on each child something remarkable. These objects came to be known as 'tokens'.

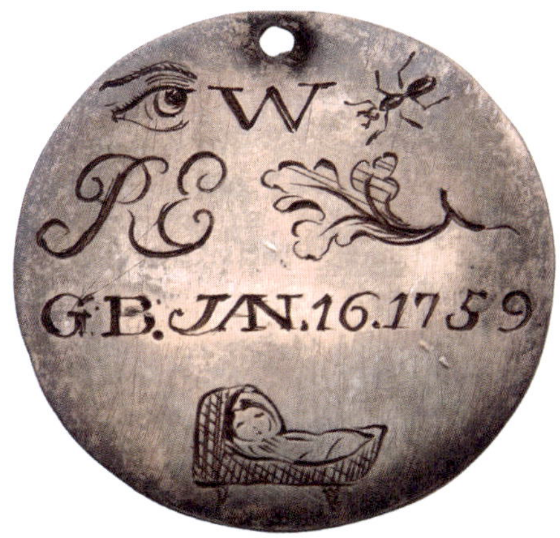

Metal token engraved with the rebus: 'I want relief', *c.* 1759 – for foundling known only as 'G.B'.

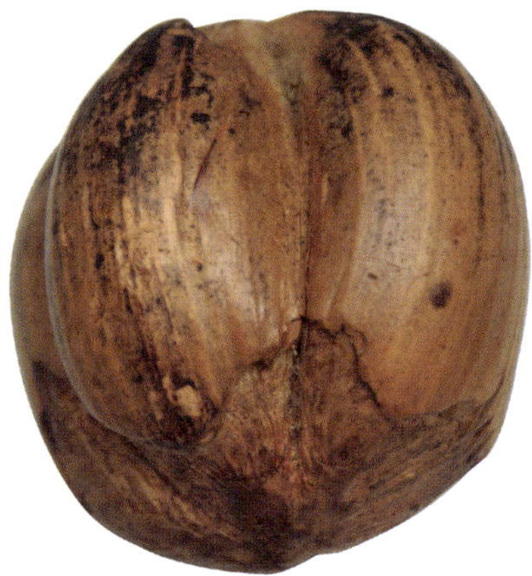

Hazelnut token, pierced for a string or cord, left at the Foundling Hospital with a child at admission, 1752.

The tokens were to be used as further identification when the child was reclaimed. Most of the tokens were written notes or scraps of fabric and ribbon, but there is also a range of everyday objects and mysterious little things, including coins, buttons, a hazelnut, a child's tiny ring, padlocks, keys, coral necklaces and the heart-breaking medal disc engraved with a rebus that reads 'I want relief.'

The hard tokens were placed inside the paper billet, which was folded into an envelope and sealed with wax. The child's serial number was written on the outside.[37] The soft tokens – a snippet of cloth, a brocade ribbon, a piece of embroidery, a baby's cap, a baby's sleeve – were pinned on the billet itself before being folded into an envelope. The envelopes were never to be opened unless the mother came back to reclaim her child. The wax seals were to be respected. But like secrets that insist on telling, envelopes beg to be opened.

Dickinson has pencilled next to the cut-and-torn gummed seal of a recycled envelope: 'We should respect the seals of others.'

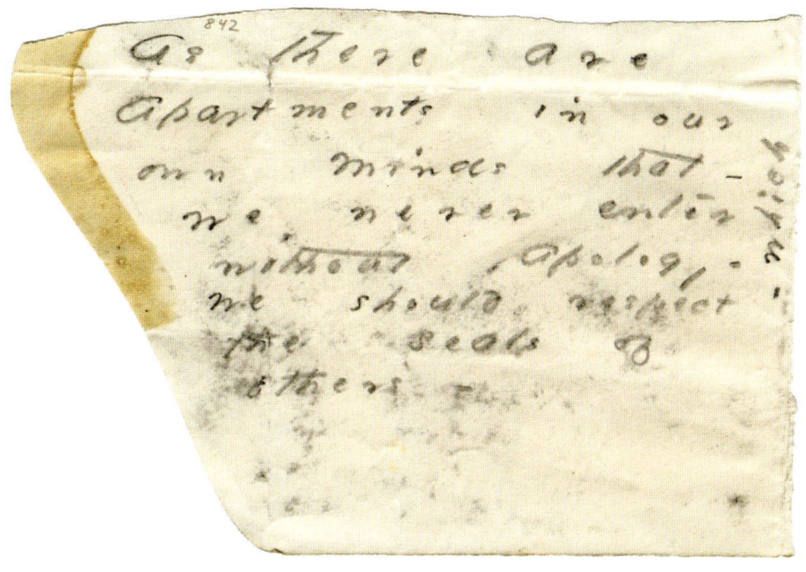

Emily Dickinson, 'As there are/ Apartments in our/ own Minds',
n. d., envelope poem.

A 842

As there are
Apartments in our
own Minds that –
we never enter
without Apology –
we should respect
the seals of
others –

– which

Emily Dickinson, 'As there are/ Apartments in our/ own Minds',
n. d., facsimile.

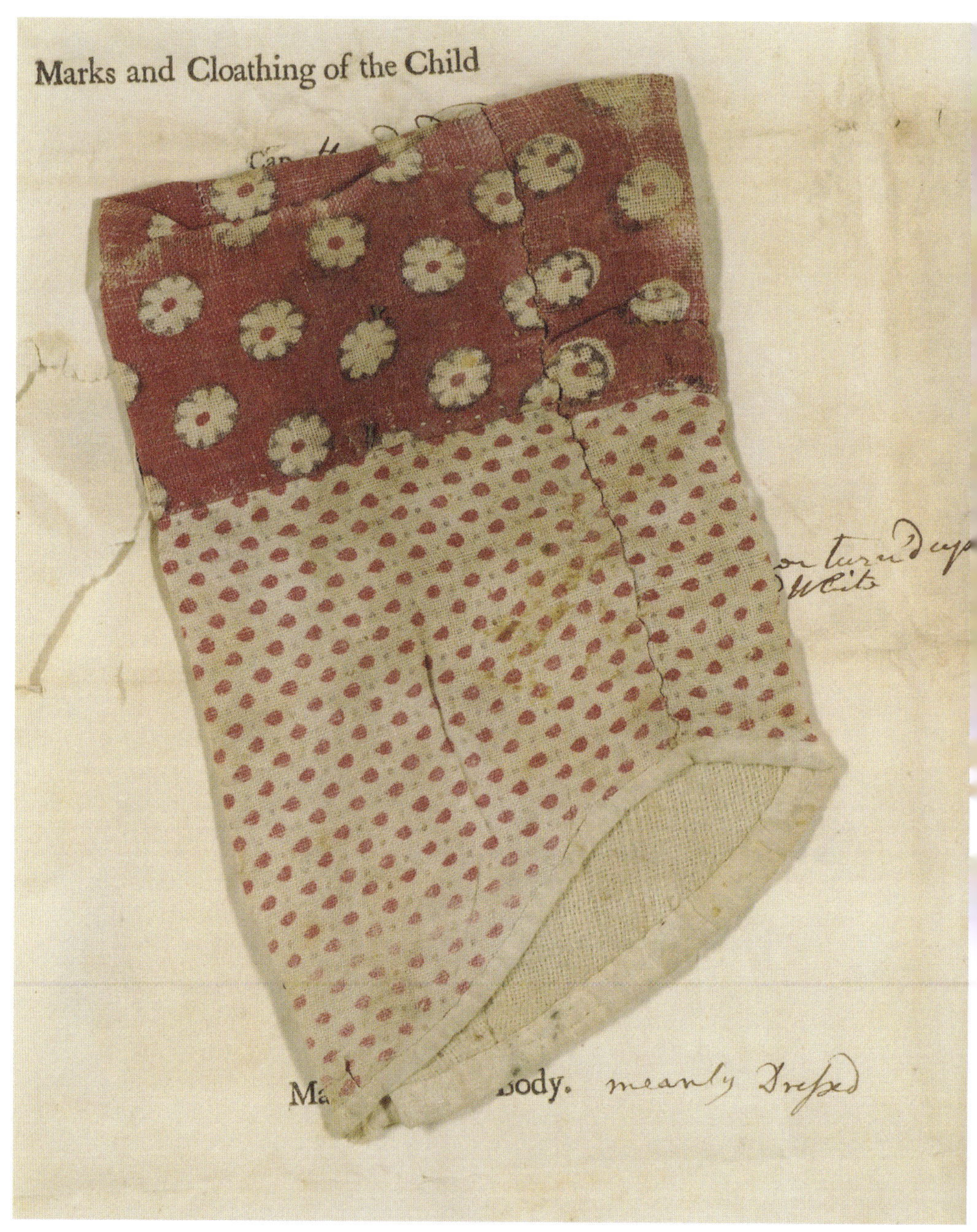

Baby sleeve, attached to billet, 'Foundling 235, a boy admitted 23 May 1746'.

'I'm nobody ! Who are you? Are you—Nobody—too?'

> Throughout the perod from 1741 to 1760, the process of giving over an infant to the Hospital was an anonymous one. It was a form of adoption, whereby the Hospital became the infant's parent and its previous identity was effaced . . . Although admission to the Hospital before 1760 was anonymous, the mother retained the right to reclaim the child if her circumstances changed. In practice such cases were few. Only 152 children were reclaimed out of the 16,282 admitted between 1741 and 1760.[38]

Few children made it back to their broken envelope.

Heartbreaking is to understand that in the interest of further anonymity, infants were erased of their names and named anew. Good intentions aside, the child is left a blank page.

'I'm Nobody! Who are you?
Are you—Nobody—too?'[39]

The caul presents itself as an always-tearing envelope

There are about 5,000 material objects that have survived which were used as identifiers for children accepted between 1741 and 1760. Most of them are flat swatches of textiles. There are also ribbons. For a handful of children, their tokens 'consist of a complete sleeve, or cap'.[40] The sleeves were separate pull-on items that were worn when the child was wrapped in 'bands of fabric called rollers, or dressed in a looser, long wrapping garment with armholes called a mantle'.[41] Like the baby's sleeve made from linen printed with red dots, free in their marking. The dots remind me of those that I used to make with the tiny pink eraser at the end of my yellow wooden pencil by dipping it into paint and using it as a makeshift rubber stamp. Its red cotton (or linen) cuff, printed with red-eyed white flowers encircled in brown, brings back happy memories of a dress made for me by my mother when I was a child. The sleeve came in with 'Foundling 235, a boy admitted 23 May 1746'.[42] The mother probably sewed the sleeve herself. The first cut was umbilical. The loveliness of the object shows her aesthetic taste and that the 'poor did not live in black and white'.[43]

The three-dimensional tokens 'were removed for display at the Foundling Hospital in the middle of the nineteenth century, when the billets, which had originally been folded up with tokens inside, were flattened for binding into ledgers now known as the billet books'.[44] The hard tokens were captivating for display purposes and, practically speaking, they were 'too bulky to interleave in the bound volumes'.[45] No one thought to make a note about whom the hazelnut belonged to, nor any of the other hard tokens, not even

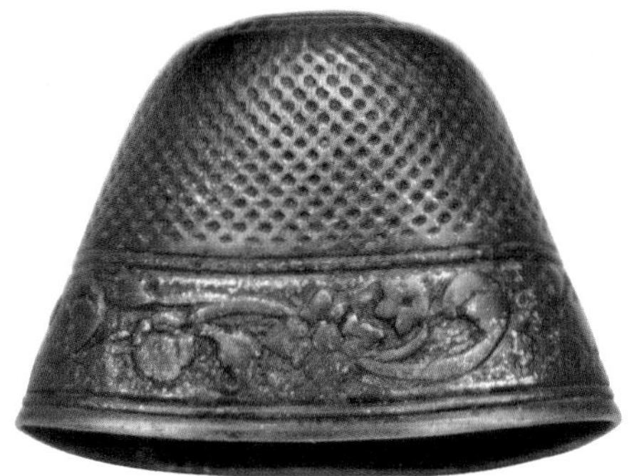

Thimble token left at the Foundling Hospital with a child at admission, 1759.

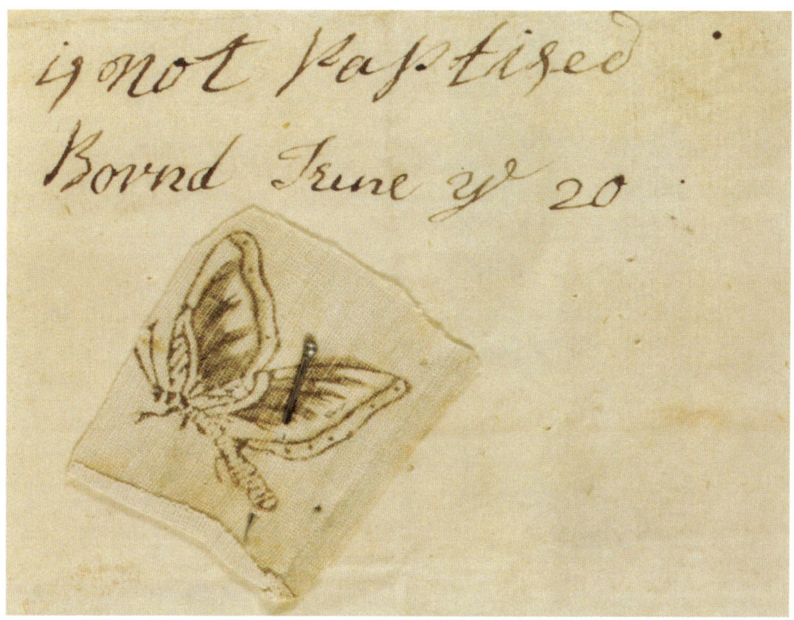

Fabric swatch of a butterfly, pinned to a billet, 'Foundling 1908, a boy admitted 23 June 1758'.

the smashed thimble. These hard objects became foundlings in the truest sense of the word: deserted with no one to claim them.

The fabrics, ribbons, caps and sleeves remain pinned to the unfolded billets. These slim objects were able to avoid binding problems, thereby escaping being severed from their histories, their children.

A brown butterfly on cotton or linen, pinned to its billet as if by the hand of the lepidopterist: 'Foundling 1908, a boy admitted 23 June 1758'.[46]

– Egg.
– Caterpillar.
– Pupa.
– Butterfly.

– Doll.
– Boy.
– Not baptised.
– 90018.

A pinned print of a brown acorn: ‘Foundling 9324, a boy admitted 22 July 1758’.[47]

– Fall from a tree.
– On the ground, stone-still.
– Shock at being chosen from other acorns left untouched.
– The strange tickly feeling of being eaten from the inside by the elongated snout of a weevil.
– The resulting lightness of being.
– Eaten, he will not be able to grow into a three-hundred-year-old oak tree and put forth large branches so that birds can sing and nest.
– 9324

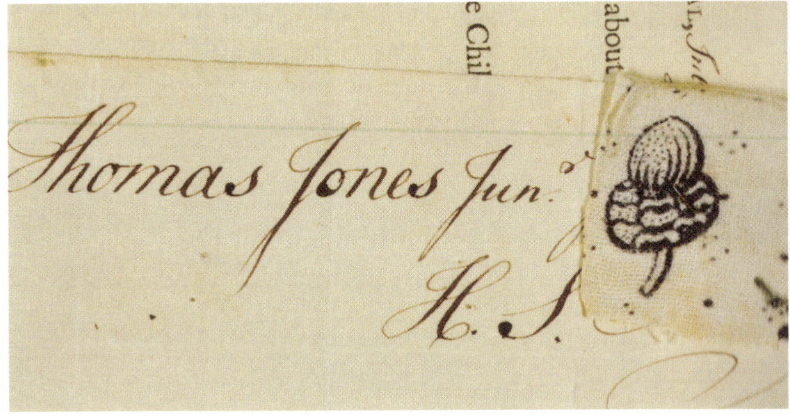

Fabric swatch of an acorn, pinned to a billet, ‘Foundling 9324, a boy admitted 22 July 1758’.

A yellow ribbon, the bright yellow of a mustard flower, upon which is written 'My Name is Andrews'.

I suddenly remember a minuscule mustard seed in a small, round glass casing, no bigger than a dime, on a delicate chain, to be worn around my neck. Such pendants were very popular in the 1960s. A gift from 'Nana'? My Aunt Jo? I don't know. My 'token' is severed from its past. As a child, I was indifferent to it. I could not understand its meaning. The tiny seed, so unremarkable, like a 'sleepy' from my eye in the morning, when the Sandman had visited. I did not like it. Its metaphor, I later learned, is from the Gospel of Mark, which states that the kingdom of God 'is like a mustard seed, which, when sown upon the ground, is the smallest of all seeds on earth; yet when it is sown it grows up and becomes the greatest of all shrubs, and puts forth large branches, so the birds can make their nest in its shade' (Mark 4:30). I try to find it in my box of 'things' – it is not there, as I knew it wouldn't be. I am relieved. One does not always want to touch the past.

Startling is the token of a baby's caul, appearing like ancient gossamer fabric. The caul is the amniotic sac. Transparent. Water-filled. First-home-envelope. Only on very rare occasions are babies born *en caul*. When born *en caul* the infant can spectacularly emerge, completely enclosed in the amniotic sac. Untorn. As if in a clear balloon. Or, the child can be born with the torn amniotic sac veiling their face or other parts of their body.

To be born with the caul is auspicious, good luck. Sailors believed it would protect you from drowning.

After 1760, a petitioning system was put in place and tokens were no longer required. Nevertheless, mothers voluntarily provided them during the four decades that followed.

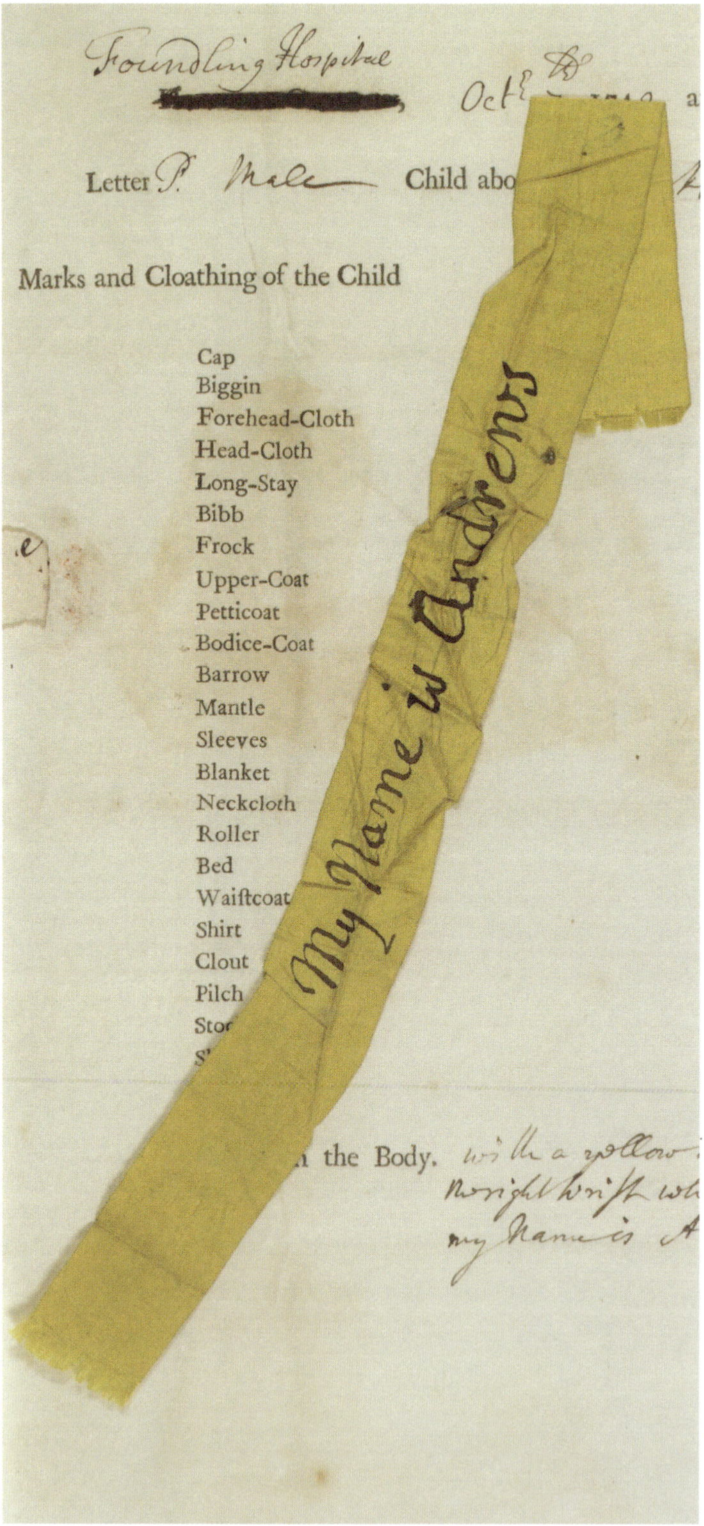

Foundling Hospital

Octr 7 1740 a

Letter P. Male Child abo

Marks and Cloathing of the Child

Cap
Biggin
Forehead-Cloth
Head-Cloth
Long-Stay
Bibb
Frock
Upper-Coat
Petticoat
Bodice-Coat
Barrow
Mantle
Sleeves
Blanket
Neckcloth
Roller
Bed
Waiſtcoat
Shirt
Clout
Pilch
Sto
S

My Name is Andrews

n the Body. with a yellow
Ronight Wrist wh
my Name is A

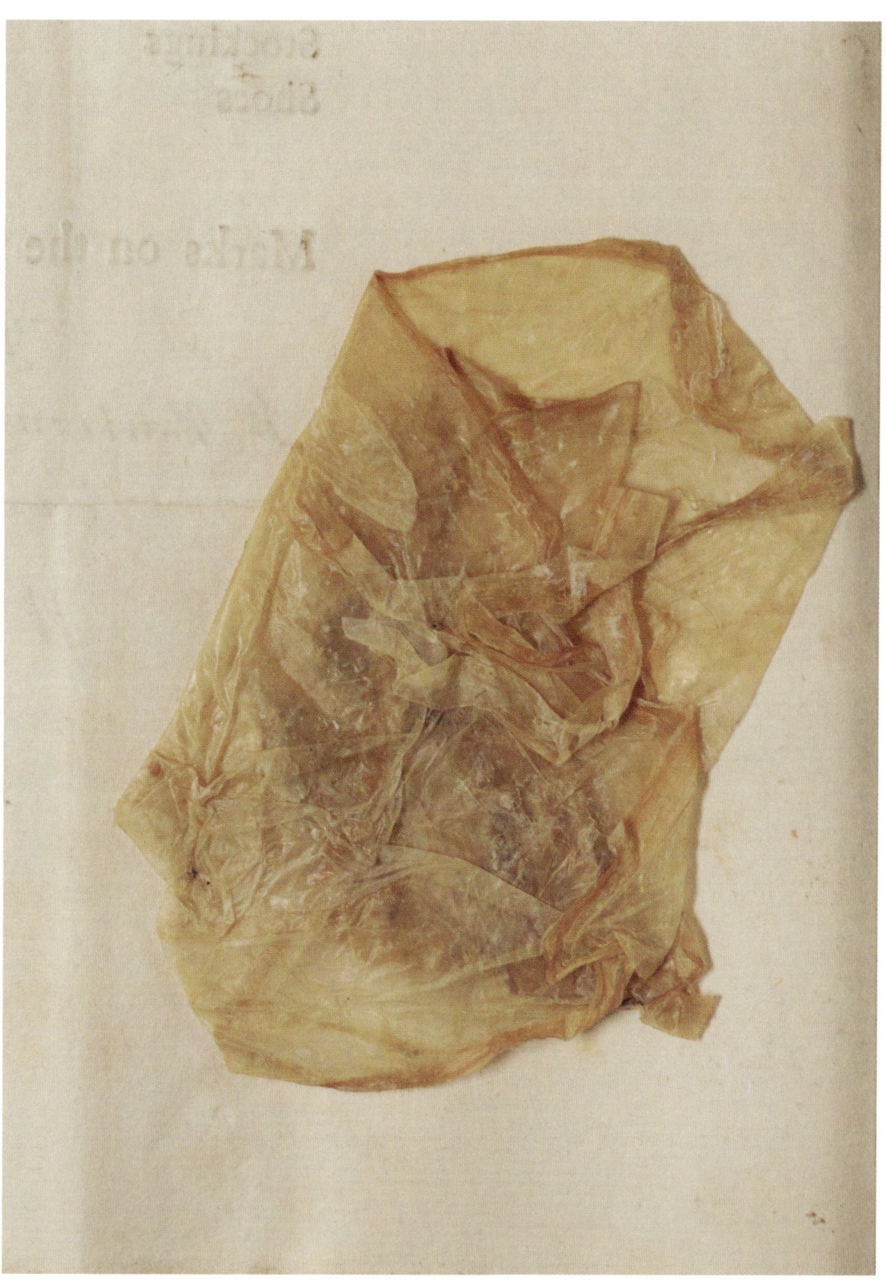

An infant's caul accompanying Child 5588, renamed Robin Carr and admitted 30 August 1757.

Opposite:
Yellow ribbon, upon which is written 'My Name is Andrews', pinned to a billet.

Amulets.

Magic.

Hope.

The hazelnut is forever sealed.

The caul presents itself as an always-tearing envelope.

Hope leaves the attic

The tiny patchwork needle case (called a 'housewife'), with patterns of several sorts, including pink-and-white stripes and wee white flowers outlined in navy blue – forget-me-not-notes sown – was a go-between for that rarer-than-rare reunion.

The mother was Sarah Bender. The boy, admitted on 11 February 1767, was christened Charles. Before she cut her tiny needle-scabbard into two separate halves, she stitched its solid grey-blue patch with red thread to make a heart and to proclaim each of their names in one tiny place with the initials '**S**'(arah) and '**C**'(harles). These stitches are difficult to see – to read – to bear.

Cut into two –

Needle stories.

Scissor stories.

For the reunion, I picture Sarah with her half, with her halved heart in her pocket, when she comes for Charles. He is eight years older than the last time that she saw him. For eight years he has been called Benjamin Twirl.

'Hello Charles,' Sarah says with a warm smile.

Hope leaves the attic.

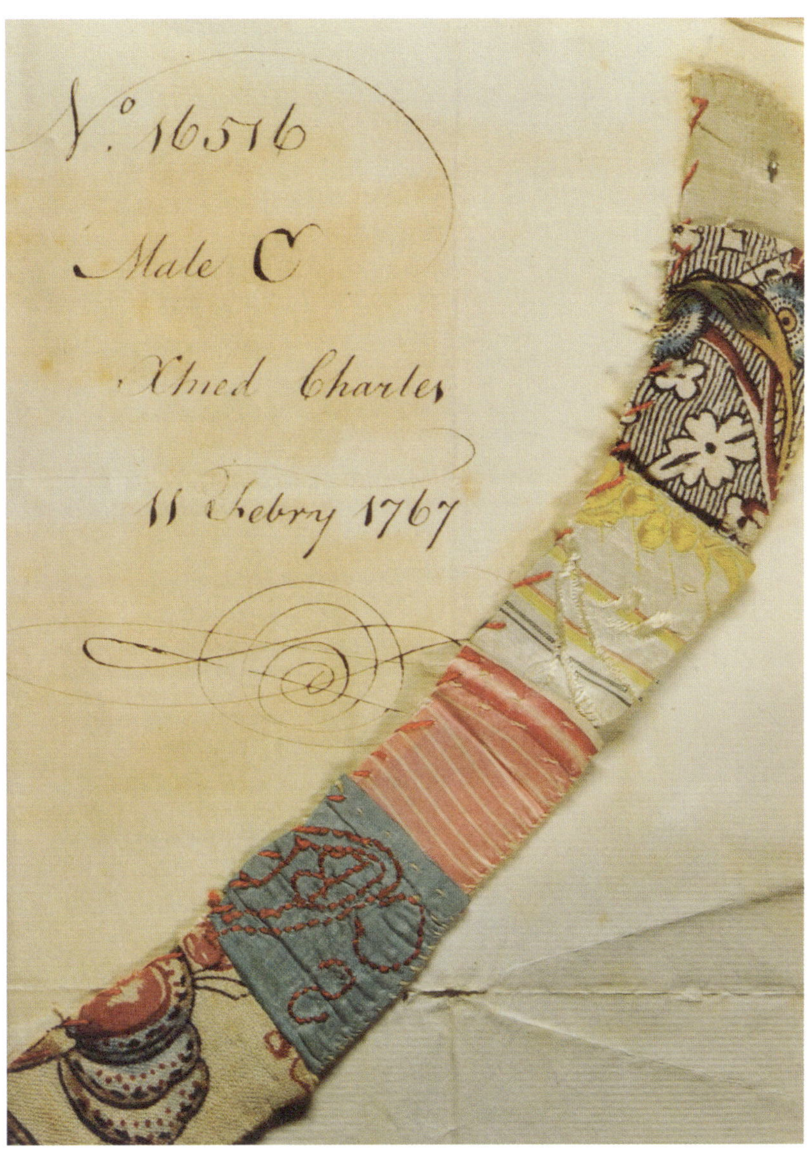

Needle case, pinned to a billet, accompanying a boy admitted 11 February 1767.

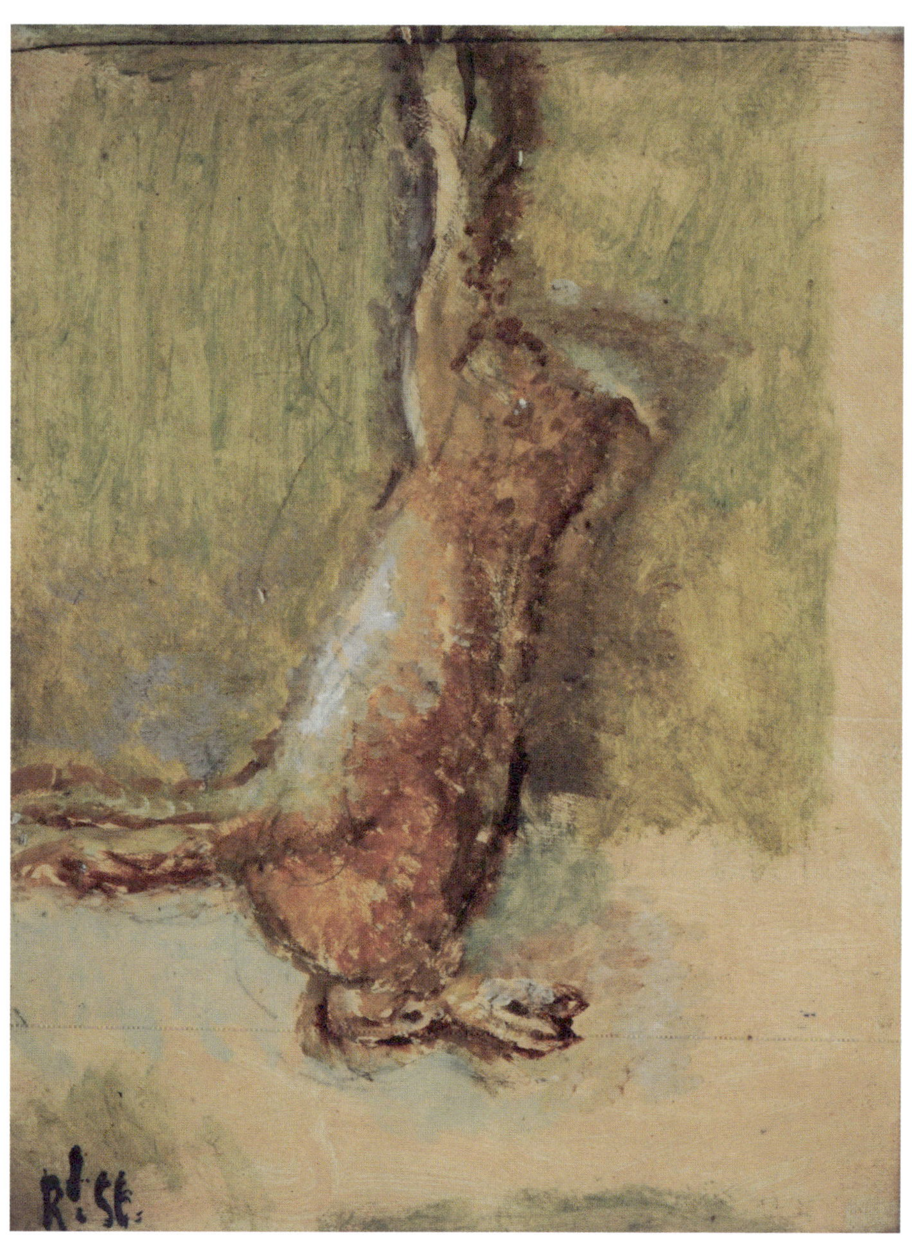

Walter Richard Sickert, *A Dead Hare*, n.d.,
oil on panel.

CHAPTER FIVE

Two Hares Falling Out of Breath

The truth is a category that remains in suspension while we're alive.
– JAVIER MARIAS, *Thus Bad Begins*

The blood of the hare is added at the end

This is Walter Sickert's oil sketch, a little sliver of a painting entitled *A Dead Hare*.[1] The Hare lives, at least when I last checked, in a storage closet at a small museum in Sheffield, England. The exact date of the sketch is sketchy (somewhere between 1927 and 1942). Smaller than an 8-by-10-inch sheet of paper, this hare is smaller than a hare. The animal is roughly outlined: a quick poem of swift brushstrokes, without much detail. A sketch is unpretentious – a rough draft of a more finished work of art that is yet to come.

A Dead Hare was painted by a self-styled enigmatic artist who is famous for his depictions of brutality, as in his four 'Camden Town Murder' paintings from 1908. In 1907 Sickert painted a picture of his bedroom at 6 Mornington Crescent, London, and entitled it Jack the Ripper's Bedroom. (Sickert's landlady suspected that the previous tenant may have been the Ripper.) Sickert courted association with Jack the Ripper, as a 'party trick' – like pulling a rabbit out of a hat.[2] Believing that a rabbit comes out of a hat and that Sickert is Jack the Ripper are fantastic tales, requiring (to quote Samuel Taylor Coleridge) 'the willing suspension of disbelief . . . which constitutes poetic faith'.[3] Like overlooking, but not denying, the fact that your delicious stew is made from a real rabbit. (Perhaps that is why the 'Utopians' of Thomas More's island made it a law that all slaughtering should take place out of town.) Or like believing in the reality of a photograph but not denying that it is just an image on flat paper, the latter a subject that I will return to when discussing Richard Learoyd's very large photograph *Hare 1*, 2012 (121.7 × 121.7 cm).

In Sickert's painting, the killing has happened. The freshly caught hare is not yet a meal. It may be cooked up as a jugged hare, a traditional British dish for which a whole hare is cut into pieces, 'larded here and there', marinated, and cooked in red wine and juniper berries in a tall jug that stands in a pot of water.[4] Often the blood of the hare is added at the end.

Too close to hear. Hear.

More elaborate recipes for jugged hare call for making a sauce to be poured over the dish at the time of serving, consisting of the hare's blood, its pulverized liver and cream. In Judaism, to combine milk with blood is taboo. Or as Deuteronomy 14:21 has it: 'You shall not boil a kid in its mother's milk.' But Sickert's hare is not yet cut up: it is not yet larded here and there; not yet cooked with red wine and juniper berries; not yet sauced in its own blood. Hanging in a larder by its hind legs, it is a sketch of a dish yet to come.

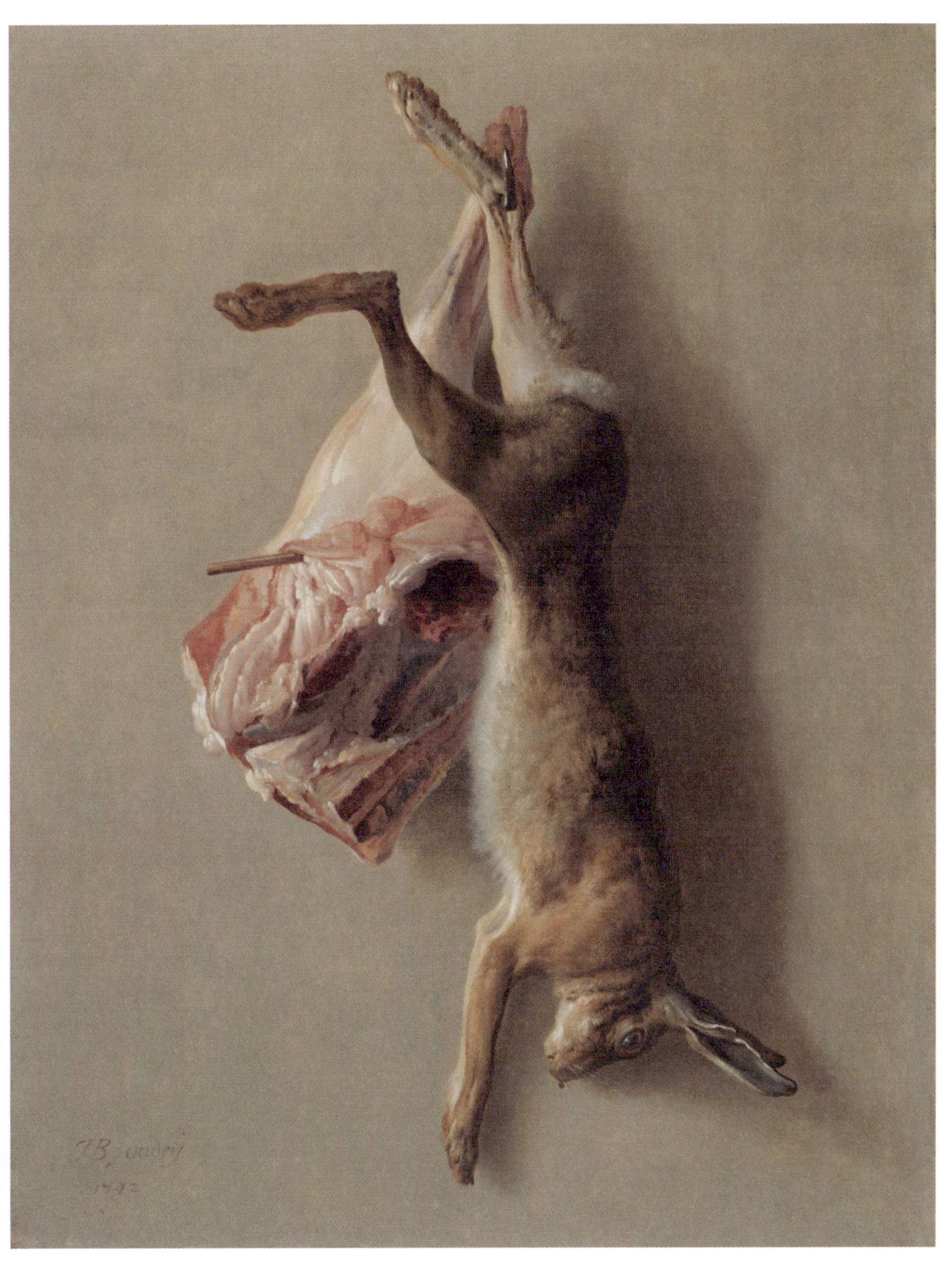

Jean-Baptiste Oudry, *A Hare and a Leg of Lamb*, 1742, oil on canvas.

Much different is Jean-Baptiste Oudry's 1742 life-size painting *A Hare and a Leg of Lamb*. Here, the lean hare – not yet skinned, not yet cut up in pieces – hangs next to a hefty slab of lamb, pink and fatty. Oudry, the animal painter of his time, who made use of a camera obscura for realistic accuracy and who was married to the daughter of a mirror-maker, gives his hare a finished look. He also gets close to the end of the story, frankly picturing what is in store for the hare. Together they hang, the hare and the lamb, like a couple of butchered Bluebeard wives in the locked closet of the Grimms' gruesome tale. Missing is the stewpot or jug. But we get the picture. Turn the painting 90 degrees anticlockwise, and the hare becomes 'posed ready to run', as if trying to escape the knife and the stewpot.[5]

A jugged hare in a broth of red wine and juniper berries, perhaps with some of its own blood added at the end, or even more elaborately sauced with its pulverized liver and cream, is marvellously dished up as a 'culinary sign'.[6] French philosopher Louis Marin's *La parole mangée et autres essais théologico-politiques* (The Word Eaten and Other Theological-Political Essays) claims that the marvel of the culinary sign is dependent on its being concealed and supported at once.[7] (Etymologically, the word 'marvellous' comes from *mirabilia*, which is Latin for a miraculous event and is a rich term in fairy tales, religious experience and surrealism – as in the work of André Breton and Georges Bataille.) 'The power to transform what is generally edible into culinary works of art that will be consumed within a social context' gives access to the magic of the signifier.[8] As a case in point, Marin gives the example of Robert sauce in Charles Perrault's 'The Sleeping Beauty in the Wood', which he refers to throughout the text as 'marvelous'. In the tale, the wicked queen mother, an ogress with a taste for eating children, commands her steward to kill her little granddaughter Dawn, exclaiming, 'I want to eat her with onion and mustard sauce.'[9] (Robert sauce is a classic made from chopped onions cooked in butter and a reduction of white wine, pepper, demi-glace and mustard. It is perfect with pork and other grilled meats, including, in this case, small children.) But the steward, who cannot bear to murder four-year-old Dawn, tricks the queen mother by killing a lamb instead as a substitute. When the lamb is served up to the ogress à la sauce Robert, the Queen Mother finds the dish delicious and is happily convinced that she is eating her granddaughter. Likewise, the ogress delights in eating what she believes to be her three-year-old grandson Day and her twenty-something daughter-in-law à la sauce Robert (rather than a tender young goat and the hind of a doe).[10]

In Marin's words:

> The cultural sign of cooking (Robert sauce) transcends the opposition between human meat and animal meat. It renders both the former and the latter unrecognizable, at least from the perspective of the ogress. Speaking literally, the sign transsignifies, rather than transubstantiates. It transforms both what is inedible according to social prohibition, as well as what is edible according to the rules governing culture, into a prepared dish that is ready to be eaten.[11]

Transsignification goes beyond the mystery of transubstantiation. As Marin continues,

> Contrary to the eucharistic sign, however, which involves bread concealing the transubstantiated body of Jesus, the culinary sign involves letting the sauce conceal the animal meat, which itself continues to exist while it supports the saucy sign: Rather than transubstantiation, we have transsignificance . . . this is what constitutes the marvelous nature of the tale, compared to the miracles of theology. Considered according to its specificity, the culinary sign, and particularly the Robert sauce in 'Sleeping Beauty in the Forest,' would be the distinctive mark of the marvelous.[12]

Although the ogress of 'Sleeping Beauty in the Forest' does not actually eat her grandson, her granddaughter and her daughter-in-law, it is possible, thanks to the Robert sauce, for her and readers of the story 'to mediate between fresh human meat and fresh animal meat'.[13] When the ogress eats the little farmyard lamb, she can believe that she is eating a little girl belonging to the royal family. Unaware that her steward has rustled up some delicious substitutes (lamb, young goat and the hindquarters of a doe) to placate her, it is in good faith that the ogress dines on Day, Dawn and Aurora. In the words of Marin, this appears to be true 'prima facie' – on the face of it, or we might say on the taste of it – unless proven otherwise.[14] 'The art of cooking is structured like a language.'[15] Or as Jeremiah 15:16 has it, 'When your words came, I ate them.' Jugging a hare, or covering lamb, goat, doe, child or young woman with Robert sauce, turns meat into a delicious dish, makes a change, makes a narrative. And you can make the narrative without eating anything as exotic.

Growing up as a middle-class American child, I found my mother's Southern fried chicken to be especially delicious. I liked to eat the skin, savouring the small liver (my father and I would split it), and gnaw on the bones with ogress relish. The coating of the chicken in egg, cornmeal, milk and flour, with plenty of salt and pepper, and then frying in oil, made a marvellous dish; it at once concealed the chicken meat while supporting the culinary sign of Southern fried chicken, transsignifying the chicken into my mother (at least in retrospect). Mine was a fantasy of eating the mother. Proust ate his mother as a madeleine; I ate mine as a cut-up fried chicken, liver and all. My love consumes like the hateful mouth of the ogress who fantasizes about eating her grandchildren and daughter-in-law. I have an oral fixation. I understand, like Karl Abraham's patient, that 'loving somebody' is 'exactly the same as the idea of eating something good'.[16] I invert the famed line, 'My father, he ate me' (from the Grimms' 'Juniper Tree') into 'My mother, I ate her.'

As a child, my mother was a song-singing Southern-Baptist girl growing up in the pines of a no-place in Arkansas during the Great Depression – a hungry cotton-picking child. She wore dresses that her mother sewed out of empty flour sacks. The family's paltry crop fell to only six cents a pound in 1931, which was the year that my mother began picking cotton at age five. Poverty meant that she was expected to eat suppers of skinned squirrel covered in fatty gravy: her failing Robert sauce. It did not work for her: the abject gravy was as inedible as the squirrel. She developed a severe aversion to gravy. That is why my mother did not smother our Southern fried chicken, as is traditionally practised, in a white gravy made from bacon grease, flour, milk, salt and pepper. Nevertheless, for me, Southern fried chicken remains a saucy Saussurean-Southern-Baptist sign that mediates between my mother and a whole 'fryer' (a chicken suitable for frying), covered in a golden crust and something more.

Although there were no slaves on my mother's sparse cotton farm, or any help of any kind, my maternal grandfather's hungry squirrel-shooting and my maternal grandmother's necessary smothering of the measly meat (to make believe what lie beneath was chicken or rabbit, with a distinctly nutty flavour) is necessarily soused by Southern history's most metonymic sign: always already there slavery. It may *not* have gravy poured over it, generously thickened with flour: but it's there in the recipe, the history.

Even if it is oral.

Aural.

Too close to hear.

Here.

Dead forever?

Sickert's hare is not a rabbit.

Rabbits are very different to hares. Unlike rabbits, who are born blind and without fur, the hare is 'born fully furred, able to see, and able to move about soon after birth'.[17] With a touch of Peter Rabbit anthropomorphism, hares are born 'with their clothes on, with full sight and ready to go'.[18]

The fast hare is always on the run, with no place to go – for hares do not burrow underground like rabbits. Despite the March Hare, hares have no *Alice's Adventures in Wonderland* hole to fall into. Hares have long been associated with a keen eye and with wakefulness, even in sleep. As the Roman author Aelian wrote in his *On Animals*, the hare 'sleeps with its body alone while it continues to see with its eyes . . . enjoying this advantage over all other animals'.[19]

The hare's strong ties with seeingness may have prompted Joseph Beuys to assert, 'I am not a human being, I am a hare.'[20] In his 1965 performance *How to Explain Pictures to a Dead Hare*, the artist crawls along the floor, moving the legs of the floppy dead animal, animating it like a marionette, bringing it back to life. He shows the hare pictures. Beuys sets the hare running and looking again, as if awakened.

In 1882 Marey created chronophotography, which utilized a kind of machine gun to shoot sequential photographs in rapid succession that were then put together into a composite image depicting motion. As Marey wrote: 'I have a photographic gun which has nothing murderous about it, and which takes a picture of a bird flying or an animal running in less than 1/500 of a second. I do not know if you can imagine such a speed, but it is something surprising.'[21] For Marey, the rabbit is shot with a gun that results not in the stillness of death, but the awakening of cinema.

Carried away, I see the word 'RISE' in Sickert's sketchy signature in the bottom left corner, as if the hare and even the artist could rise from the dead. (In 1927 Sickert abandoned his first name, Walter, in favour of his middle name, and thereafter chose to be known as Richard Sickert.)

Sickert's dead hare floats in the middle of things. If only the canvas could be tilted 90 degrees anticlockwise, it, too, might leap away: like Beuys's dead hare, like animals moved by Marey's

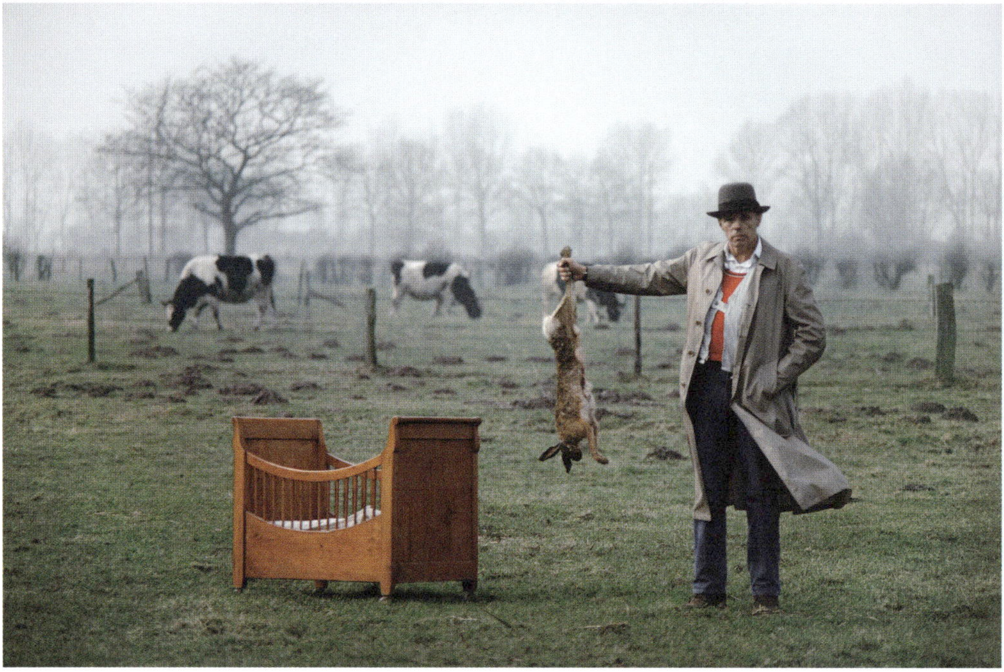

Gerd Ludwig, *Joseph Beuys with Cradle and Hare in Mehr near the Dassendokshof*, 1978, photograph.

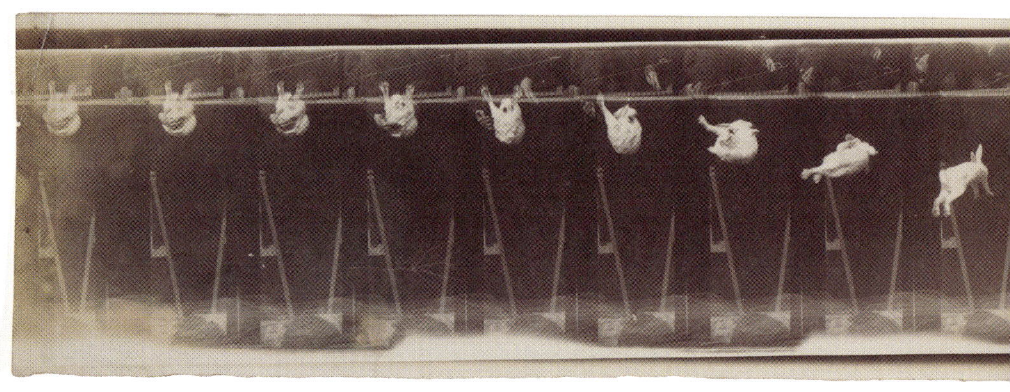

chronophotography, like the awakening of Sleeping Beauty in the forest after a hundred years, like Samantha Sweeting's 2007 video *Run Rabbit, Run Rabbit, Run, Run, Run*. In the last, Sweeting's hand gently draws the front paws of the dead rabbit towards its hind legs, as if it were preparing for a leap. Then she gently pulls the front paws and the hind legs away from each other: the rabbit soars on an invisible magic carpet. It is as if she has massaged the rabbit back to life, like rubbing a magic lamp to get the genie out. The scene has a touch of Marey with the odour of grass. *Run Rabbit, Run Rabbit, Run, Run, Run* is a filmic image of the suspension of disbelief. The rabbit is not dead, forever.

In Marcel Proust's *In Search of Lost Time*, the character Bergotte famously goes to see the little patch of yellow in Vermeer's *View of Delft*. Upon seeing it, Bergotte collapses and dies. Marcel wonders at the loss of Bergotte after he falls dead from the settee to the floor: 'He was dead. Dead forever?'[22]

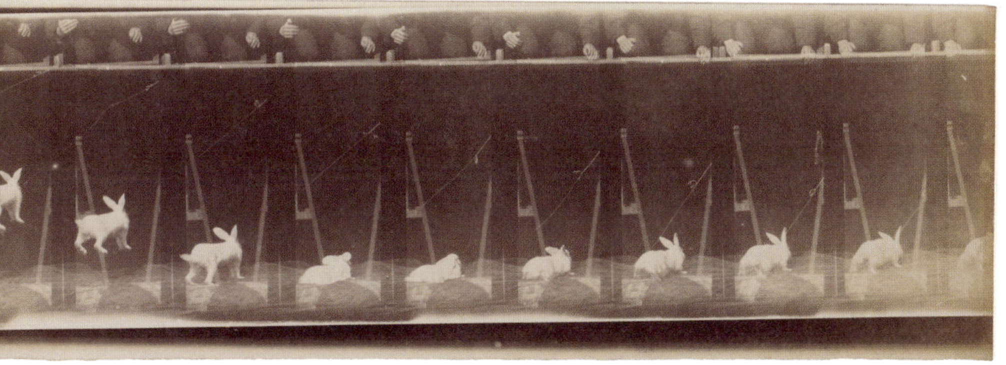

Étienne-Jules Marey, *Rabbit – Evolution of the Fall*, 1894, albumen print.

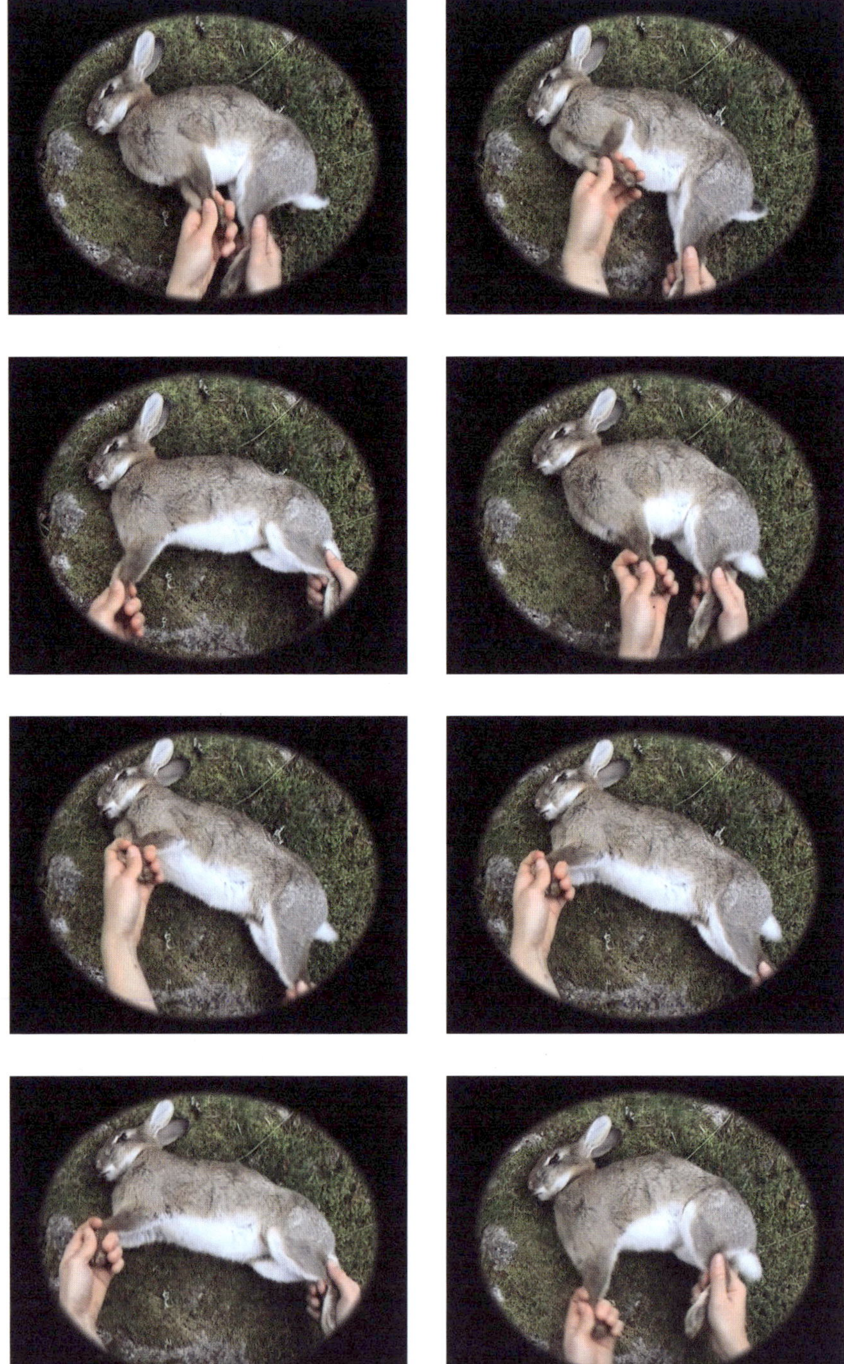

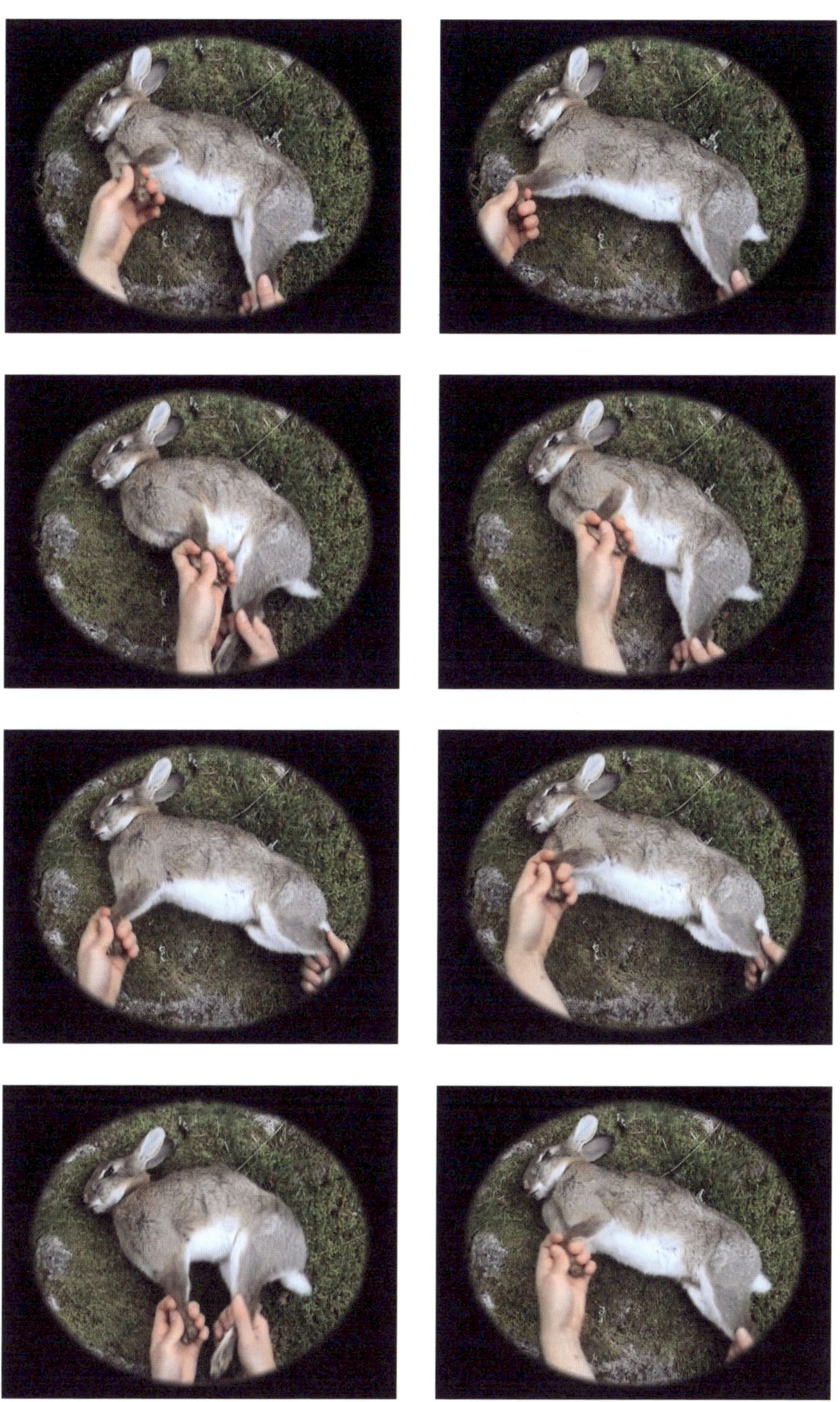

Stills from Samantha Sweeting, *Run Rabbit, Run Rabbit, Run, Run, Run*, 2007, video.

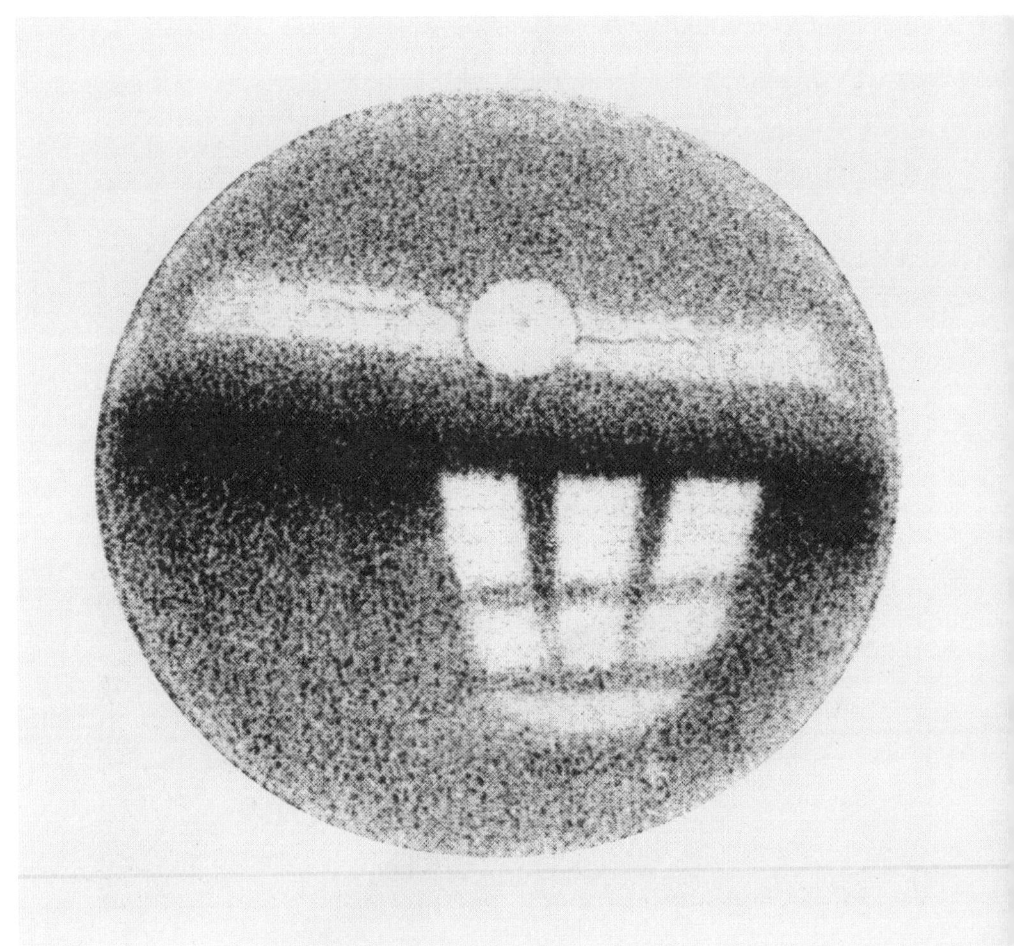

Wilhelm Kühne's rabbit optogram, 1878.

As if in a fairy tale

In a willing suspension of disbelief, photographs keep the dead alive.[23] They are associated with a magical 'return of the dead'.[24] In the middle of *Camera Lucida*, Roland Barthes claims: 'The realists do not take the photograph for a "copy" of reality, but for the emanation of past reality: a magic, not an art.'[25] Throughout *Camera Lucida* are many allusions to the magic of photography, including as an 'eidolon' (a phantom or spectre); as like the 'princess falling asleep in Sleeping Beauty', in which 'Time is engorged'; as like the young automaton (that Barthes finds so enchanting, falls in love with) in Fellini's *Casanova*; and as like 'St Veronica's napkin', miraculously 'not made by the hand of man', as '*acheiropoietos*'.[26]

This desire to magically defeat death through photography must have fuelled Wilhelm Kühne's claim in 1878 that he had found a picture – a kind of photogram, a cameraless (thereby, more magical) photograph – of a window on the retina of a dead rabbit. He called this magical manifestation an optogram, which was like a photogram.[27] Kühne believed and was determined to prove that the eye captured a final, eternal image before death, asserting that the window in the rabbit's eye was the last image that it saw before dropping dead. The image remained forever stuck on its eye; as if an acheiropoieton, as if in a fairy tale.

The body loses itself and experiences an internal transformation of suspension

Richard Learoyd has pictured a larger-than-life dead hare. Death is clear through the hare's deteriorated eye, which looks like cherry compote – abjectly edible. Looking at this photograph, I am reminded of the first three lines that fall from the dark, nightly, mothy-mouth strings of Jean-Luc Nancy's *The Fall of Sleep*: 'I'm falling asleep. I'm falling into sleep and I'm falling there by the power of sleep. Just as I fall asleep from exhaustion.'[28] The original French title of Nancy's book is *Tombe de Sommeil*, which translates as 'Tomb of Sleep', 'Tombstone of Sleep' or 'Monument of Sleep'.[29] French readers will feel the title's connection to the verb *tomber*, 'to fall'.[30] '*Tomber de sommeil* (literally, "to fall from sleep") is an idiomatic expression meaning "to drop from exhaustion, to be falling asleep on one's feet."'[31]

Significantly, for Nancy, sleep is undifferentiated from death. 'Like death, sleep, and like sleep, death – but without awakening.'[32] To suspend the fall is to will oneself to disbelieve in the catastrophe to come (death). It is a refusal of the categorization of death as different from sleep. Sleep is a fall into another world, in which the body loses itself and experiences an internal transformation of suspension.

'In the puppet or in the god'

Learoyd's dead hare is suspended by the process of his photography, as if caught in the middle of a cat's cradle of strings. In the traditional string game, players begin by making the figure of a 'cat's cradle'. Then, each player takes a turn rearranging and looping and tightening the strings to make a new figure, including 'diamonds', 'cat's eyes', 'fish in a dish' and 'candles'. One string can be made into so many things. The game ends when a player makes a mistake, creating a dead-end figure. The point of the play is to avoid dead ends.

The hare's body is loose, like a marionette, and is held delicately by strings that look to be made of milk, as if taken from Alonso Cano's 1650 painting *The Miraculous Lactation of St Bernard* (in which a statue of the Virgin comes to life and shoots a thin stream of milk into the lips of the saint). Its form, floppy and soft like an infant, suggests a pietà. Though not a lamb, the hare invokes stories of the Virgin and Christ, and the latter's martyrdom.

Learoyd's *Hare 1* has what Heinrich von Kleist names 'grace'. Its body hangs pure, 'never guilty of affectation', like the grace that can be found in the mute gestures of the marionette.[33] Marionettes 'do not think, so there is no affectation in them. They are like a man in a state of innocence before he was expelled from Eden and knew he was naked and a philosopher.'[34] Therefore, according to Kleist, 'grace appears most purely in that human form which either has no consciousness or an infinite consciousness. That is, in the puppet or in the god.'[35]

'Sprinkle flour over it and make it visible'

More disturbingly, the strings of Learoyd's hare also hang the body like a noose. The hare is lynched, like the slave Solomon in Steve McQueen's beautiful-horrific film *12 Years a Slave* (2013). The film visualizes Solomon Northup's first-hand account of being 'a free black man who was kidnapped into slavery in 1841

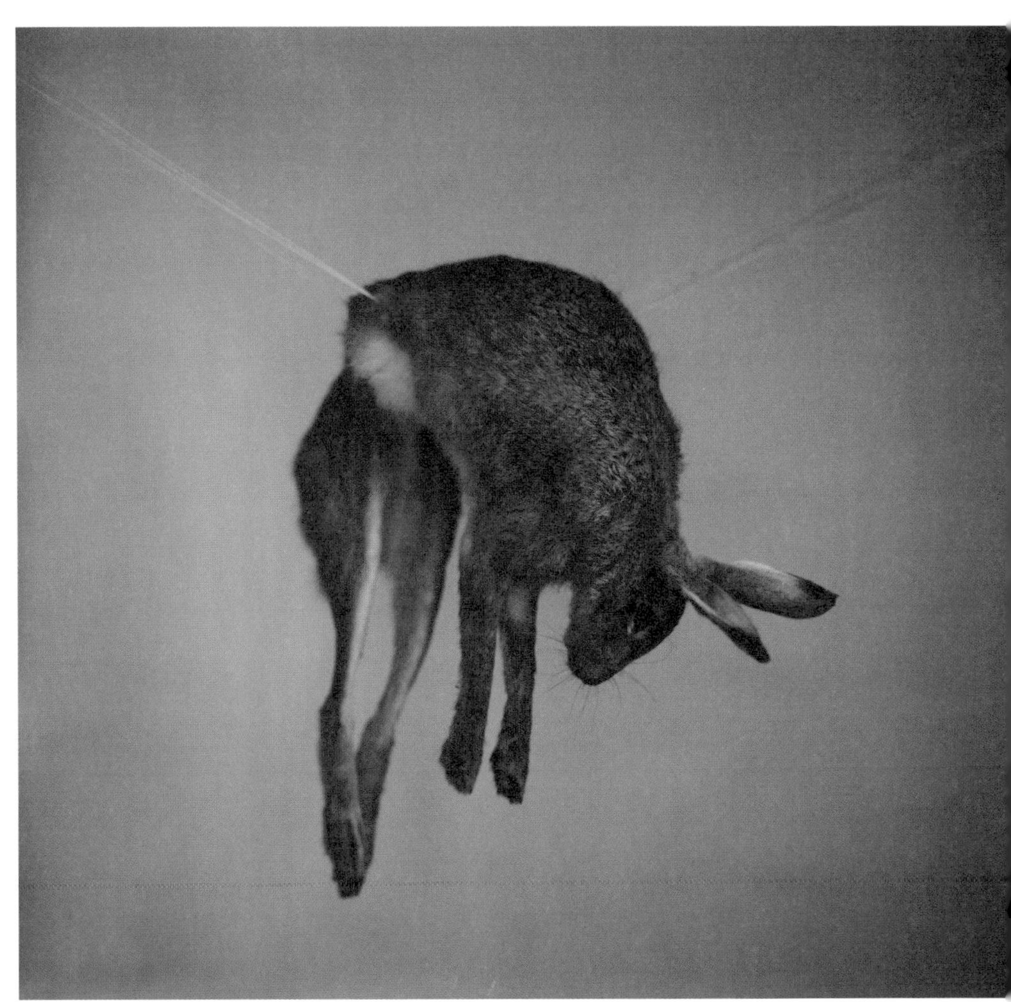

Richard Learoyd, *Hare 1*, 2012, photograph.

and forced to work on a Louisiana plantation.'[36] Although the book *Twelve Years a Slave* was a 'bestseller in its own time' (first published in 1853), it fell into obscurity.[37] That was, until a dusty copy of Northup's memoir was handed to Sue Eakin one summer in 1931 at the Bunkie Louisiana library. Eakin was a twelve-year-old white girl. At the time of her first reading, her life on earth equalled the years of Northup's enslavement.

Twelve years young for her.

Twelve years of forever for Northup.

Eakin would become a historian, dedicating her life to the book and racial equality – despite physical threats. Her 'weapon of choice was history' and Solomon Northup her 'obsession.'[38] When Eakin 'invited a black choir to sing at the Haas Auditorium, in Bunkie . . . a burning Cross landed in her front yard.'[39] But she did not let such terrorizing acts destroy her.

On his first reading of *Twelve Years a Slave*, McQueen found that 'every page was a revelation' – noting 'I felt so angry and upset with myself. Why didn't I know this book? Then I realized no one I knew knew the book. I had to make this into a film. So it became my passion.'[40]

Eakin's obsession.

McQueen's passion.

What surprised McQueen the most in translating Northup's story from page to screen was 'seeing the images. All I wanted to do was see those images . . . When I read the book. I wanted to see those images. Slavery is like the elephant in the room, and what you do is sprinkle flour over it and make it visible.'[41]

'Horrific things happen in beautiful places'

In a particularly haunting scene in the film, Solomon, with a rope strapped around his neck and tied to the branch of a tree, must stand on tiptoe to avoid hanging to death. Slaves are working all around him. Only one slave has enough courage to bring Solomon a drink of water. The audience is put into the position of considering how involved they would get. Would you just walk by? 'The whole movie is a call to arms.'[42]

Solomon barely dances to barely stay alive. A black Pavlova before Pavlova on desperate pointe. Unspeakables. The resonant sound of Solomon's choking breath terrifies. Around him hangs the strange fruit of Spanish moss – another metonymic sign for the South and, in turn, for slavery, for lynching, for terror, for the Fall of Man – which s(w)ings to the tune of Billie Holiday's 'Strange Fruit', which was written by a Jewish high-school teacher from the Bronx.[43]

I cannot close my eyes to what will always hang from the trees of the American South, where I lived for so long (North Carolina). Where my mother was born (Arkansas). Where I live and write now (Florida). I look out of my Florida window and see Spanish moss *swingin' in the Southern breeze*, along with a giant blue heron and invisible alligators in the wetlands beyond.

My 'Image-repertoire'.[44]

STEVE MCQUEEN: 'Horrific things happen in beautiful places.'[45]

The camera-mouth-room

Learoyd's *Hare 1* is a tender rendition of fur, marionette, pietà, the films of Marey, the folklore of raining animals, optography and lynchings in the American South.[46] The hare's body suspended on a string – like discarded clothing or a shed cocoon or strange fruit – wears death and life at once. The strings ensure that the hare will not fall, keeping the animal suspended, physically and metaphorically.

Learoyd's giant photographs are unique images made with a specifically built camera:

> The camera is the size of a small room, in which the artist pins direct colour positive paper (known as dye destruction, Cibachrome or Ilfachrome) to the back wall and views the image, much as inside a camera obscura. An image cast by a lens fixed to the front wall is projected onto the paper and the resulting exposed sheet is fed directly into a print processing machine connected to the walk-in camera/ dark room. The fact that this process is a direct positive on a large scale, with no print enlargement from a negative or transparency, results in an image of astounding clarity, detail and lack of film-grain. The effect is almost hyper real.[47]

Like magic, his subjects appear, as acheiropoieta.

This Pietà-hare appears to 'float' in the air, as if without a tactile paper support.[48] Like seeing an apparition. The very scale of Learoyd's hare (nearly 4 feet tall) adds to its remarkable immaculateness: even at this size, no detail is lost, no flaw appears.

To make the photograph, Learoyd stands inside his gigantic walk-in camera, a kind of camera obscura, from which he sees his shadow-subjects, like a shackled prisoner of Plato's cave. The process requires Learoyd to keep his subjects still in their pose for the eight-minute exposure. Outside of the cave, his subjects wait (dead, asleep, always still, often appearing frozen) until they are fully swallowed (rather than shot) by the camera-mouth-room.

A chance to eat again of the tree of knowledge

The difference between animal and human meat in the marvellous tale of 'Sleeping Beauty in the Forest' (between lamb and girl, between tender young goat and boy, between doe and young mother) is a metaphorical transcendence of oppositions, suspended by Robert sauce. Likewise, Learoyd's photograph transcends its own oppositions (between dead and alive, between awake and asleep, between falling and being suspended) by way of its own saucy sign: a unique photographic process without a negative or a positive or even a grain, giving us food for thought, a chance to eat again of the tree of knowledge.

> The Fall is not a past event, it is the human situation, our terrible urge to take thought, to divide, categorize and explain.
>
> – IDRIS PARRY, *Essay on Dolls*

CHAPTER SIX

Lolita's Gray Eyes

Her dream-gray[1] gaze never flinches.
Ninety pounds is all she weighs
With a height of sixty inches.
VLADIMIR NABOKOV, *Lolita*

She is 4,380 days old.

Like a photograph emerging out of its developer in a darkroom lit with red lights, like the albino eyes of a white rabbit, from yesteryear, she comes to me. Only her pool is not shallow. It is deep.

From the bottom of the blackened pool, she beats her way up – fluttering her guppy-tail feet to the pulse of the silent siren-sung melody quavering from the watered-silk castratos in the wings. Naked. Her bones poke out kiddishly. Anorectically. Her very white skin, like the moon in a black sky, takes on that new-baby-opalescent-greyness eyed in the first seconds of life, before oxygen pinks the child with blood. Her memory hole is not yet safeguarded by thick black thistledown, as was her mother's before her.

Little mole-hill breasts.

The 'erotics of tininess'.[2]

I really like her – Lolita – the gray one between the covers of Nabokov's book. Not as America's most famous adolescent – vibrantly found in film, fashion and hearsay – where her after-life is imagined as juicy, beautiful, delicious, shiny and fresh. In the USA and the UK, she wears American Apparel short pleated skirts and cropped fuzzy sweaters. So clean and shiny. So un-Lolita. In Japan, she is fashioned as Sweet, Gothic and Punk Lolita, wearing, of all things, Victorian and Rococo-inspired clothes. Petticoats. Crinolines. Bloomers. Bonnets. Lace. Big puffy sleeves. More Alice-meets-Fragonard than Lolita. (Although I must admit I am drawn to Mamechiyo's *obi*, with its anthropomorphic white-rabbit girls, worn with a creamy-pink-and-white-striped kimono with a lace collar. I could do without the lace.)

My Lolita.

My Lolita.

My Lolita.

At the tip of my tongue.

I want to protect you.

I like you, like an adolescent girl likes another adolescent girl. So much so that I write of you (and to you) in a juvenile first person.[3] Cocooning you in your true gray.

Lolita, I write you in gray pencil: the colour of your eyes.

I have gone gray, Lolita

Lolita, I know your eyes are 'clouded-glass gray'.[4] I know that your 'dream-gray gaze never flinches' [257].

I know that you grew up in a house 'dingy and old, more gray than white' [38].

Lolita, your surname seems to say it all: Haze.

And, who could forget that you died in a town named Gray Star?

'A gray star is one veiled by haze.'[5]

You are a gray American girl, ever since 1955,[6] with nothing but youth to fill your time.

Like you Lolita, I too, am an 'only' (child), born just two years after you.

If I had not been an only child, I don't think that I would have been so terrified to turn thirteen?[7] Were you terrified, as well?

If I had not been an only child, would I have failed to notice childhood slipping away?[8] Did you watching it slipping away as well?

Lolita, I am gray like you, but with my own particular palette. I grew up in California, where the smog sat heavy and motionless in the Santa Clara Valley. On weekday mornings, my yellow high-school bus meandered through the haze, as I sat on the sticky, vinyl seat, putting on thick mascara, Dr Pepper lip gloss, rose oil, brushing my hair, even tying my shoes. I was always untidy and late for the bus, waving it down at the very last minute, catching it just before it flew around the corner. I finished dressing on the bus.

In the family room of our suburban house, I watched the shooting of Bobby Kennedy by Sirhan Sirhan and all six U.S. landings on the moon: all in gray. It was not until I grew up and left home that my parents replaced our black-and-white television with colour. Seeing it, I felt inexplicably betrayed by its blaring hues. (Like adulthood.) I missed the softness, even the boredom, of seeing the world in gray.

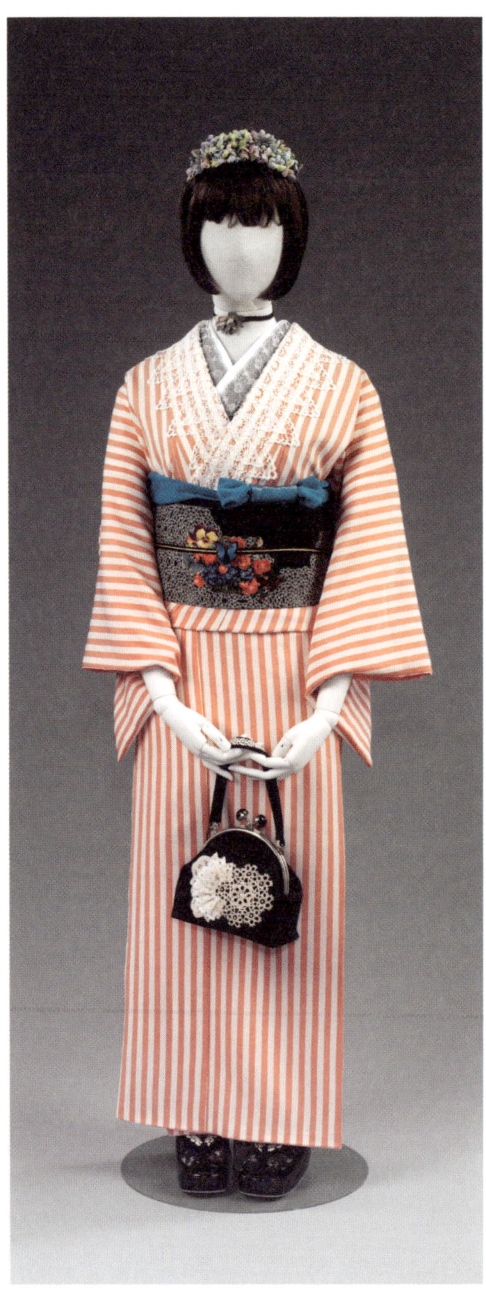

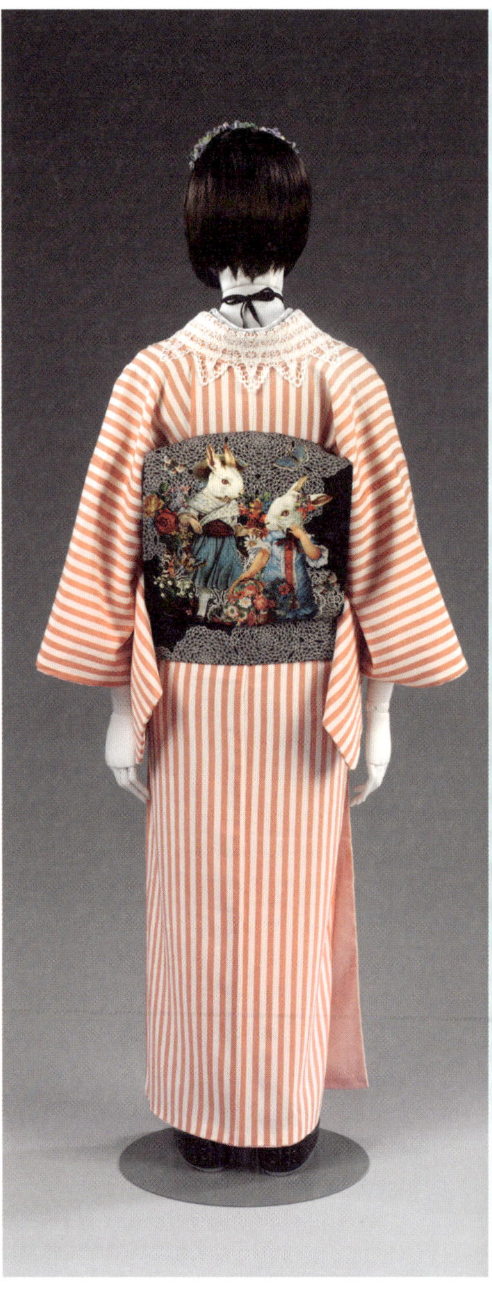

'Japanese Lolita': front, *obi* (sash) designed by Mamechiyo Modern, 2011, silk crêpe; on display from 23 April 2012 to January 2013 in the 'Kitty and the Bulldog Lolita Fashion and the Influence of Britain' exhibition at the V&A; 'Japanese Lolita': back, *obi makrura* (pillow) wrapped by *obi* (sash).

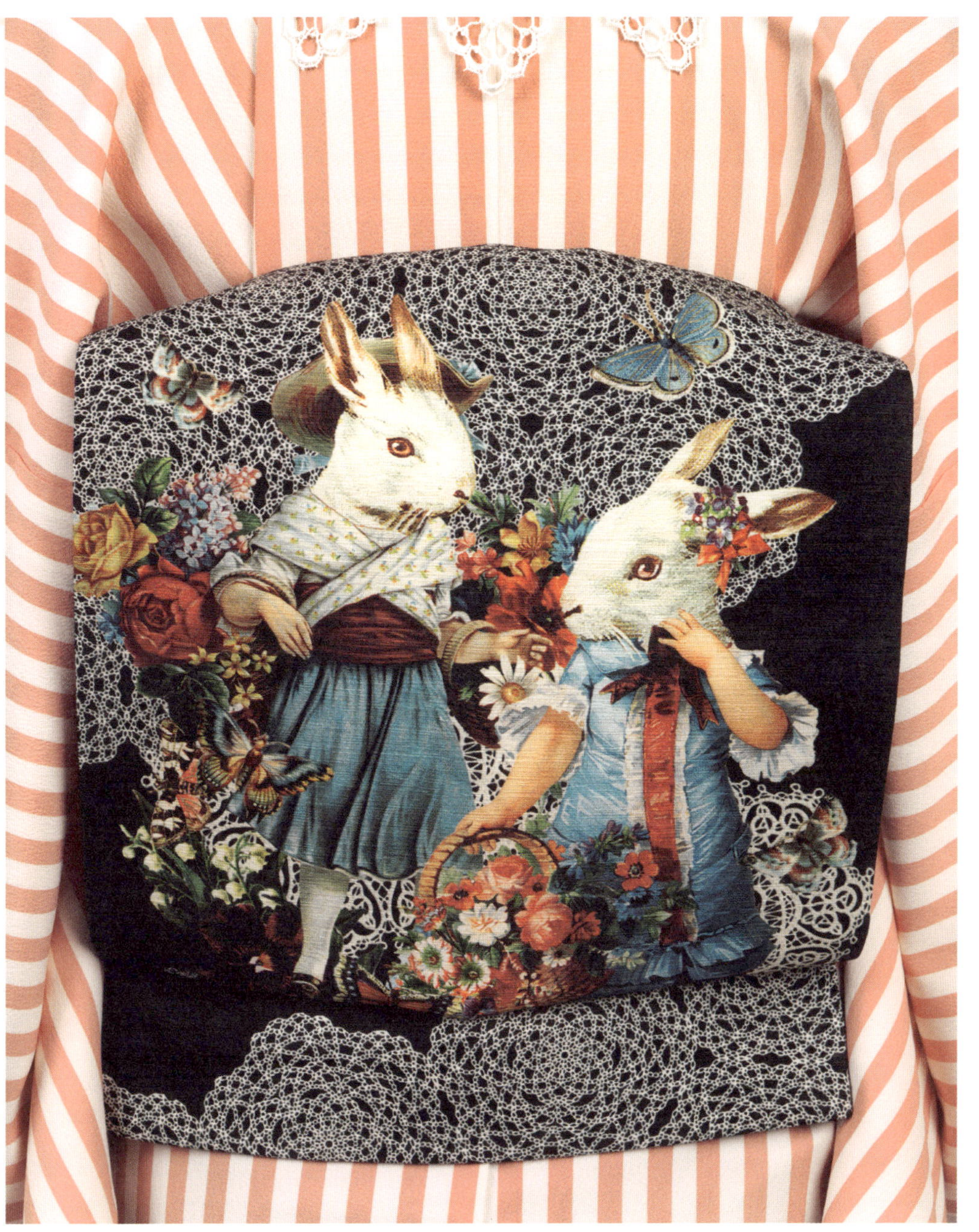

'Japanese Lolita': detail of *obi makrura* (pillow) wrapped by *obi* (sash).

And now today, I find that softness in my own hair. I have gone gray, Lolita.

Totally, going around, ya ya, man, bummer, fox, tough, drag, like

I like, I really like you, my Lolita, my Lolita – with your 'soot-black lashes' and 'pale-gray vacant eyes' [46]. Not like Humbert Humbert likes you – your obsessed pursuer, who is 'like one of those inflated pale spiders you see in old gardens' [51] – but as a girl, really likes another girl.[9] I like you adolescently – for being like me, but not the same.[10]

Like.

Alike.

Liking.[11]

I like your unrefined teenage vocabulary, stippled with words like *revolting*, *super*, *luscious*, *goon*, *drip*. When I was twelve, I talked like that too. Like you, but not the same. I said: *cool*, *doofus*, *nerd*, *chick*, *spaz*, *neat*, *jock*, *for sure*, *no dah*, *you know*, *Deadhead*, *narc*, *totally*, *going around*, *ya ya*, *man*, *bummer*, *fox*, *tough*, *drag*, *like*.

Proof that we are alive

Between you and me, in the cold morning air: breath clouds.

Gray dandelion puffs with the scent of us.

Proof that we are alive.

I found it

I write you with the gray pencil lead of 'The Ugly Duckling'. The 'hideous gray' one not yet a swan.[12] Ugly and beautiful. Like you, Lolita. You have an 'intoxicating brown fragrance' – nevertheless you 'should wash' your 'hair once in a while'. [45].

I worked hard to find your smudgy pencil-lead gray, but I found it.

Like you

Gray is the colour of ash, lead, flint, an overcast sky. Gray can be a rabbit, a dog, a fox, a Persian cat or a shark. Gray is a roly-poly pill bug, pencil lead, castles, a wolf.

Gray is mostly too undecided to be a sure symbol, save for ageing. Gray is not direct, is between black and white, like an adolescent between adult and child.

Gray tends towards expansion, like an elephant's hide, like a skyscraper's height, like a blanket of dust, like the magnitude of the moon.

Gray makes time felt, as in Joseph Beuys's *Felt Suit* (1970).

Although often as big as an elephant, gray is mousy.

A goose can be gray and so can a swan and a pearl.

Gray is dust, cement, stone, wool, a battleship, everyone's hair, at least those with the good luck to eventually grow old (save for Marcel Proust, who claimed his hair did not turn gray), the Zone System of black-and-white photography, a complexion that is not well, a name (as in Effie Gray, who married the painter Millais). Some of the squares in the series of paintings by Josef Albers,

Josef Albers, *Homage to the Square: With Rays*, 1959, oil on masonite.

entitled *Homage to the Square*, are gray. There is one particular image, *Homage to the Square: With Rays*, painted in 1959, just four years after your birth, that I like to daydream about. Squares of field-yellow, morning-sun-yellow and butter-yellow – and a centre square in fog-gray. The yellow makes the gray sing.

Like the marigold-yellow that chirrups and hovers on the wingtip of the chained European goldfinch – a common little pet of the time – whose golden notes are made brighter by the soft feathery daubs of mouse-gray, khaki-gray, charcoal gray, in a small *trompe-l'œil* painting by Carel Fabritius.

Like the unchained little Lawrence's goldfinch, with wing and breast patches of yellow in its mostly gray feathering, who fluttered into our garage on my twelfth birthday. Such adventitious things do happen.

Gray is *Attracted to Light* – the soft gray photograph of a moth by the Starn Twins, with thin, dust-powdered wings the colour of cream spotted by drops of pewter. It's a toned silver print on Thai mulberry paper, printed as large as a pillowcase. The moth's wings, writ large, spread flat and open across an electric-light moon, a luminous nimbus. The light holds back the black night, which seeps through along the picture's edges. Fine T-shaped, nickel-plated pins fasten the creature-as-picture to the wall. The Starn Twins like to poke pins into their photographs. I like the star of their name, veiled by the haze of all the things I like about you. Twins always feel eternally adolescent to me, even when they have grown old. Like you.

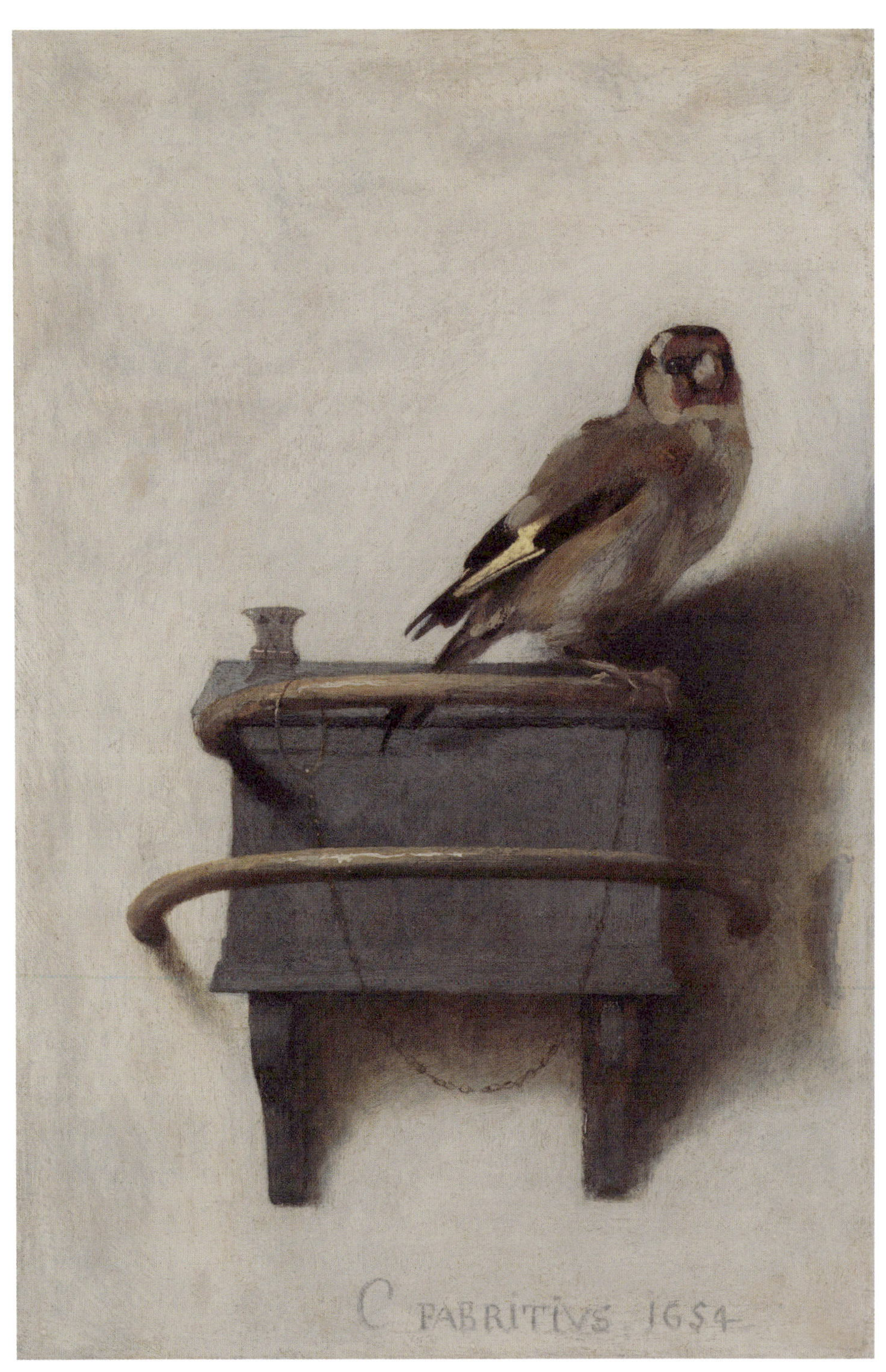

Carel Fabritius, *The Goldfinch*, 1654, oil on panel.

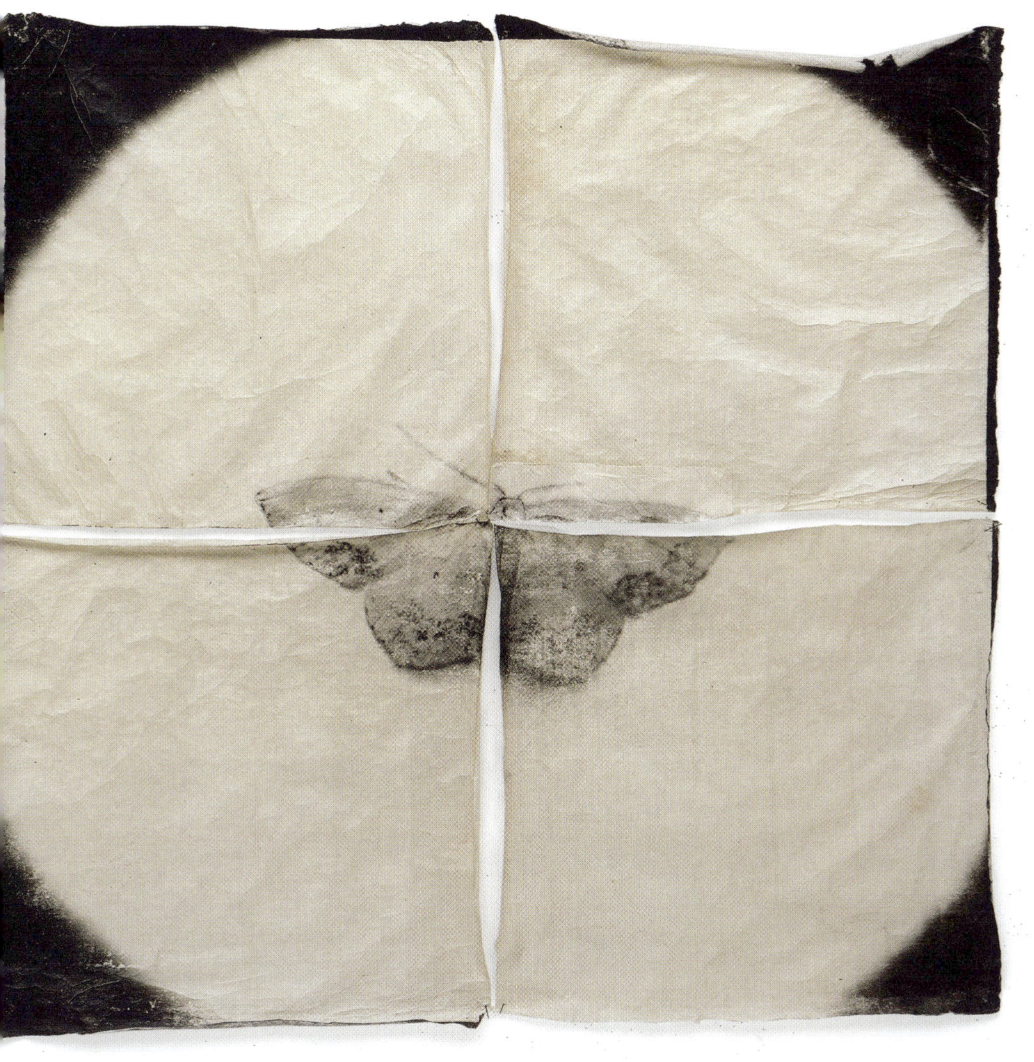

Doug and Mike Starn, *Attracted to Light B*, 1996–2000, toned silver prints on Thai mulberry paper.

'Snug-fitting bodices and generously full skirts'

Gray is James McNeill Whistler's *Harmony in Grey and Green: Miss Cicely Alexander* (1872–4). The wall behind her is a patina of gray and gray-green velvety moth-wing smudges. The realness of her girlness is in her admirable, frankly cross pout. It seems she was able to sustain it for the two years of posing. As the grown Cicely told Whistler's biographers, she considered herself a 'victim all through the sittings or rather standings, for he never let me change my position, and I believed I sometimes used to stand for two hours at a time. I know I used to get very tired and cross, and often finished my days in tears . . . I was a very grumbling, disagreeable girl.'[13] It's been said that 'it would be difficult to cite another example of a portrait in which the sitter scowls at the artist.'[14]

Cicely's white dress is crisply starched with pleated veins, filled with air, like a fresh moth who has just burst from its cocoon. The painter with the famed signature – who made his initials into a butterfly ideograph with the flair of Japonisme – wanted her dressed in the perfect dress, so he called on his mother Anna (also famously painted in gray[15]) to contact Cicely's mother to find pure white muslin. She writes in a letter: 'It should be without blue, as purely white as it can be.'[16]

> At this point Whistler takes the pen from his mother's hand and continues, giving detailed instructions, including a map as to where the fine Indian muslin he prefers can be purchased. He proceeds to design the dress in detail: 'The

> dress might have frills on the skirts and about it – and a fine little ruffle for the neck or else lace – also it might be looped up from to time with bows of pale yellow ribbon . . . the little dress afterwards [should be] done up by the laundress with a little starch to make the frills and skirts etc stand out – of course not an atom of blue!' He added a little sketch.[17]

The transparent gray-green gossamer of Cicely's sash is made of pupa remnants, appearing more like a butterfly's chrysalis sac than the remains of a moth's cocoon. Heaped on a seat behind her is the bulk of what is decidedly a discarded cocoon – like a coat. The charcoal-gray felt hat in her hand is like the head of a moth, its pale green-gray-yellow plume a feathery antenna.

Tiny butterflies flit about her. Like delicate miniature marionettes, their strings are invisible. The two butterflies above Cicely's head are butter-yellow; one has dipped its wings in monarch russet. Above the yellow-centred daisies – whose stems are so delicate and slight that the flowers appear to fly and float through the air – is a white butterfly, whose open white wings express gray-blue eyes.

The bows on her velvet slippers are floral butterflies. She has a light step.

Whistler's gray butterfly signature is flat on the wall, like a spider in waiting. The strong body is more of a dragonfly. Butterfly-man-spider-dragonfly. When further developing his signature, Whistler sometimes added a stinger. He had a bellicose side.

When you are 'twelve years and seven months old' [107–8], H.H. – the self-proclaimed spider – goes shopping for you, Lolita.

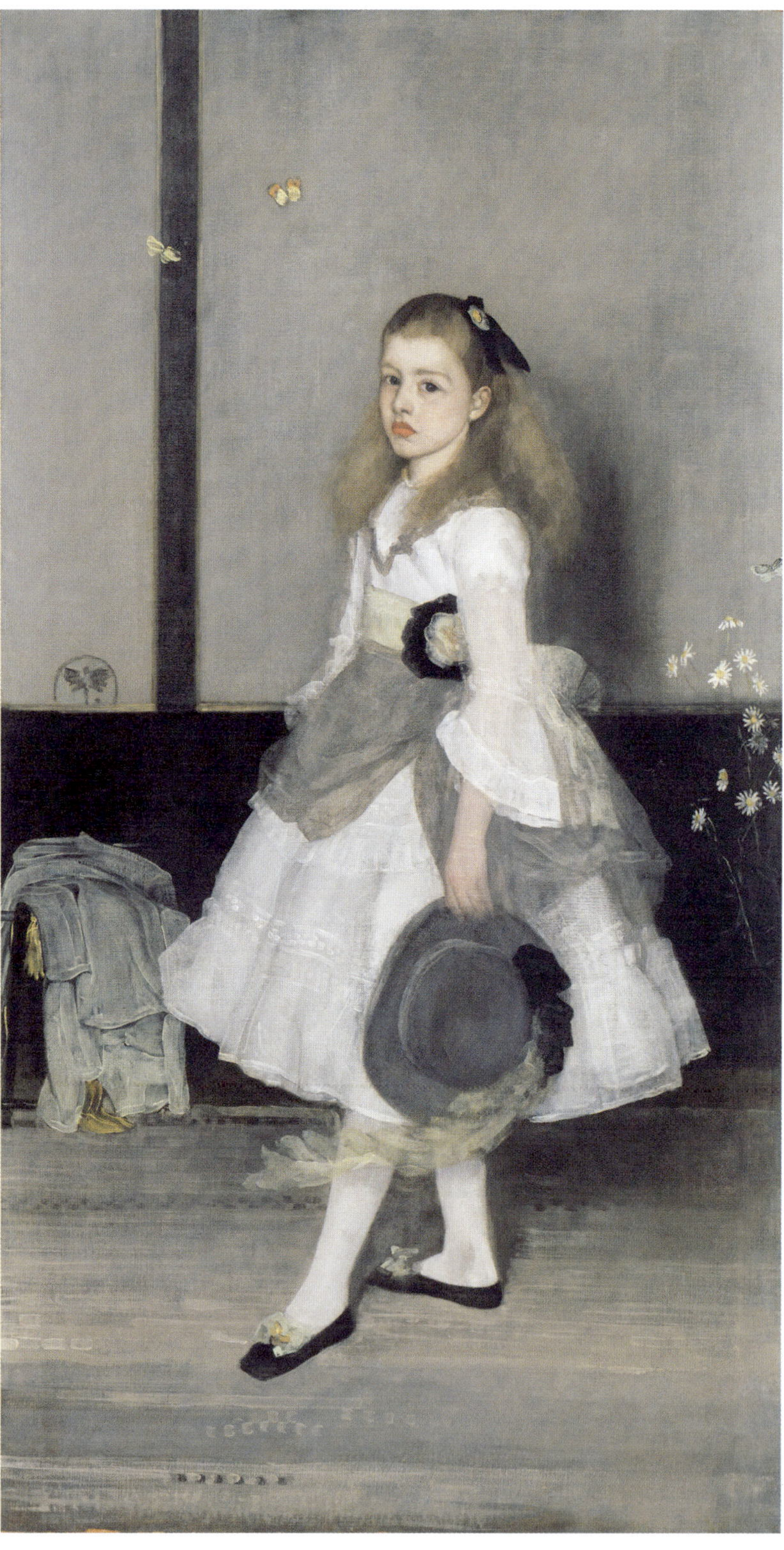

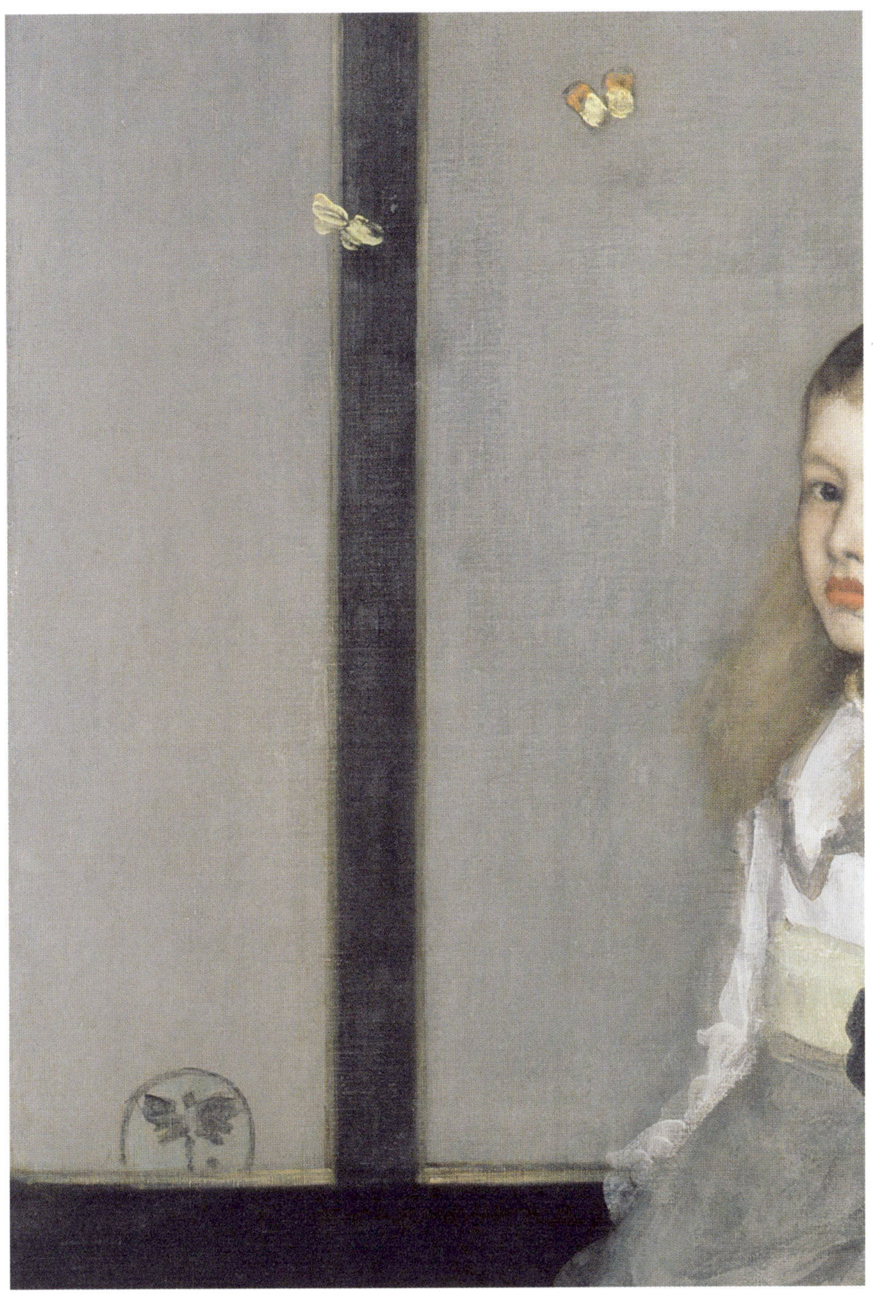

James McNeill Whistler, *Harmony in Grey and Green: Miss Cicely Alexander* (detail of signature).

James McNeill Whistler, *Harmony in Grey and Green: Miss Cicely Alexander*, 1872–4, oil on canvas.

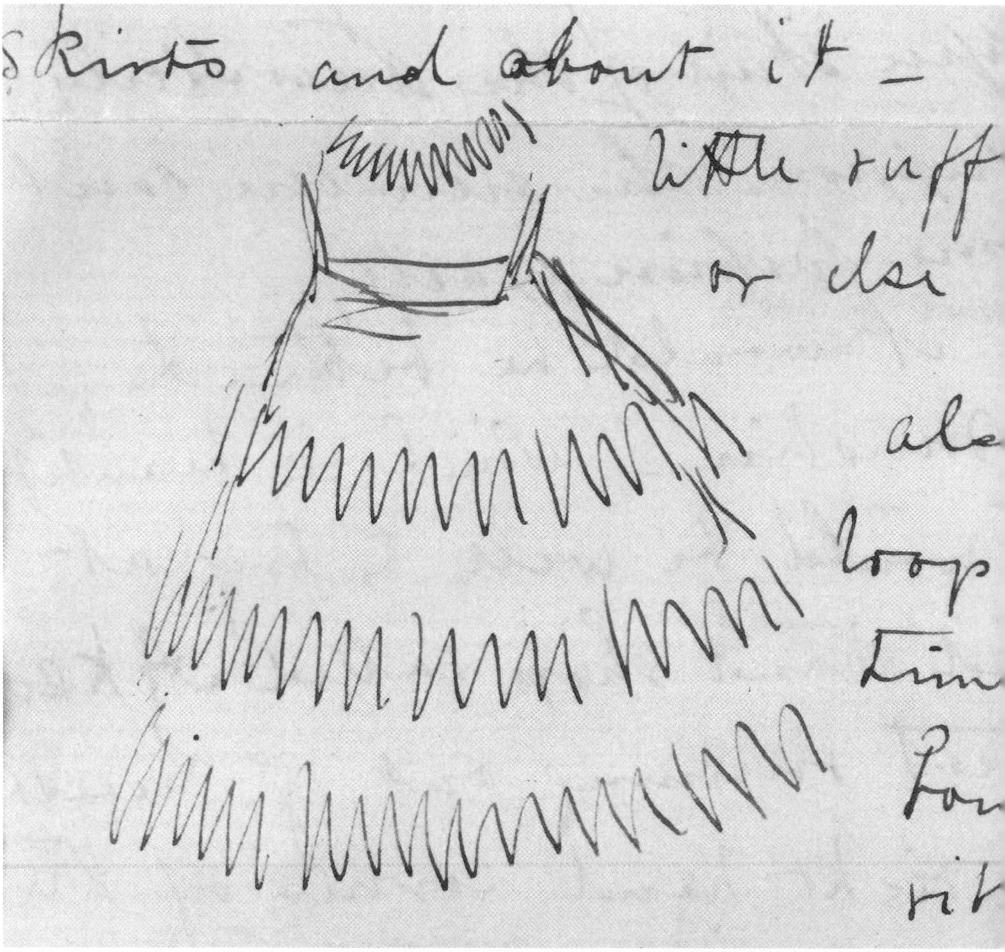

Skirts and about it –
little ruff
or else

Whistler's sketch of how he imagined Cicely Alexander's dress for her portrait as part of his letter to Mrs Alexander, 26 August 1873.

He has an eerie eye for girl-fashion with the same scissoring precision as the thread-counting Whistler. To get the perfect fit, H.H. brings along your exact measurements – as recorded in an 'anthropometric entry' by your mother on your twelfth birthday in her copy of *Know-Your-Child* [109]:

> hip girth, twenty-nine inches; thigh girth (just below the gluteal sulcus), seventeen; calf girth and neck circumference, eleven; chest circumference, twenty-seven; upper arm girth, eight; waist, twenty-three; stature, fifty-seven inches; weight seventy-eight pounds; figure, linear; intelligence quotient 121; vermiform appendix present, thank God [109].
>
> H.H. has a predilection for 'check weaves, bright cottons, frills, puffed-out short sleeves, soft pleats, snug-fitting bodices and generously full skirts!' [109]

A mouthful of gupa

Gray is Giotto's grisaille, in the mostly blue frescoes of Cappella degli Scrovegni.

On the lower walls below the star-studded lapis lazuli canopy of the Scrovegni Chapel, seven vices and seven virtues are 'painted in mineral shades of gray'.[18] Here, with more *trompe-l'œil* play, evil and good are not black and white, are beguiled gray. Around the sinful neck of *Infidelitas* (Idolatry) hangs an idol (doll) from a rope.

With one eye wide open and the other shut tight, *Infidelitas* worships his plaything. Yoked by the belief that youth can be lassoed. Like a cross-eyed Humbert Humbert, nictating with desire.

The 'doll' holds a small tree in her hand: she's a wood nymph.[19]

Lolita, you were 'Dolly at school' [11] just as you are 'Dolores on the dotted line' [11].

In Latin, doll is *pupa*. Hence the French *poupée*.

A pupa is also the chrysalis of those insects that undergo complete metamorphosis (*holometabolous*), like moths, and butterflies. Moving from egg to larva to pupa to imago (adult), these insects grow to look nothing like their newborn selves. Pupas, like human adolescents, are one with their rooms (their close-fitting cocoons, their snug chrysalises). They take a long while to finally come out, suddenly emerging as young adults, with the surprise of a moth or a butterfly.

Complete metamorphosis, as told through the proboscis of the entomologist, is a scientific version of the ugly duckling becoming a beautiful swan. (Andersen's tale rolls off of Humbert Humbert's punning proboscis when he asks us to consider: 'the ugly dumplings in black stockings and white hats that are metamorphosed into stunning stars of the screen' [19].)

Lolita, you are a new beast freed from your original signifier of 'girl'. You are girl + pupa.

A portmanteau creature.

A mouthful of gupa.

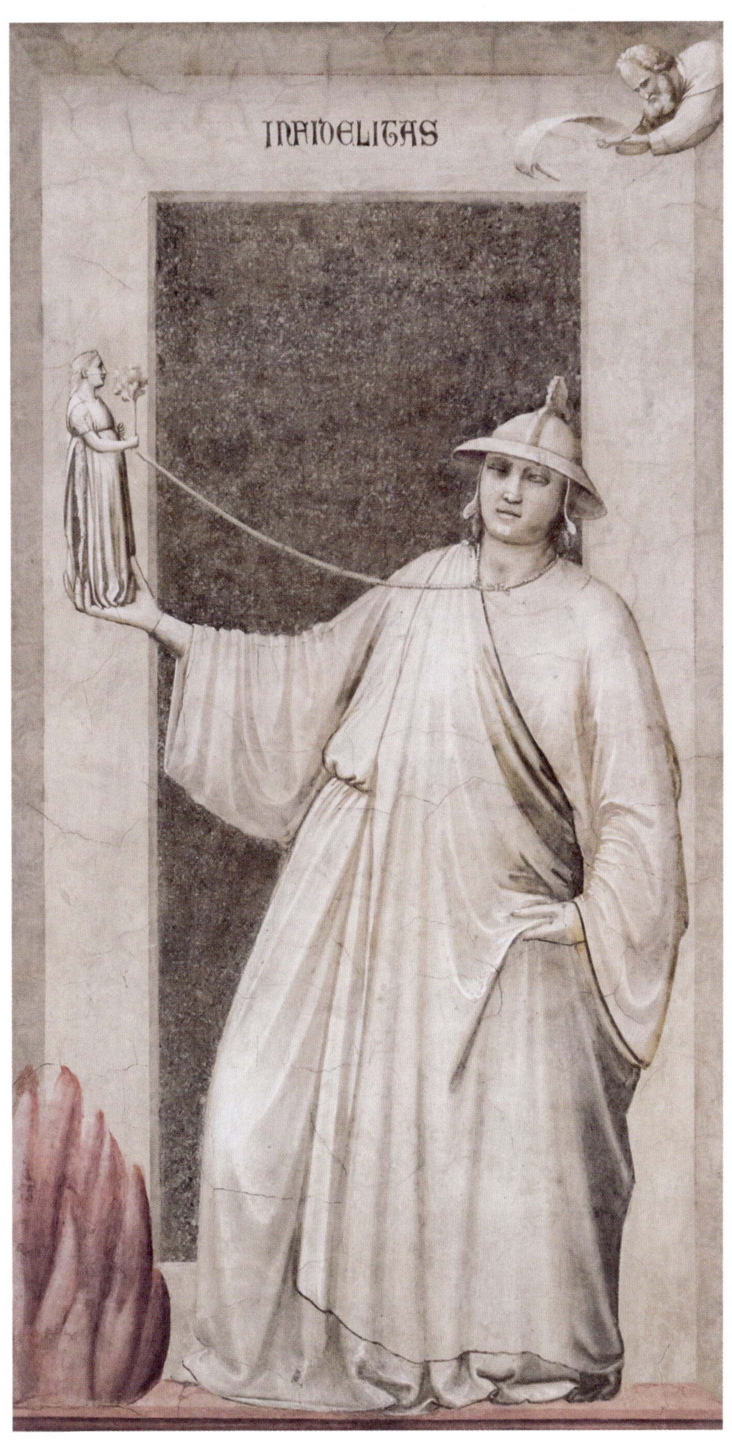

Giotto, *Idolatry*, *c.* 1305, marble imitation, Arena Chapel.

I like Alice, just as I like you

I feel 'a breeze from Wonderland' [131].

Lolita, do you know that Lewis Carroll invented the portmanteau word? You know, like 'mimsy' for 'miserable' and 'flimsy'.[20]

Did you know that Nabokov once referred to Carroll as the original Humbert Humbert?[21]

Did you know that Nabokov translated *Alice's Adventures in Wonderland* into Russian in 1923?

Did you know that 'Alice' was a real little girl named Alice Liddell and that Lewis Carroll gave her the original handwritten manuscript as a Christmas gift in 1864?

Have you read *Alice's Adventures in Wonderland*?

I like Alice, just as I like you.

Butterfly hunting

Lolita, your author was a famed entomologist, who had a remarkable passion for collecting butterflies.

Did you know he wrote you on the road while hunting butterflies? He took to his pen 'in the evenings or on cloudy days', when the butterflies were reluctant to come out or were in hiding.[22] His clever wife Véra did all the driving, as he hunted (and wrote you) state by state, across America.

'Véra famously saved [you] "Lolita" from incineration in a trash can when he wanted to destroy it [you].'[23]

Thank you, Véra. Thank you for liking ugly things.

I was starting to like ugly things more and more

When I was five years old, the big tree in our backyard became filled with mysterious and enchanting gray cocoons. My kind and benevolent father cut off a few select branches, rich with flight yet to come, and placed them in a huge clear glass jar for me. I proudly brought my portable hothouse, filled with branches and cocoons, to my kindergarten. The cocoons looked like the rows of neatly crinkled brown curls in Diego Velázquez's strange portrait of the Infanta of Spain. Pinned to her huge head of coiffured hair are more than a dozen silk butterflies (or moths), as if recently hatched.

But my cocoons, unlike the Infanta's hair, seemed to be in eternal hibernation. The jar was their block of ice, seemingly keeping them frozen. My classmates gave up any hope that they would ever hatch. Then suddenly, one evening, a thaw. I entered the classroom to discover that the cocoons had hatched. Not as the beautiful butterflies of my imagination, but as mammoth moths with furry antennae. They were the size of small birds, with ocular patterns on their huge wings, which appeared like disembodied eyes, like owls hiding in a dark forest. I hated them. But the boys in the class loved their abjectness and begged for them as surreal gifts. P-l-e-e-e-a-s-e. P-l-e-e-e-a-s-e. P-l-e-e-e-a-s-e.

From afar, I chose a boy to take the whole jar. That night, the Sandman came to me. I did not dream of Hoffmann's wicked Sandman taking my eyes out and placing them in a bag to take home to his eye-eating children, with 'crooked beaks, like owls, with which to peck out the eyes of naughty human children' who lived on the 'crescent moon'.[24] But I did have a nightmare of moths

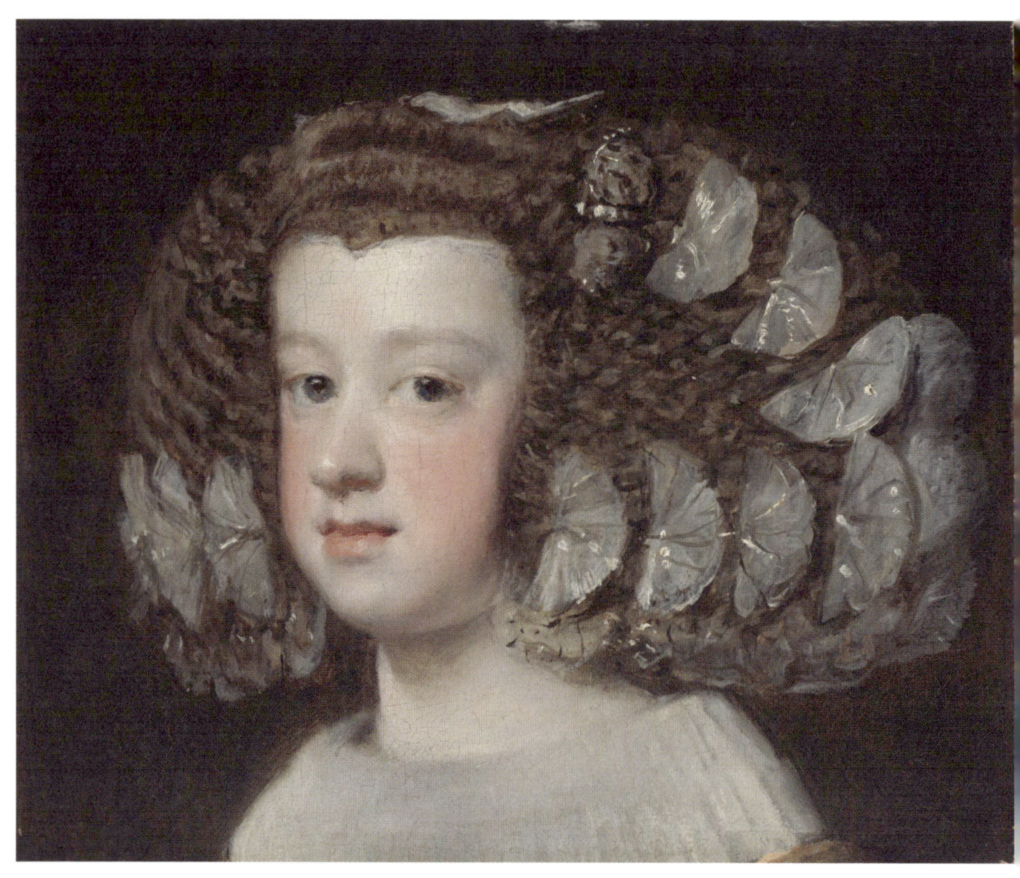

Diego Velázquez, *María Teresa, Infanta of Spain*, 1651–4, oil on canvas.

metamorphosing into owls. I awoke before the nocturnal beasts got to my eyes.

Four years after my horrific kindergarten experience, my gut was turned inside out by metamorphosis once again. This time it happened when my fourth-grade teacher showed our class a time-lapsed educational film of a caterpillar turning into a chrysalis, only to emerge from its casement as a monarch butterfly. (I bet, Lolita, you saw the same film too. In school, back then, we all learned the same things in a curriculum of sameness.)

Like playing rock paper scissors, metamorphosis all comes from the same hand. The same hand makes the caterpillar, the chrysalis and the butterfly: caterpillar pupa butterfly. But unlike rock paper scissors, the metamorphosis of a monarch butterfly, at least for the girl still in me, is ugly and abject. Like finding the skin formed from overheating the milk in a mouthful of hot cocoa.

While watching the film, the smushy caterpillar made me ill.

And the pupa made me ill.

And the folded and moist butterfly made me ill.

And the discarded pupal case, like the dried glue that I enjoyed peeling off the tips of my fingers – which was also like the embryonic sacs of the kittens I once saw being born – which was also like the jellyfish washed up on the beach that I sometimes accidentally stepped on – made me especially ill.

Yet I really liked watching this American educational horror flick. I could not help from looking. I was changing.

I was starting to like ugly things more and more.

You are my gray nymphéa

Humbert Humbert calls you a 'perfect little nymph' [198] – 'the loveliest nymphet' [44]. He sees you as a 'sleepy nymphet' [108] and claims you as 'not human, but nymphic' [18]. Your 'dear dirty jeans' smell of 'orchards' in 'nymphetland' [94]. H.H. suffers madly from the malady of nympholepsy, belonging to a group of 'lone voyagers' known as 'nympholepts' [19].

Nymph punning is a Humbert-Humbert Humming of zoological, botanical, biological and mythological notes at once.

Your author/pursuer knew that a nymph is a word used not only for pupa, but for an undeveloped bug. Different from moths and butterflies, ladybirds and beetles (and other such bugs) undergo *incomplete* metamorphosis (*hemimetabolism*). They forego pupation. Nymphs are bug-children and bug-teenagers, not yet adults.

Lolita, did you know that Nymphalidae is the largest family of butterflies, which includes monarchs among its 6,000 species? One of your author's butterfly discoveries is known as 'Nabokov's Wood-Nymph', and belongs to the family Nymphalidae, bringing wonder to me, the girl connoisseur.[25]

Although now rare, your author knew that 'nymphae' once referred to the female genitals (labia minora). '*Nymphæ* are little pieces of Flesh in a Woman's Secrets,' writes Steven Blankaart in his 1684 *A Physical Dictionary*.[26] (Yuck.)

And your author knew that nymphéa is the scientific name for water lilies – from the family *Nymphaeaceae*. (In his poem 'Lilith' – a very early nymphéa bloom of you, Lolita – Nabokov writes: 'showing a russet armpit, in a doorway/ there stood a naked girl./ She had a water lily in her curls.'[27] Although I would not recommend that you read it, Lolita. It's not very good.)

Above the water, nymphéas offer petals of pure pretty femininity – but upon closer study, one discovers the frightening tangle of dark roots half hidden in the murky waters below. Nymphéas are like mermaids, hiding their darker, uglier sexuality, their tuber rhizomes (like fishy tails), below the surface. Fittingly, H.H. buys you a *deluxe* edition of Andersen's *The Little Mermaid* for your thirteenth birthday. (But weren't you too old for that sort of thing?)

A white lotus (the most popular of the nymphéas) is traditionally an image of purity and innocence, if you forget the slimy parts below. Slimy + purity = Slimurity. A good word for describing a real, growing, living nymphéa.

As H.H. himself learns about you, while the two of you were lodging at the Enchanted Hunters hotel, you had already lost your virginity at summer camp to a young boy, when you were only eleven years old.

Lolita, you are not innocent and not, not innocent.

You are my gray nymphéa.

Gray is your lotus

In Peter Henry Emerson's 1886 photograph, a gray figure in a gray hat picks in gray boat picks gray nymphéas out of the gray water (like photographs being pulled out of the fixing bath) among rushes of gray. The lilies will be used in the large gray bow net (which can be seen behind the oarsman) as bait for catching the gray fish, which remain unseen.

Gray is your lotus.

Girtree

And your author knew that a nymph was girly mythological spirit of lissom beauty and sprightly youth who inhabited watery and woodsy places.

Apollo's first love was lovely *nymphey* Daphne, the child of the river Penéüs. Jealous of Apollo, Cupid shot the god with an arrow made of gold, which filled him with unquenchable desire for the virgin Daphne. To make matters worse, spiteful Cupid shot Daphne with a heavy arrow made of gray, glum lead that made her have no desire at all.

Lolita, when H.H. comes crawling on his knees to your chair, you give him 'one look – a gray furry question mark of a look: "Oh no, not again"' [193]. And, 'oh *no*', you say with a 'sigh to heaven', your 'soot-black lashes matted', your 'grave gray eyes more vacant than ever' [287].

Francesca Woodman, with her unescapable foresty name, who took her first photographs at age thirteen, shoots herself with her camera as if it were loaded with arrows of Cupid's glum lead and becomes a Daphne tree. Surrendering to roots, her gray arms are wrapped in white birch bark like fingerless gloves, like shackles, her hands raised above her head. She says: 'Take me, but you will have to take me as a gray tree.'

Around the Woodman-nymph, I hear the timbre of trees murmuring support: 'Better to be a tree, then have to fuck Apollo.'

Woodman is held, in gray emulsion, between girl and tree. Girl + tree = Girtree.

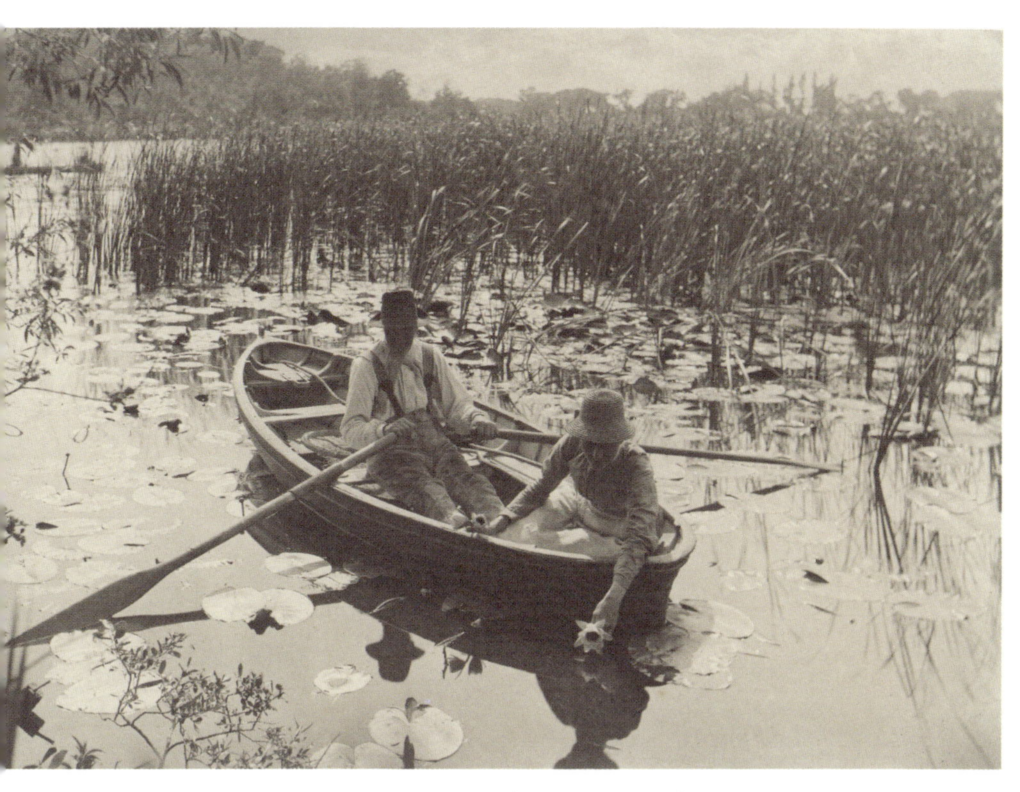

Peter Henry Emerson, *Gathering Water-Lilies*, 1886, photograph.

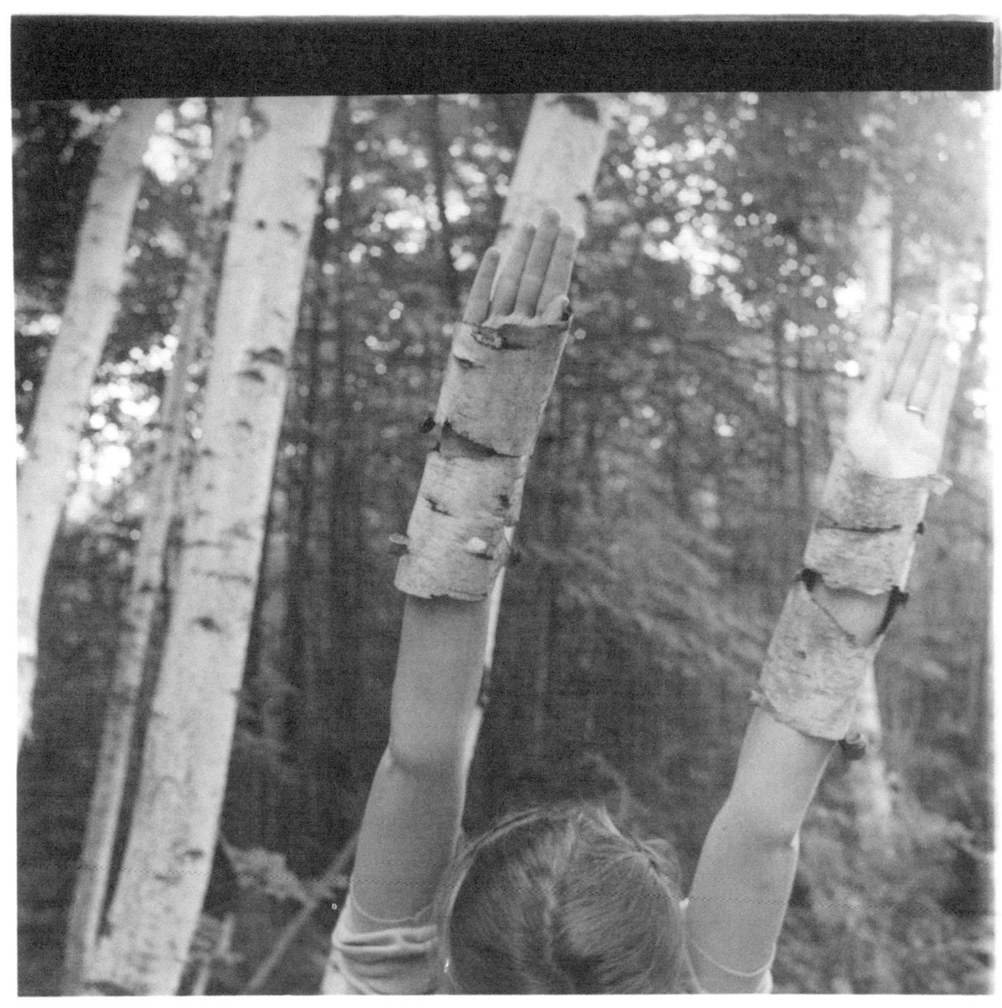

Francesca Woodman, *Untitled (MacDowell Colony, Peterborough, New Hampshire)*, 1980, gelatin silver estate print.

This is not true

Lolita, your author frolics with you as pupa – as nymph – as doll – as chrysalis – as butterfly – as girleen of the forests, rivers and seas – as water lily.

'Oh, my Lolita, I have only words to play with!' [34] Humbert Humbert exclaims.

In school, we were taught to say: 'Sticks and stones may break my bones, but words will never hurt me.'

This is not true.

The metamorphosis fails

By the end of the novel, you are still only seventeen. An adolescent pupa forever. Married and pregnant with your own little doll.

You died before your author/lepidopterist could pinch your thorax so that he could spread your wings enough to be pinned. You died in childbirth, on Christmas day, in the town of Gray Star.

Failed fecundity.

Your baby was unable to emerge alive from your womb. A stillborn girl. Unpinked with life. Presumably a gray little thing.

The metamorphosis fails.

I like you

You, my Lolita, are the failed echo of an earlier story written by your author, in Russian, in 1928, entitled 'Christmas': a tale of hibernation and successful metamorphosis. A dark story of a moth (the night-time butterfly). A story of a boy. I love the story, but not as much as I like you.

'Christmas' – with its snowdrifts reaching all the way to the window, tilted mirrors like ice, dazzling frost, the green paws of fir trees under bright plump loads of snow, and the delicate icy moon – is a fairy tale. Like the 'Snow Maiden', the Russian tale of a girl named Snegurka, who is made of snow. Or Andersen's 'The Snow Queen,' in which Gerda's hot tears melt Kai's lump-of-ice heart back to life. Enchantments from your author's childhood.

The story begins shortly before Christmas. Sleptsov has returned from Petersburg to his manor house, where he spends his summer holidays. It's winter. Sleptsov will stay just a couple of days. Ivan, his portly valet, has settled his master in the annex (rather than the big house), where it's easier to keep Sleptsov warm by lighting the Dutch stoves in the smaller, living space. The main house has been left alone: cold – on hold – in hibernation – like a great sleeping bear waiting for summer. The paintings are covered over with curtains of 'gray squares',[28] like blankets.

Nabokov-the-wordsmith has carefully chosen the name Slept(sov): seeing that sleep quietly rested in the protagonist's name.[29]

Two days before, Sleptsov's beloved son died in Petersburg. The boy died, 'after having babbled in his delirium about school, about his bicycle, about some great Oriental moth'.[30] The boy, like Nabokov, liked to hunt butterflies and moths.

It is night. The sorrow is too great. It is very cold outside. Sleptsov is sitting on a plush-covered chair. He despondently raises his hand and notices 'a drop of candle wax had ... stuck and hardened in the thin fold between two fingers. He spread his fingers and the little white scale cracked.'[31]

On Christmas Eve, Sleptsov leaves the warmth of the annex and enters the big house, stepping into the cold room, which had been his boy's study in the summer months. It is frozen in time – exactly as it was before death. Sleptsov discovers 'a note-book, spreading boards, supplies of black pins and an English biscuit tin that contained a large exotic cocoon which had cost three rubies. It was papery to the touch and seemed to be made of a brown folded leaf'.[32] Sleptsov gathers the 'biscuit tin with the pear-shaped cocoon' and other objects belonging to the boy and returns from the cold big house to the warm annex: 'chilled, red-eyed, with gray dust smears on his cheek'.[33] The boys' objects are inspected, and the father grieves. The clock ticks. Finding life 'devoid of miracles',[34] Sleptsov presses his eyes shut.

> At that instant, there was a sudden snap – a thin sound like of an overstretched rubber band breaking. Sleptsov opened his eyes. The cocoon in the biscuit tin had burst at its tip, and a black wrinkled creature the size of a mouse was crawling up the wall above the table . . . It had emerged from the chrysalid because a man overcome with grief had transferred a tin box to his warm room and the warmth had penetrated its taut leaf-and-silk envelope . . . And its wings – still feeble, still moist – kept growing and unfolding, and now they were developed to the limit set for them by God, and there, on the wall instead of a little lump of life, instead of a dark mouse, was a great *Attacus* moth like those that fly, birdlike, around lamps in the Indian dusk.

> And then those thick black wings, with a glazy eyespot on each and a purplish bloom dusting their hooked foretips, took a full breath under the impulse of tender, ravishing, almost human happiness.[35]

'Christmas' is full metamorphosis.

This was not your achievement Lolita.

You refused to come out of your room, your cocoon.

Like a Russian nesting doll, a pupa within a pupa within a pupa – there is no development. *Mise en abyme*: a girl within a girl; a daughter within a daughter; a story within a story.

Your metamorphosis fails, that is its success.

You stay as gray as an ugly duckling.

I like ugly things.

I like you.

Afterword

[ ]

Like Caravaggio's St Matthew – cloaked in an orange, as orange as the orange trees in Rome – I have a desire, even 'a lust', to write, to float, like the angel above St Matthew.[1] I touch the angel's billowing bedsheets of narrative. The angel falls through the envelope of space.

[ ].

Between God and earth: brackets through which only angels can travel. The angel's huge dark, nearly black wings tipped in warm orange-brown are ripped by wind. They are soaked by thunderous rain. They do not have the scent of Icarus (of softened yellow beeswax, of feathers on the waves). The angel-boy no longer hovers magically. He lands broken – a touch of blood on a wing – as Hugo Simberg's *The Wounded Angel.* I secure her blindfold over her eyes.

[ ].

I touch the blank space that Anne left in 'Kitty' on 1 August 1944, after the final line of the diary – 'if only there were no other people in the world'.[2]

[ ].

I try my hand at play. But the marbles Anne left with her neighbour before she went into hiding are cold. Not warm.

[ ].

I unearth my mother's Shirley Temple doll. Deteriorated, mud-covered-unrecognizable. I try to resuscitate her. Actually, there was nothing there.

[ ].

No more photos of Anne, after she went into hiding at age thirteen.

[ ].

A dusty copy of Solomon Northup's memoir, *Twelve Years a Slave*, was handed to Sue Eakin during the summer of 1931, at the Bunkie Louisiana library. She was twelve years old. Her years on earth equalled those of Northup's enslavement. She would become a historian, and would bring the book out of hiding.

[ ].

Richard Learoyd's huge 4-foot-tall grainless photograph of a dead hare hanging from strings is a tender rendition of fur, marionette, pietà, the films of Marey, the folklore of raining animals, optography. And . . . a meal of jugged hare cooked in red wine with juniper berries and served with a sauce of *taboo*: the hare's own blood, its pulverized liver and cream.

[ ].

Food for thought.
The word eaten.

[ ].

Solomon Northup hanging from a tree in Steve McQueen's *12 Years a Slave*: Spanish moss *swingin' in the Southern breeze.*

'Horrific things happen in beautiful places.'[3]

[ ].

Sally Mann photographed her Mississippi tree – its bark scarred with a slash that marks its wound as mouth – a botched attempt to cut it down – a grimace of refusal. Who knows what fortuitous accidents Mann's old lens will make. Likewise, her photographic process is cranky – wet-collodion messy. Mann does not confess her sins to Jesus, but she does pray to the angel of *uncertainty*. The angel of serendipity.

I touch the mouth of Mann's Mississippi tree in hopes that Gee-Gee – Virginia Franklin Carter – will speak to me. 'I put my hand for a moment across my eyes',[4] like Proust trying to understand 'the three trees'. I stretch my ear. 'Ears do not have eyelids.' I hear a mur-mur from Gee-Gee as tree.

[ ].

Or is it Emily Dickinson?

'Nature is a Haunted House – but Art – a House that tries to be haunted.'[5]

[ ].

Lolita is twelve at the start of Nabokov's novel. Throughout the novel she is associated with the colour gray. From her hazy gray name (Dolores Haze on the dotted line) – to her eyes of gray-glass – to her death in a town called Gray Star.

Lolita was saved from the gray cinders by Véra, Nabokov's clever wife. Proust's 'good angel of certainty' must have flown down and lent her a helping hand.

I like Lolita adolescently, like an adolescent girl likes another girl. I write of her/to her/with her . . . adolescently. No metamorphosis. She's not a novel. She's an essay written in gray (pencil). 'Imagine a type of writing so hard to define its very name should be something like: an effort, an attempt, a trial. Surmise or hazard, followed likely by failure.'[6] I use my eraser – and scissors too: we make paper poupées together. We're 'onlies'. No siblings get in the way. We have our own rooms.

[ ].

Simberg's wounded angel curls into herself making her wings arch up behind, like gigantic brackets, separating her from the surrounding text of the world.

Her wings look like lungs.

Wings as lungs give flight to the breath of life.

To inspire is to resuscitate.

A torn envelope.

A hazelnut.

A diary in a red-plaid cover.

Two hares out of breath.

The gray eyes of Lolita.

A scarred live oak.

Serendipitously.

REFERENCES

Preface: My Early Education in Serendipity

1 Vladimir Nabokov, 'From Nabokov's Cornell lectures, March 1951', in *Nabokov's Butterflies: Unpublished and Uncollected Writings*, ed. Brian Boyd and Robert Michael Pyle (Boston, MA, 2000), p. 473.

Introduction: From a Smashed Thimble to Two Hares Falling Out of Breath

1 Robert K. Merton and Elinor Barber, *The Travels and Adventures of Serendipity: A Study in Sociological Semantics and the Sociology of Science* (Princeton, NJ, 2004), p. 1.

2 Ibid., pp. 1–2. Walpole is sloppy in his retelling. The animal was a camel, not a mule.

3 Ibid., p. 6. In French 'serendipity' is *sérendipité*, retaining the link to the Persian tale. In Spanish, *casualidad* (coincidence). In German, *glücklicher Zufall* (lucky coincidence).

4 Ibid., p. 9.

5 Ruth Mack, 'The Castle of Otranto', in *Horace Walpole's Strawberry Hill*, ed. Michael Snodin (New Haven, CT, and London, 2009), p. 8.

6 Laetitia Matilda Hawkins, as quoted by T. H. White, *The Age of Scandal: An Excursion through a Minor Period* [1950] (London, 2011), pp. 89–90.

7 Matthew M. Reeve, 'Gothic Architecture, Sexuality, and License at Horace Walpole's Strawberry Hill', *Art Bulletin*, XCV/3 (September 2013), pp. 411–39 (p. 411).

8 Ibid., p. 426.

9 Simon Swynfen Jervis, 'Horace Walpole and Strawberry Hill', *Burlington Magazine*, CLII/1286 (May 2010), pp. 321–4 (p. 322).

10 Michael Snodin, 'Going to Strawberry Hill', in *Horace Walpole's Strawberry Hill*, ed. Snodin, p. 16.

11 Horace Walpole, in *The Yale Edition of Horace Walpole's Correspondence*, ed. William Sheldon Lewis et al., 48 vols (New Haven, CT, 1937–83), letter to Horace Mann, 27 April 1753, vol. XX, p. 372 and letter to George Montagu, 8 June 1754, vol. IX, p. 162. *Syringa* is the genus of lilacs, those blueth, gloomth, strongly-fragranted flowers.

12 See Carol Mavor, *Blue Mythologies: Reflections on a Colour* (London, 2013), pp. 52–3.

13 Margaret K. Powell, 'The "Curious Books" in the Library at Strawberry Hill', in *Horace Walpole's Strawberry Hill*, ed. Snodin, p. 236.

14 Ibid.

15 Ibid.

16 Michael Ann Holly, *The Melancholy Art* (Princeton, NJ, and Oxford, 2013), p. 114. Holly is working closely with the work of Johann Joachim Winckelmann.

17 Peter Stallybrass, 'Against Thinking', *PMLA*, CXXII/5 (2007), pp. 1580–87.

18 Jean-Luc Nancy, *God, Justice, Love, Beauty: Four Little Dialogues*, trans. Sarah Clift (New York, 2011), p. 26.

19 Anne Carson, *The Beauty of the Husband* (London, 2001), p. 5.

20 Brian Dillon, *Essayism* (London, 2017), p. 12.

21 The French Philosopher Roland Barthes, who has been a lifelong influence on my work, describes a 'writerly' approach to writing as 'the novelistic without the novel, poetry without the poem, the essay without the dissertation, writing without style, production without product, structuration without structure', *S/Z*, trans. Richard Miller (New York, 1974), p. 5.

22 Emily Dickinson, *The Complete Poems of Emily Dickinson*, ed. Thomas Johnson (Boston, MA, New York, London, 1961), poem 405, p. 193.

23 Marina Warner, *Forms of Enchantment: Writing on Art and Artists* (London, 2013), p. 9.

24 Donna Haraway, 'Do It Yourself! A New Film on the Life and Work of Donna Haraway', interview by Hestia Peppe, *Frieze*, 18 March 2019, p. 7, at www.frieze.com.

25 Ibid.

1 To Angelize

1 An earlier version of this painting was rejected by church officials for its depiction of St Matthew as appearing ignorant, with his dirty bare feet exposed. The angel is shown taking his hand and guiding it to make letters, as one would do with a child. This first version made its way to Berlin and was destroyed by a fire in 1945. Documentation of it exists. See, for example, Irving Lavin, 'Divine Inspiration in Caravaggio's Two *St Matthews*', *Art Bulletin*, LVI/1 (March 1974), pp. 59–81. In Lavin's text the paintings are referred to as *St Matthew Composing His Gospel*, versions one and two.

2 Anne Hollander, 'The Fabric of Vision: The Role of Drapery in Art', *Georgia Review*, XXIX/2 (Summer 1975), p. 438.

3 Peter Stallybrass, 'The Materiality of Writing', lecture for CIDRAL (the Centre for Interdisciplinary Research in Arts and Languages) at the University of Manchester, 5 May 2010.

4 Lavin, 'Divine Inspiration in Caravaggio's Two *St Matthews*', p. 64.

5 Hollander, 'The Fabric of Vision', p. 414.

6 Ibid., p. 415.

7 Sigmund Freud, 'Delusions and Dream in Jensen's "Gradiva"' [1906], in *The Standard Edition of the Complete Psychological Works of Sigmund Freud*, trans. James Strachey et al., vol. IX (London, 1959), pp. 7–95.
8 I thank Elizabeth Howie for this observation. She talked me through the painting while we observed it together in Rome.
9 Roland Barthes, 'To Write: An Intransitive Verb?', in *The Rustle of Language*, trans. Richard Howard (Berkeley and Los Angeles, CA, 1989), p. 18.
10 Ibid.
11 Ibid., p. 19.
12 Roland Barthes, *Michelet*, trans. Richard Howard (Berkeley and Los Angeles, CA, 1992), p. 25.
13 A sacred spring believed to be a fountain of knowledge that inspires whoever drinks from it.
14 Sappho, *If Not, Winter: Fragments of Sappho*, trans. Anne Carson (London, 2003), p. 55.
15 *Oxford English Dictionary*, s.v. 'muse (n.1)', March 2024, https://doi.org/10.1093/OED/9635249654.
16 Page duBois, *Sappho* (London, 2015), p. 72.
17 Sappho 'is not a person, not even a character in a drama or a fiction, but a set of texts gathered in her name . . . We know her work only in fragments . . . we have only ruins . . . lines painstakingly reconstructed from ancient papyri exhumed from Egyptian sands.' Page duBois, *Sappho Is Burning* (Berkeley and Los Angeles, CA, 1995), p. 3.
18 Carson, *If Not, Winter*, p. xi.
19 Ibid., p. 58.
20 Luce Irigaray, *An Ethics of Sexual Difference*, trans. Carolyn Burke and Gillian C. Gill (Ithaca, NY, 1993), pp. 15, 12.
21 Ibid., p. 16.
22 Ibid., p. 15.
23 Luce Irigaray, 'The Invisible of the Flesh: A Reading of Merleau-Ponty, *The Visible and the Invisible*, "The Intertwining – The Chiasm"', in *An Ethics of Sexual Difference*, p. 174.
24 T. J. Clark, *Heaven on Earth: Painting and Life to Come* (London, 2018), p. 45.
25 Ateneum Art Museum, *Ateneum Guide* (Helsinki, 2010), p. 57.
26 Caravaggio used swan wings for the angel in the first version of *Inspiration of St Matthew*. See Ann Sutherland Harris, *Seventeenth-Century Art and Architecture* (London, 2004), p. 42.
27 Lance Olsen, 'The Wounded Angel', *Iowa Review*, XXXIII/1 (2003), p. 111.
28 Marcel Proust, *In Search of Lost Time*, vol. V: *The Fugitive*, trans. C. K. Scott Moncrieff and Terence Kilmartin, revd D. J. Enright (New York, 1993), p. 879. Proust is discussing the angels in Giotto's Arena Chapel.
29 Olsen, 'The Wounded Angel', p. 111.
30 Ibid., p. 112.

31 Ibid., p. 115.

2 Moeder, Maman, Mom – Anne Frank, Chantal Akerman, Dorothy Aileen Ashcraft

1 Margaret Atwood, 'What Happened', in *The Animals in That Country* (Boston, MA, 1968), p. 27.

2 There are many versions of Anne Frank's journal, beyond its countless translations into other languages.
A version: The handwritten journals began in the plaid diary and continued in three other notebooks.
B version: After hearing a request on *Radio Oranje* for stories of the occupation to be kept and published after the war, Anne begins to rewrite the original entries from her diary as a novel. She wants them to be published after the war. These pages are the B Version.
C version: After the war, Anne's father Otto Frank combines the A and B versions and publishes the combined texts as *The Secret Annexe* (25 June 1947).
Critical Edition: Contains versions A, B and C, as well as related articles.
Definitive Edition: This is the expanded edition compiled by Mirjam Pressler, which works with and expands Otto Frank's original selection. It contains approximately 30 per cent more material and has been approved by the Anne Frank Fonds (Anne Frank Foundation). I have used the Definitive Edition for all my references to Anne Frank's diary.

3 I first saw the video as part of an installation: *Chantal Akerman*, 11 July–14 September 2008, Camden Arts Centre, London. The opening room featured a text in French, by Akerman, projected on two large banderoles of white gauze. The streaming words moved quickly. A doleful violin could be heard. The words, quotes from *To Walk Next to One's Shoelaces in an Empty Fridge*, magically spun out from the fabric. Sophie Arkette describes the watery effect as almost womb-like: 'As the sentences move, one after another, reflections of the words magnified can be seen on the walls behind. For the viewer, to be at the centre of this installation is to be swimming in words and meaning.' *Studio International*, 13 August 2008, www.studiointernational.com/chantal-akerman.

4 Anne Frank, *The Diary of a Young Girl*, ed. Otto H. Frank and Mirjam Pressler, trans. Susan Massotty, intro. Elie Wiesel, trans. Euan Cameron (London, 2019), p. 73. All further citations will be noted by page number only, in brackets, in the body of my text.

5 Elie Wiesel, introduction to ibid., p. vii.

6 Chantal Akerman, *Marcher à côté de ses lacets dans un frigidaire vide* (To Walk Next to One's Shoelaces in an Empty Fridge), 2004. Courtesy of the Camden Arts Centre, London. The idiom 'marcher à côté de ses lacets dans un frigidaire vide' means 'to be completely out of it'.

7 Interview by Julia Weiner with Chantal Akerman, 'My Family and Other Dark Materials', *Jewish Chronicle*, 11 July 2008, at www.thejc.com.

8 Dorothy Allison, *Bastard out of Carolina* (New York, 1993), p. 224.
9 From my mother's recorded journal, 4 February 1992, as transcribed by Stefania Olafsdottir. All quotes from this recording appear in this same format (with the speaker's name in bold) as if the lines were the script of a play.
10 Akerman, 'My Family and Other Dark Materials'.
11 This description of a bruise is fed by Han Kang's *The Vegetarian*, trans. Deborah Smith (London, 2015).
12 Marguerite Duras, *The War: A Memoir*, trans. Barbara Bray (New York, 1986), p. 62.
13 Wiesel, 'Introduction', *The Diary of a Young Girl*, p. xi.
14 Julia Kristeva, 'The Adolescent Novel', in *New Maladies of the Soul*, trans. Ross Guberman (New York, 1995).
15 Wiesel, 'Introduction, *The Diary of a Young Girl*, p. xi.
16 Sarah Kofman, *Rue Ordener, Rue Labat*, trans. Ann Smock (Lincoln, NE, and London, 1996), p. 3.
17 Roland Barthes, *The Pleasure of the Text*, trans. Richard Miller (New York, 1975), p. 66.
18 Marcel Proust, *In Search of Lost Time*, vol. III: 'The Guermantes Way', trans. C. K. Scott Moncrieff and Terence Kilmartin, revd D. J. Enright (New York), p. 174.
19 Adam Phillips, *On Kissing, Tickling and Being Bored: Psychoanalytic Essays on the Unexamined Life* (Cambridge, MA, 1993), pp. 68–78.
20 The French vocabulary list was on display when I visited the Anne Frank House in 2016.
21 As quoted by Peter Gay, *The Bourgeois Experience: Victoria to Freud*, vol. II: *The Tender Passion* (London, 1986), p. 82.
22 Richard Learoyd, *Richard Learoyd, Giant Camera*, online interview, SFMOMA (San Francisco Museum of Modern Art), www.sfmoma.org, October 2014.
23 Marie Darrieussecq, *Tom Is Dead*, trans. Lia Hills (Melbourne, 2009), p. 73.
24 Autobiography (or even the more literary 'memoir') cannot touch real emotions like fiction: *autofiction* (a portmanteau of *autobiographie* and *fiction*) is a French response to this paradox. Serge Doubrovsky is credited with developing this term. The genre is associated with such French authors as Marguerite Duras and Hervé Guibert.
25 Julia Kristeva defines 'women's time' as outside of the linear time of history and politics – interiorized, multiple, cyclical, monumental (eternal). See 'Women's Time', in *The Kristeva Reader*, ed. Toril Moi (New York, 1986), pp. 187–213.
26 Chantal Akerman, 'Chantal Akerman on *Jeanne Dielman*', interview for *Criterion Collection*, 2009, www.youtube.com.
27 Ibid.
28 Sally Mann, *What Remains* (Boston, MA, New York, London, 2003), p. 6.
29 Gaston Bachelard, *The Poetics of Space*, trans. Maria Jolas (Boston, MA, 1994), p. 234.

30 Marguerite Duras, *Hiroshima mon amour; Text by Marguerite Duras, for the Film by Alain Resnais*, trans. Richard Seaver (New York, 1961), p. 91.
31 Ernst Bloch, *The Principle of Hope*, vol. I, trans. Neville Plaice, Stephen Plaice and Paul Knight (Cambridge, MA, 1986), pp. 65–7.
32 Akerman, 'My Family and Other Dark Materials'.
33 Marguerite Duras, *Wartime Notebooks*, ed. Sophie Bogaert and Olivier Corpet, trans. Linda Coverdale, as included in *The Lover, Wartime Notebooks, Practicalities*, with an introduction by Rachel Kushner (New York and London, 2018), p. 293.
34 Ibid., p. 294.
35 Ibid.
36 Ibid.
37 Ibid., p. 297.
38 Ibid., p. 290.
39 Akerman, 'My Family and Other Dark Materials'.

Postscriptum: Written After: Moeder, Maman, Mom; or, I sang so hard I almost exploded

1 Chantal Akerman, in Griselda Pollock, 'The Long Journey: Maternal Trauma, Tears and Kisses in a Work by Chantal Akerman', *Studies in the Maternal*, II/1 (2010), pp. 1–32 (p. 8).
2 Chantal Akerman and Claudine Paquote, *Chantal Akerman: Autoportrait en cineaste* (Paris, 2004), p. 72. The English translation of the French is from Pollock, 'The Long Journey', p. 15.

3 Sally Mann's Scarred Tree – *Tête-à-Tête with Proust's 'Three Trees'*

1 The Narrator of *In Search of Lost Time* is never clearly named and is conventionally referred to as the Narrator. Yet there are two instances in the novel where Proust plays, perhaps accidentally, with the Narrator as 'Marcel'. Since the *Search* borders on memoir, novel and philosophy, there are solid arguments for using 'the Narrator' and 'Marcel'. For *Serendipity*, I am choosing to 'favour the convention of referring to the first person protagonist of Proust's novel as "Marcel"'. See Roger Shattuck, *Proust's Way: A Field Guide to 'In Search of Lost Time'* (New York, 2000), p. 33.
2 Marcel Proust, *In Search of Lost Time*, vol. I: *Swann's Way*, trans. C. K. Moncrieff and T. Kilmartin, revd D. J. Enright (New York, 1992), p. 60. There are six volumes to the Random House (American edition); the British edition has different pagination.
3 Ibid., p. 64.
4 Ali Smith, 'May', in *The Whole Story and Other Stories* (London, 2003), p. 53.
5 *Mother Land* was the title of an exhibition (and accompanying catalogue) of Mann's landscapes shown at Edwynn Houk Gallery, New York, 25 September–8 November 1997. See also Carol Mavor, 'Mother Land Missed: The Becoming

Landscapes of Clementina, Viscountess Hawarden, and Sally Mann', in *Singular Women: Writing the Artist*, ed. Kristen Frederickson and Sarah E. Webb (Berkeley, Los Angeles, CA, and London, 2003), pp. 66–79.

6 Sally Mann, 2001, from an interview originally published on PBS (the U.S. public broadcasting channel) in September 2001; republished by PBS for their series entitled *Art 21: Art in the Twenty-First Century*. The transcript can be read online at www.pbs.org/art21/artists/mann/clip2.html.

7 Sarah Greenough, 'Writing with Photographs: Sally Mann's Ode to the South, 1969–2017', in *Sally Mann: A Thousand Crossings* (Washington, DC, and New York, 2018), p. 41.

8 Ibid.

9 Jean-Luc Nancy, *Listening*, trans. Charlotte Mandell (New York, 2007), p. 2.

10 Correspondence through email with Sally Mann, July 2010. The poem is entitled 'Anecdote of the Jar' (1923) as found in Wallace Stevens, *Harmonium* [1923] (London, 2001), p. 92.

11 Mann, 2001, PBS interview.

12 Ibid.

13 Ibid.

14 Masahiko Abe, 'Placing a Tree in "Anecdote of the Jar"', *Wallace Stevens Journal*, XXVIII/2 (Fall 2004), pp. 322–8 (p. 328).

15 See Carol Mavor, 'Winnicott's ABCs and String Boy', in *Reading Boyishly: Roland Barthes, J. M. Barrie, Jacques Henri Lartigue, Marcel Proust, and D. W. Winnicott* (Durham, NC, and London, 2007), pp. 57–75.

16 Roland Barthes, 'Toys', in *Mythologies*, trans. Richard Howard and Annette Lavers (New York, 2012), p. 59.

17 Ibid.

18 Ibid.

19 Ibid., p. 60.

20 In the novel *Beautiful World, Where are You?* (New York, 2021), p. 83, Sally Rooney's character Eileen writes an email to Alice, with a 'new theory':

> Human beings lost the instinct for beauty in 1976, when plastics became the most widespread material in existence . . . I know we have good reason to be sceptical of aesthetic nostalgia, but the fact remains that before the 1970s, people wore durable clothes of wool and cotton, stored drinks in glass bottles, wrapped food produce in paper and filled their houses with sturdy wooden furniture. Now a majority of objects in our visual environment are made of plastic, the ugliest substance on earth, a material which when dyed does not take on colour but actually exudes colour, in an inimitably ugly way.

21 Barthes, 'Toys', p. 61.

22 Melissa Block, 'From Lens to Photo: Sally Mann Captures Her Love', NPR, www.npr.org, 17 February 2011, for the NPR show *All Things Considered*.

23 Nancy, *Listening*, p. 31.
24 As Leon S. Roudiez writes of Julia Kristeva's use of *jouissance*: in her 'vocabulary, sensual, sexual pleasure is covered by *plaisir*; "jouissance" is total joy or ecstasy . . . also, through the working of the signifier, this implies the presence of meaning (*jouissance=j'ouïs sens*=I heard meaning), requiring it by going beyond it.' Roudiez, 'Introduction' to Julia Kristeva's *Desire in Language: A Semiotic Approach to Literature and Art*, ed. Leon S. Roudiez, trans. Thomas Gora, Alice Jardine and Leon S. Roudiez (New York, 1980), p. 16.
25 See Rosalind E. Krauss, 'Yo-Yo', in Yves-Alain Bois and Rosalind E. Krauss, *Formless: A User's Guide* (New York, 1999), pp. 219–23.
26 Sally Mann, *Deep South* (New York, Boston, MA, and London, 2005), p. 49.
27 Craig Owens, 'Photography "en abyme"', *October*, 5 (Summer 1978), p. 75; Krauss, 'Yo-Yo', pp. 219–23; Roman Jakobson, 'Why Mama and Papa?', in *Selected Writings*, vol. I (The Hague, 1962), pp. 538–45.
28 Owens, 'Photography "en abyme"', p. 75.
29 Barthes, 'Myth Today', in *Mythologies*, p. 219. Barthes is playing with Saussurean linguistics here. He is claiming that a tree is no longer quite a tree, especially when it is expressed in a poem by the French little girl Minou Drouet: a *cause célèbre* of the 1950s. The once-famous child-writer is nearly forgotten today. Her most famous poem was entitled 'Tree That I Love'. See Carol Mavor, *Aurelia: Art and Literature Through the Mouth of the Fairy Tale* (London, 2017), pp. 238–9.
30 Greenough, 'Writing with Photographs', p. 50.
31 Mann, quoted ibid.
32 Ibid.
33 Jean Cayrol's *Nuit et brouillard* (Paris, 1997). The line in French is: 'Nous ne pouvons que vous montrer l'écorce', p. 24. The text became the voiceover for Alan Resnais' famed film *Nuit et brouillard* (Night and Fog), 1955.
34 Walter Benjamin famously described Eugène Atget's pictures of Paris streets, devoid of people, as 'scenes of crime'. Benjamin makes no reference to Atget's trees. Nevertheless, I think that Atget also photographed many of his trees as 'scenes of crime'. See Benjamin, 'The Work of Art in the Age of Mechanical Reproduction', in *Illuminations: Essays and Reflections* (New York, 1969), p. 226. One can see Atget's photographs of 'crime-scene' trees, taken at Parc de Sceaux, Saint-Cloud, Versailles and so on, reproduced in John Szarkowski's *Atget* (New York, 2000).
35 Mann, *Deep South*, pp. 50–52.
36 Proust, *In Search of Lost Time*, vol. II: *Within a Budding Grove*, p. 407.
37 Ibid.
38 Ferdinand de Saussure, *Course in General Linguistics*, ed. Charles Bally and Albert Sechehaye with the collaboration of Albert Riedlinger, trans. and annot. Roy Harris [1996] (Chicago and La Salle, IL, 1997), p. 69.

39 Ibid.
40 Nancy, *Listening*, p. 2.
41 Mann, 2001, PBS interview.
42 Ibid.
43 Jean Paul Sartre, *Nausea*, trans. Robert Baldwick (London, 2000), pp. 183, 185.
44 Here I am twisting the words of Barthes, like kudzu, from his discussion of the Winter Garden photograph. See his actual words in *Camera Lucida: Reflections on Photography*, trans. Richard Howard (New York, 1982), p. 73.
45 Sally Mann, *What Remains* (Boston, MA, New York, London, 2001), p. 6.
46 Proust, *In Search of Lost Time*, vol. VI: *Time Regained*, p. 531.
47 I borrow this phrase from Joan Copjec's essay 'Sartorial Superego', as found in her *Read My Desire: Lacan Against the Historicists* (Cambridge, MA, and London, 1994), pp. 65–116.
48 Proust, *In Search of Lost Time*, vol. II: *Within a Budding Grove*, p. 404.
49 Ibid., p. 405.
50 Words of Tristan in Wagner's *Tristan and Isolde*, as quoted by Nancy in *Listening*, p. 46.
51 Kudzu was introduced from Japan to the United States in 1876.
52 Nancy, *Listening*, p. 26.
53 Gilles Deleuze, *Proust and Signs: The Complete Text*, trans. Richard Howard (Minneapolis, MN, 2000), p. 12.
54 Proust, *In Search of Lost Time*, vol. II: *Within a Budding Grove*, pp. 405–6.
55 Ibid., p. 407.
56 Ibid., p. 405.
57 Dickinson, as quoted in Fred Rush's review of the exhibition *Sally Mann: A Thousand Crossings*, 23 August 2018: 10.3202/caa.reviews.2018.194, accessed 8 January 2024. The quote is from a letter to Thomas Wentworth Higginson, 1876, letter 459A, in *Emily Dickinson: Selected Letters*, ed. Thomas H. Johnson (Cambridge, 1971), p. 236. See Susan Howe's discussion of the quote in *My Emily Dickinson* (New York, 1985), p. 13.
58 Nancy, *Listening*, p. 14.
59 Ibid., pp. 27–8 (my emphasis).
60 Mann, describing the wet-collodion process in Malcolm Daniel's 'Torn from Time Itself: Sally Mann's New Avenues from Old Processes, in *A Thousand Crossings*, p. 251.
61 Mann, as quoted in Greenough, 'Writing with Photographs', p. 41.
62 Proust, *In Search of Lost Time*, vol. I: *Swann's Way*, pp. 9, 7, 5, 7.
63 Roland Barthes, 'An Idea of Research', in *The Rustle of Language*, trans. Richard Howard (Berkeley and Los Angeles, CA, 1989), p. 273.

4 Making Poems Out of What Is Not There: The Envelopes of Emily Dickinson and London's Foundling Hospital

1 Patrick Syme, *Werner's Nomenclature of Colours* (London, 2017), n.p., Section 26. First published in Edinburgh in 1821.

2 Emily Dickinson, *The Complete Poems of Emily Dickinson*, ed. Thomas Johnson (Boston, MA, New York, London, 1961), poem 1578, p. 654.

3 Ibid., poem 1574, p. 653.

4 Ibid., poem 254, p. 116.

5 Ibid., poem 526, p. 257.

6 I am grateful to Alice Butler's inspiring work on envelopes, which has breathed new life into this work. I am especially grateful for her invitation to do a writing workshop at The Courtauld (May 2022) centred on the themes of this chapter. All of the seminar participants helped me to open many envelopes and to cautiously respect their seals, including Lauren Elkin, Rebecca Hurst, Rebecca Birrell, Catherine Grant and Esther Teichmann. Also I must pay homage to students who took my 'Afterlife' course over the years while I was teaching at the University of Manchester and the University of Copenhagen.

7 Dan Chiasson, 'Emily Dickinson's Singular Scrap Poetry: On Letters, Envelopes and Chocolate Wrappers, the Poet Wrote Lines that Transcend the Printed Page', *New Yorker*, www.newyorker.com, 27 November 2017. Along with the envelope scraps, poems were written on all kinds of scavenged paper: the backs of letters, a bit of newspaper, a baking chocolate wrapper.

8 Marta Werner and Jen Bervin, with a preface by Susan Howe, *The Gorgeous Nothings: Emily Dickinson's Envelope Poems* (New York, 2013).

9 Syme, *Werner's Nomenclature of Colours*, Section 50.

10 Ibid., Section 28.

11 Marta Werner, 'Itineraries of Escape: Emily Dickinson's Envelope Poems', in *Gorgeous Nothings*, p. 200.

12 Helpful indexing and maps of the envelopes abound in *Gorgeous Nothings.*

13 Jen Bervin, 'Studies in Scale', ibid., p. 8.

14 Dickinson, letter to Thomas Wentworth Higginson, 7 June 1862, http://archive.emilydickinson.org.

15 Chiasson, 'Emily Dickinson's Singular Scrap Poetry'.

16 Helen Hunt's letter to Emily Dickinson, 3 February 1885. See Werner and Bervin, *Gorgeous Nothings*, p. 220.

17 Bervin, 'Studies in Scale', p. 12.

18 Emily Dickinson, 'Untitled', *c.* 1864, in *The Complete Poems of Emily Dickinson,* ed. Johnson, poem 921, p. 433.

19 Bervin, 'Studies in Scale', p. 12.

20 Dickinson, *The Complete Poems of Emily Dickinson*, ed. Johnson, poem 921, p. 433.

21 Bervin, 'Studies in Scale', p. 12.

22 From 'Nabokov's Cornell lectures, March 1951,' in Nabokov's Butterflies, ed. and anno. Brian Boyd and Robert Michael Pyle (Boston, MA, 2000), p. 473.
23 Julia Meech-Pekarik, 'Early Collectors of Japanese Prints and The Metropolitan Museum of Art', *Metropolitan Museum of Art*, XVII (1984), pp. 93–118 (p. 99).
24 Jane Gallop, 'Annie Leclerc Writing a Letter, with Vermeer', *October*, XXXIII (Summer 1985), pp. 103–17 (p. 107).
25 Syme, *Werner's Nomenclature of Colours*, Section 40.
26 See Marta Werner, *Dickinson's Birds*, an online visual and sound archive curated by Werner, Caroline McGraw, Danielle Richards and Will Sikich, 2023: https://dickinsonsbirds.org/project.
27 Dickinson, envelope poem A109, Werner and Bervin, *Gorgeous Nothings*, pp. 26–7.
28 Dickinson envelope poem A140, Werner and Bervin, *Gorgeous Nothings*, pp. 34–5.
29 Dickinson envelope poem A514, Werner and Bervin, *Gorgeous Nothings*, pp. 150–51.
30 Dickinson, envelope poem A821, Werner and Bervin, *Gorgeous Nothings*, pp. 172–3.
31 Louisa Norcross, 'Housework Defended', *Woman's Journal*, 26 March 1904, p. 98. As quoted in Gary Scharnhordst, 'A Glimpse of Dickinson at Work', *American Literature*, LVII/3 (October 1985), pp. 483–5 (p. 485).
32 Roland Barthes, *The Pleasure of the Text*, trans. Richard Miller (New York, 1975), pp. 66–7.
33 Dickinson, envelope poem A320, Werner and Bervin, *Gorgeous Nothings*, pp. 82–3.
34 Ibid.
35 The first infants were accepted in 1741. In 1954 the last residential pupil was placed in foster care. More than 25,000 children were cared for over the two centuries that the Foundling Hospital was in operation.
36 See the Foundling Museum exhibition 'Tiny Traces: African and Asian Children at London's Foundling Hospital', 30 September 2022–19 February 2023, at https://foundlingmuseum.org.uk.
37 Maria Zytaruk, 'Artefacts of Elegy: The Foundling Hospital Tokens', *Journal of British Studies*, LIV/2 (April 2015), pp. 320–48 (p. 320).
38 John Styles, *Threads of Feeling: The London Foundling Hospital's Textile Tokens, 1740–1770* (London, 2010), p. 13. Styles's fine research and sensibility have been instrumental to this chapter and my understanding of the tokens.
39 Ibid., pp. 13–14.
40 Ibid., p. 53.
41 Ibid.
42 Ibid., p. 75.
43 Ibid.
44 Ibid., p. 17.

45 See London's Foundling Museum website, https://foundlingmuseum.org.uk.
46 Styles, *Threads of Feeling*, p. 68.
47 Ibid.

5 Two Hares Falling Out of Breath

1 In 1927 Walter Richard Sickert (1860–1942) abandoned his first name in favour of his middle name. Given the signature at the bottom of the painting, we know that the work was done after that date.
2 Judith Mackrell, 'Walter Sickert and the Dance of Death', *The Guardian*, www.theguardian.com, 19 March 2012.
3 The phrase was coined by Samuel Taylor Coleridge in 1817 with the publication of his *Biographia Literaria; or, Biographical Sketches of My Literary Life and Opinions*. See Coleridge, 'Biographia Literaria, in *The Major Works*, ed. H. J. Jackson (Oxford, 2008), p. 314.
4 Hannah Glasse, *The Art of Cookery Made Plain and Easy* (Mineola, NY, 2015), p. 91. The Dover book is a reprint of the 1805 edition published in the United States by Cottom and Stewart; the book was first published in England in 1747.
5 Simon Carnell, *Hare* (London, 2010), p. 146.
6 Louis Marin, *Food for Thought*, trans. and afterword by Mette Hjort (Baltimore, MD, 1989), p. 145.
7 The title of Marin's book has been rendered as *Food for Thought* in its English-language edition; however, I prefer the more literal translation, which emphasizes the consumption of language like food, as well as Marin's interest in theology, especially the sacrament.
8 Marin, *Food for Thought*, p. 117.
9 Charles Perrault, 'The Sleeping Beauty in the Wood', in *The Complete Fairy Tales*, trans., intro. and notes by Christopher Betts (Oxford, 2009), p. 94.
10 'To hate is to love' is a cliché that turns on food in the psychoanalytic theory of Melanie Klein. For Klein, the feeding breast is a good and bad object: an object full of milk, hence an object to be loved; an object unavailable for milk, hence an object to hate and destroy. See, for example, Melanie Klein, 'Envy and Gratitude', in *The Writings of Melanie Klein*, vol. III: *Envy and Gratitude and Other Works, 1946–1963* (New York, 1975), p. 183. Of note, Klein's own reputation is that of a monster-ogress, causing Jacques Lacan to refer to her as 'an inspired gut butcher' 'projecting . . . monsters into the womb of the nursing mother'. See Julia Kristeva, *Melanie Klein*, trans. Ross Guberman (New York, 2001), p. 230. If to love someone is like having something good to eat – as is argued in Daniel Birnbaum and Anders Olsson, *As a Weasel Sucks Eggs: An Essay on Melancholy and Cannibalism*, trans. Brian Manning Delaney (Berlin, 2008), pp. 59–60 – then perhaps to hate someone can taste pretty good too.
11 Marin, *Food for Thought*, p. 145.
12 Ibid., p. 146.
13 Ibid., p. 145.

14 Ibid.
15 Ibid., p. 118.
16 Karl Abraham as quoted in Birnbaum and Olsson, *As a Weasel Sucks Eggs*, p. 59.
17 Carnell, *Hare*, p. 31.
18 Ibid.
19 Aelian, cited in Carnell, *Hare*, p. 7.
20 Joseph Beuys, cited in Carnell, *Hare*, p. 162.
21 Étienne-Jules Marey, letter to his mother of 3 February 1882, as translated in *A New History of Photography*, ed. Michel Frizot, trans. Susan Bennett, Liz Clegg, John Crook and Caroline Higgitt (Cologne, 1998), p. 248.
22 Marcel Proust, *In Search of Lost Time*, vol. v: *The Captive*, trans. C. K. Scott Moncrieff and Terence Kilmartin, revd D. J. Enright (London, 2000), p. 208.
23 This is a continual theme throughout Proust's *Search*. See, for example, my *Reading Boyishly: J. M. Barrie, Roland Barthes, Jacques Henri Lartigue, Marcel Proust and D. W. Winnicott* (Durham, NC, 2007), and Georges Brassaï, *Proust in the Power of Photography*, trans. Richard Howard (Chicago, IL, 2001).
24 Roland Barthes, *Camera Lucida: Reflections on Photography*, trans. Richard Howard (New York, 1981), p. 9.
25 Ibid., p. 88.
26 These references appear in Barthes' *Camera Lucida* on pages 9, 91, 116 and 82, respectively.
27 One is reminded of Albrecht Dürer's famous watercolour of a living hare, *Young Hare* (1502), featuring a clean 'window' of light in its eye. The tamed hare (or could it have been stuffed?) was painted indoors. The window in its eye is real; with careful inspection, the transom and mullion are clearly reflected.
28 Jean-Luc Nancy, *The Fall of Sleep*, trans. Charlotte Mandell (New York, 2007), p. 1.
29 These alternative renderings of the title appear in Mandell, 'Translator's Note', ibid., p. ix.
30 Ibid.
31 Ibid.
32 Ibid., p. 41.
33 Heinrich von Kleist, 'On the Marionette Theatre', in Idris Parry, *Hand to Mouth and Other Essays* (Manchester, 1981), p. 15.
34 Idris Parry, 'Preface', *Essays on Dolls: Heinrich von Kleist, Charles Baudelaire, Rainer Maria Rilke*, trans. Idris Parry and Paul Kegan (London, 1994), p. vi.
35 Kleist, 'On the Marionette Theatre', p. 18.
36 Henry Louis Gates Jr and Steve McQueen, '*12 Years a Slave*: A Conversation with Steve McQueen', *Transition*, 114: *Gay Nigeria* (2014), pp. 185–96 (p. 185).
37 Ibid., p. 185.
38 Ibid.
39 Michael Schulman, 'The Historian Who Unearthed "Twelve Years a Slave"', *New Yorker*, www.newyorker.com, 7 March 2014.

40 Gates and McQueen, '*12 Years a Slave*', p. 186.
41 Ibid., p. 188.
42 Ibid., p. 194.
43 Abel Meeropol wrote the poem and published it under the title 'Bitter Fruit' in 1937, before the famed Billie Holiday recording of it as 'Strange Fruit'. Meeropol, a soft-hearted communist, also ended up adopting the sons of Julius and Ethel Rosenberg.
44 Roland Barthes, *A Lover's Discourse: Fragments*, trans. Richard Howard (London, 2002). Throughout this book, Barthes uses the phrase as a way to explain how we personalize our experiences of the world.
45 McQueen speaking in Gates and McQueen, '*12 Years a Slave*', p. 192.
46 According to Wikipedia: 'Raining animals is a rare meteorological phenomenon in which flightless animals fall from the sky. Such occurrences have been reported in many countries throughout history. One hypothesis is that tornadic waterspouts sometimes pick up creatures such as fish or frogs, and carry them for up to several miles. However, this aspect of the phenomenon has never been witnessed by scientists.' See 'Rain of Animals', https://en.wikipedia.org, accessed 11 October 2023.
47 Summary information for Richard Learoyd's photograph 'Agnes with Eyes Closed', Victoria and Albert Museum, London, https://collections.vam.ac.uk, accessed 8 January 2024.
48 Martin Barnes, 'Richard Learoyd: Present Tense', in *Richard Learoyd, Day for Night* (New York, 2015), n.p.

6 Lolita's Gray Eyes

1 Of note, since this chapter is on *Lolita* – a book written by Nabokov while living in the USA and teaching at Cornell – my spelling of 'gray' will be almost uniformly American 'gray', rather than UK 'grey', unless the colour is sourced from a British quote or title of a painting.
2 This phrase belongs to the scholar and writer Eva-Lynn Jagoe, who used it as a doctoral student at Duke University, 1993.
3 I am grateful to Alice Butler for her work, which makes use of the direct form of the letter as a method of writing to her subjects, along with other authors, who use the letter form more loosely. Most especially Yiyun Li's *Dear Friend, from My Life I Write to You in Your Life* (New York, 2017) and *Where Reasons End* (New York, 2019). And, of course, Anne Frank's journal, a series of 'Dear Kitty' letter-essays written by an adolescent.
4 Vladimir Nabokov, *The Annotated Lolita*, ed. Alfred Appel Jr (New York, 1970), p. 206. Further quotes from the book will be in brackets in the body of the text.
5 Appel, note for ibid., n. 6/8, p. 324.
6 The book was written in English, and first published in English (although in Paris), in 1955. It was published in the United States in 1958 and in England in 1959.

7 Alexandra Schwartz, 'Onliness', *New Yorker*, www.newyorker.com, 18 July 2013.

8 Ibid.

9 The spider is 'prominent amongst the butterfly's natural enemies', writes Appel in *The Annotated Lolita*, n. 44/5, p. 356.

10 See Jonathan Flatley's discussion of 'liking' through the work of Andy Warhol in 'Like: Collecting and Collectivity', *October*, CXXXII: *Andy Warhol* (Spring 2010), pp. 71–98.

11 Ibid., p. 73. According to Flatley, the childlike 'liking' for affinities is a 'positive' emotional response. Flatley's reworking of the word 'like' has been very influential to this chapter.

12 Hans Christian Andersen, 'The Ugly Duckling', in *Hans Christian Andersen Fairy Tales*, trans. Tiina Nunnally, ed. Jackie Wullschlager (New York, 2004), p. 152.

13 Cicely Alexander, as quoted in 1908 by Elizabeth Robins Pennell and Joseph Pennell, *The Life of James McNeill Whistler*, 2 vols (London and Philadelphia, PA, 1921), vol. I, pp. 173–4.

14 Richard Dorment in Dorment and Margaret F. MacDonald, *James McNeill Whistler* (London, 1994), p. 147.

15 *Arrangement in Grey and Black: Portrait of the Painter's Mother*, 1871, oil on canvas.

16 Whistler to Mrs Alexander, 26 August 1873, letter in the British Museum, Dorment and MacDonald, *James McNeill Whistler*, p. 146.

17 Ibid., p. 246.

18 Sophie Duval, '"Some dear or sad fantasy": Faith, Idolatry, Infidelity', in *Proust and the Arts*, ed. Christie McDonald and François Proulx (Cambridge, 2015), pp. 23–39 (p. 27).

19 Ibid.

20 See the *Oxford English Dictionary* and Lewis Carroll, *The Annotated Alice*, ed. Martin Gardner, expanded and updated by Mark Burstein (New York, 2015), pp. 176, 179, 253.

21 '"I always call him Lewis Carroll Carroll," says Nabokov, "because he was the first Humbert Humbert."' Appel, *The Annotated Lolita*, n. 133/1, p. 377.

22 Vladimir Nabokov, 'On a Book Entitled *Lolita*', in Appel, *The Annotated Lolita*, p. 316.

23 Judith Thurman, 'Silent Partner: What Do Nabokov's Letters Conceal?', *New Yorker*, 16 November 2015.

24 E.T.A. Hoffmann, 'The Sandman', in *The Golden Pot and Other Tales*, trans. Ritchie Robertson (Oxford, 2008), p. 87.

25 Appel, *The Annotated Lolita*, n. 18/6, p. 340.

26 *Oxford English Dictionary*, s.v. "nympha (n.)," July 2023, https://doi.org/10.1093/OED/2324384448.

27 Nabokov, *Collected Poems* (London, 2012), p. 110. 'Lilith' was written in 1928.

28 Vladimir Nabokov, 'Christmas', in *Collected Stories, Vladimir Nabokov* (London, 1995), p. 133.
29 Nabokov grew up in a household that spoke Russian, French and English – he learned to read and write in English before Russian.
30 Ibid., pp. 132–3.
31 Ibid., p. 132.
32 Ibid., p. 134.
33 Ibid., p. 135.
34 Ibid., p. 136.
35 Ibid.

Afterword

1 As Susan Sontag, the great American essayist, writes: 'I lust to write', *Reborn: Early Diaries, 1947–64* (London, 2009).
2 Anne Frank, *The Diary of a Young Girl*, ed. Otto H. Frank and Mirjam Pressler, trans. Susan Massotty, intro. Elie Wiesel, trans. Euan Cameron (London, 2019), p. 334.
3 Henry Louis Gates Jr and Steve McQueen, '*12 Years a Slave*: A Conversation with Steve McQueen', *Transition*, 114: *Gay Nigeria* (2014), p. 192.
4 Marcel Proust, *In Search of Lost Time*, trans. C. K. Moncrieff and T. Kilmartin, revised by D. J. Enright (New York, 1992), vol. II: *Within a Budding Grove*, p. 405.
5 *Emily Dickinson: Selected Letters*, ed. Thomas H. Johnson (Cambridge, 1971), p. 236.
6 Brian Dillon, *Essayism* (London, 2017), p. 12.

ACKNOWLEDGEMENTS

On a modest blue-ruled sheet of everyday notepaper, lightly browned here and there with time (as if baked in the oven), a crease across its horizonal centre, probably from being stored in Emily Dickinson's pocket, the poet has pencilled Mrs Carmichael's recipe for coconut cake.

1 pound sugar –
½ – Butter –
½ – Flour –
6 eggs –
1 grated Cocoa Nut –

There are no directions given. On the flip side of the recipe Dickinson has noted:

The Things that never can come back, are several
– Childhood – some forms of Hope – the Dead –

She's probably right.

Or, wrong.

Dickinson's austere-excessive Cocoa-Nut cake could be a map leading to Serendipity 3.

In any case, it's nice to thank those that have helped you with a little cake.

I thank three women: Marina Warner for her beguiling *Forms of Enchantment* and for her willingness to give so much to my writing, without making me feel like a magpie; Page duBois for her wild, fierce, gentle, intellectual [ ] and an early education in Sappho, who will always be for me 'Like the sweet apple turning red on the branch-top, on the top of the topmost branch'; and Amy Ruth Buchanan, always hovering over my writing desk, with her own billowing bedsheet.

I thank three princesses of Serendip, who read, read, read everything I write: Fatema Albdoolcarim, Alice Butler and Rebecca Hurst.

And the magical bookmakers at Reaktion, especially Simon McFadden (who designed this book), Alexandru Ciobanu, Martha Jay and Michael Leaman.

And, as always, a little shout-out to Hayden.

Joan I. Siegel's 'Mary Cassatt: The Letter (1890–1891)', from Joan I. Siegel, *Hyacinth for the Soul* (2009), is quoted by kind permission of Deerbrook Editions.

PHOTO ACKNOWLEDGEMENTS

The author and publishers wish to express thanks to the sources listed below for illustrative material and/or permission to reproduce it. Some locations of artworks are also given below, in the interest of brevity:

Alamy Stock Photo: pp. 67 (Paradise Films/Unité Trois/Album), 79 (Paradise Films/Album); Amherst College Library, MA: pp. 115 (MS 821), 118 and 119 (MS 695), 128 (MS 320), 130 and 131 *top* (MS 450), 135 *top* (MS 842); © 2024 The Andy Warhol Foundation for the Visual Arts, Inc./Licensed by DACS, London: p. 11 (private collection); Anne Frank Fonds Basel/Getty Images: pp. 45, 52–3, 60; © ARS, NY and DACS, London 2024, photo courtesy the artists and HackelBury Fine Art, London: p. 179; Art Institute of Chicago: p. 125; © Association Marcel Duchamp/ADAGP, Paris and DACS, London 2024: p. 121 (Philadelphia Museum of Art, PA); Ateneum Art Museum, Helsinki, photo Finnish National Gallery/Hannu Aaltonen: p. 38; collection of the author: p. 57; The British Museum, London: p. 184; The Cleveland Museum of Art, OH: p. 149; courtesy Coram, formerly Foundling Hospital: p. 143; © The Easton Foundation/VAGA at ARS, NY and DACS, London 2024: p. 64 (The Museum of Modern Art, New York); Foundling Museum, London: pp. 133, 134, 136, 138, 139, 140, 142, 145; Graves Art Gallery, Sheffield: p. 146; The J. Paul Getty Museum, Los Angeles: p. 195; © The Josef and Anni Albers Foundation/DACS, London 2024, photo © 2024 The Metropolitan Museum of Art, New York/Art Resource/Scala, Florence: p. 176; Olaf Kraak/EPA/Shutterstock: p. 70; © Richard Learoyd, courtesy Fraenkel Gallery, San Francisco: pp. 61, 164; Lewis Walpole Library, Yale University, Farmington, CT: pp. 21, 22 (LWL 49 2601, vol. II); © Gerd Ludwig 1978: p. 156 *top*; © Mamechiyo Modern, www.mamechiyo.jp/@mamechiyomodern, photos © Victoria and Albert Museum, London: pp. 172, 173; courtesy Sally Mann: p. 91; © Sally Mann, courtesy Gagosian: pp. 49, 84, 92, 93, 96, 104, 107; Mauritshuis, The Hague: p. 178; photo Carol Mavor: p. 20; The Metropolitan Museum of Art, New York: p. 190; Museo de Arte de Ponce, Puerto Rico: p. 35; Philadelphia Museum of Art, PA: p. 122; private collection: p. 32; courtesy Samantha Sweeting: pp. 158, 159; San Francisco Museum of Modern Art: pp. 156–7; San Luigi dei Francesi, Rome: pp. 28, 31; Shutterstock.com: pp. 19 (Lois GoBe), 187 (Enrico Della Pietra); Tate Britain, London: pp. 75, 182, 183; from Marta Werner and Jen Bervin, eds, *The Gorgeous Nothings* (New York, 2013), courtesy the editors and New Directions Publishing: pp. 117, 129, 131 *bottom*, 135 *bottom*; © Woodman Family Foundation/ARS, NY and DACS, London 2024: p. 196.